EMILY DICKINSON

Personae and Performance

EMILY DICKINSON

Personae and Performance

Elizabeth Phillips

THE PENNSYLVANIA STATE UNIVERSITY PRESS
University Park, Pennsylvania

The right to use previously published material cited in the text is grate-
fully acknowledged: Reprinted by permission of the publishers and the
Trustees of Amherst College from *The Poems of Emily Dickinson*, edited by
Thomas H. Johnson, Cambridge, Mass.: The Belknap Press of Harvard
University Press, Copyright 1951, © 1955, 1979, 1983 by the President and
Fellows of Harvard College. From *The Complete Poems of Emily Dickinson*,
edited by Thomas H. Johnson. Copyright 1914, 1929, 1935, 1942 by Martha
Dickinson Bianchi; Copyright © renewed 1957, 1963 by Mary L. Hampson.
Reprinted by permission of Little, Brown and Company. Reprinted by
permission of the publishers from *The Letters of Emily Dickinson*, edited by
Thomas H. Johnson, Cambridge, Mass.: The Belknap Press of Harvard
University Press, Copyright © 1958, 1986 by the President and Fellows of
Harvard College. Reprinted by permission of The University of Massachusetts and Richard B. Sewall from *The Lyman Letters: New Light on Emily
Dickinson and Her Family*, Amherst: University of Massachusetts Press,
1965, Copyright © 1965 by *The Massachusetts Review*. Reprinted by permission of Yale University Press from *The Years and Hours of Emily Dickinson*
by Jay Leyda, New Haven: Yale University Press, 1960, Copyright © 1960
by Jay Leyda with credits to key sources (pp. 485–503).

Library of Congress Cataloging-in-Publication Data

Phillips, Elizabeth, 1919–
  Emily Dickinson : personae and performance.

  Includes index.
  1. Dickinson, Emily, 1830–1886—Criticism and
interpretation. I. Title.
PS1541.Z5P46 1988   811'.4   87–43121
ISBN 0-271-00625-0 (cloth)
ISBN 0-271-01645-0 (paper)

Second printing, 1996

for my niece and nephew

Stephanie and John William Roth

Contents

Preface and Acknowledgments ix

Introduction 1

1 Occupation: At Home 6

2 Duplicities and Desires 27

3 The Prickly Art of Reading Emily Dickinson:
The Terror Since September 42

4 "I wish I were a Hay": The Histrionic
Imagination 76

5 "It's easy to invent a Life": Listening to Literary
Voices 99

6 "How lovely are the wiles of Words": Trifles 133

7 "Experiment to me / Is every one I meet": Points
of View 168

8 Words Engender Poems 199

Coda 208

Notes 214

Chronology 237

Index 241

Preface and Acknowledgments

All quotations from Emily Dickinson's letters and poems are according to her spelling and punctuation.

Passages quoted from *The Letters of Emily Dickinson*, ed. Thomas H. Johnson and Theodora Ward (Cambridge, Mass., and London, 1958), are indicated by L in the text.

The dates of poems follow the corrections available in *The Manuscript Books of Emily Dickinson*, ed. R. W. Franklin (Cambridge, Mass., and London, 1981).

Points at which there are alternatives in Dickinson's wording for a poem are indicated when the text is quoted, and variants are given thereafter.

I want to thank Wake Forest University and my colleague Robert N. Shorter for arranging schedules that allowed me time to write about Dickinson; Germaine Brée for a generous critical reading of the manuscript; Maya Angelou, for sharing insights on relations between experience and poetry; Robert W. Pritchard, professor of pathology, and Richard G. Weaver, professor of ophthalmology, at the Bowman Gray School of Medicine, for advice in my study of

Dickinson's visual difficulties; William Ray and the Southern Humanities Conference for printing in its proceedings of 1977 my paper "Cliché as Poetry," which I have adapted for the last chapter of the book; and Doreen Asso and Eva Rodtwitt for reading and rereading my work.

Among the people with whom I have talked about Dickinson, I am particularly grateful for the encouraging support of Sally Barbour, Nancy Cotton, Kathleen Glenn, Iris Tillman Hill, Dolly McPherson, Gillian Overing, James A. Martin, Thomas E. Mullen, Mary DeShazer, Judith White, Edwin G. Wilson, and Emily Herring Wilson, as well as students in my classes at Wake Forest. It has also been a pleasure to work with Philip Winsor as editor, Cherene Holland as manuscript editor, and Mickey D. King as typist in preparing the copy for publication.

I am, finally, indebted to the many scholars and critics whose work has contributed to the great interest in the achievements of Emily Dickinson. Beyond the credits given in the Notes, I want to emphasize my gratitude to R. W. Franklin, Jay Leyda, and Richard Sewall for their dedication to Dickinson studies, without which my own would have been hampered.

Introduction

Emily Dickinson's apparent disregard for public acknowledgment of her work may seem pathological or protective; yet the disregard reinforces evidence of her belief in herself, and the record reveals at least inklings that there were contemporaries who recognized her worth. Helen Hunt Jackson, one of those to whom Dickinson sent poems, for instance, chided her: "You are a great poet—and it is wrong to the day you live in, that you will not sing aloud. When you are what men call dead, you will be sorry you were so stingy."[1] Attempting to encourage her to "sing aloud," Jackson included the early poem, "Success is counted sweetest / By those who ne'er succeed" (#67, c. 1859) in *A Masque of Poets* (1878), an anthology of verse that she edited for a "No Name Series" without identifying the authors. Jackson must have been gratified, and the poet must have been pleased that a reviewer of the volume attributed the poem to the grand old man of American letters, Ralph Waldo Emerson.[2]

While the attribution of Dickinson's verse to Emerson is only an ironic footnote in the history of the publication of her poems and correspondence, the judgment suggests a historical bias: a woman would not have been capable of the "mastery" of language which "Success is counted sweetest" exemplifies. Even though there were a few women who were skillful and fairly accomplished versifiers in nineteenth-century America,[3] the critic could not have known there was also another woman who commanded an authority and art that would outdistance the achievement of all of them. And, after the posthumous publication of the poems, she was never again accorded the anonymity of a mask that would make it possible for us to read any of the verse without consideration of gender. It is as a woman who is a great poet that we value her.

Despite the serious critical attention she has received, she has been stereotypically American literature's tragi-romantic heroine. Since she enjoyed being enigmatic and dodging the inquisitive, she was referred to as "the myth" while she was still alive. When people began to read the remarkable poems that seemed to reveal the private, intimate life of the poet, the myth was elaborated to satisfy the curious and to explain the exceptional woman.

Suffering the trauma of disappointment in love, according to the popular view, she put on virginal white, withdrew from "the world," and sang out her sorrow. More thorough explorations of the psychobiography also begin with the fact that there is no record of Dickinson's having married. It has been hypothesized that because of a weak mother, a strong father, and the mores of a Victorian society, the poet was sexually repressed and passive, became agoraphobic, and underwent catatonic agonies of psychological disorganization. Or, a victim of a patriarchial home and culture, she experienced the anxiety of gender and showed symptoms of anorexia nervosa, at least emotionally. Or, in love with the wrong man (a married man), she became pregnant and had an abortion. She was, it has been argued, a lesbian. It also is said that she was unable to maintain close friendships with other women. Expressing as a young woman a nostalgia for childhood and a concern about "how to grow up," she may be seen as either child-like or narcissistic. And, finally, there is the suggestion that she was manic-depressive.

Whatever the differences between these views, the poems are analyzed as evidence and proof. All of the theories derive from a common desire of readers to contest the separation between a writer's life and a writer's texts. The contradictions and disagreements between the theories, however, lead one to ask how the poet's texts can sustain all of them. Readings in which the daring innovative qualities of the poems yield to psychobiography and the belief that the subject is always Dickinson herself tend also to be reductive in relation to much that interested her. She is, moreover, nearly dispossessed of the magnitude of the work of a single woman whose sense of creative freedom was consonant with the virtuosity of the "performance."

Although she did not "sing aloud," and perhaps because she did not, she crossed the sound barrier long before other women learned to fly. Writing for pleasure, she wrote what she pleased; and growing sufficiently expert, she devoted as much energy as she could spare to the amusement that became at an undetermined time a vocation. Retracting an early willingness to see the poems in print, she continued to send them out selectively to people with whom she corresponded. If that were a way of controlling her audience, refusal to submit to the trials of publication also accounts for a trace of the amateur and the sense of conformity to no criteria but her own evident in the range of work. A single thesis cannot contain it, or her.

When she died at the age of fifty-five on May 15, 1886, the certificate stated, simply but ambiguously, "Occupation: At Home."[4] No one claimed that she was "Poet" or "Writer." The regional newspaper, the *Springfield Daily Republican* of May 18, announced the death: "At Amherst 15th, Emily E. Dickinson, daughter of the late Edward Dickinson." There was an unsigned obituary written for the paper by the poet's sister-in-law, Susan Gilbert Dickinson, who praised the "exceptional endowments," "intellectual brillancy," and "independent resources" of a woman relatively unknown even in Amherst. The tribute further remarked on "the ease" with which "she caught the shadowy apparitions of her brain and tossed them . . . to her friends," who were "charmed by their simplicity and homeliness as well as profundity," but "fretted" that she made "palpable the . . . fancies forever eluding their bungling, fettered grasp."[5] It is appropriate, in spite of the fact that the admiration is tinged with envy, that the first brief analysis of Dickinson as poet was by a woman who had known her over a period of at least thirty-six years.

It was to Susan Dickinson, Emily Dickinson's close friend who had married Austin Dickinson and become a formidable member of the family as well as an exacting critic of the poet, that she wrote, probably in 1882: "With the exception of Shakespeare, you have told me more of knowledge than any one living—To say that sincerely is strange praise" (L, 3:733).

Granted, we must surmise Emily Dickinson's habits of composition, but the evidence of her participation in the busy life of a nineteenth-century household lends credibility to the sister-in-law's impression of the artful inventiveness in the poems. Granted, too, we cannot always know which of the poems are conceptions of the "fancy" and which are a rendering of the poet's "real" life. It is, furthermore, difficult to ascertain the "knowledge" that Susan Dickinson, for example, "told" the poet; but there are still unexplored "resources," including people she knew, or Shakespeare, the Brontës, George Eliot, Nathaniel Hawthorne, the Brownings, and other writers whose company she kept that illuminate "the shadowy apparitions . . . tossed off" for friends, the poet herself, and posterity.

With these reservations in mind, then, I want to establish Dickinson in a new and original way vis-à-vis the poems. What she wrote is, of course, inseparable from what she was: child, daughter, sister, friend, and woman whose genius was a gift she developed and protected within the limits of the occupation at home. The grace of sense, the tangible sense of the world that Dickinson charged with emotion and thought in the poetry, would have been poorer and ghostlier had she been removed from the everyday life in which she took a fair share of a woman's duties. If she is also read in the perspective of that life, it is possible to distinguish between the "myth," the emotional crisis, and the actualities, such as the visual impairment that may account for the "cloistered" Dickinson of the declining years.

Eschewing the intention of writing either a biography or psychobiography, I am interested in the character of the poet manifest in the life, the conscious literary uses she made of that life, the common life she observed, and the reading she did. I want to explore ways in which she dramatized herself but also others' lives by appropriating the genre of the dramatic monologue, particularly whenever she wanted to go beyond the limits of "actual" experience and autobiography. Having found the histrionic imagination especially congenial, Dickinson disclaimed that she was always writing *in propria persona*. Like many authors, she assumed many personae; and the experiences in the poems are often transformations of episodes in the lives of personal friends, literary characters, and historical figures for whom a fictive " 'I' is only a convenient term."[6]

She not only tried out dramatic monologues but brief lyrics and various kinds of verse. She enjoyed describing "trifles" and writing poems for children. Responsive as she was to people, she sometimes experimented with points of view in characterizations of them and was a biographer of souls. Because she liked the play of language, words themselves—ordinary figures of speech—as well as the life she knew or read about also engendered poems.

Working both in the house and at writing, she had her wits about her. Freed from biographical strictures that assume a self-absorption and "direct egotism," the poems become less baffling; and many of them are opened up for our pleasure in the perceptions of a world by the woman who was Emily Dickinson.

1

Occupation: At Home

I

The prevalent opinion that Emily Dickinson withdrew into herself discounts her active and imaginative participation in life around her. "It gives a man character as a poet," Wallace Stevens observed about himself, "to have daily contact with a job."[1] For Dickinson, who had no "professional" career, the work of a "handmaiden" at home also gave her character as a poet and gave her writing character.

Reading her correspondence, we may be surprised to find her reporting, in March 1860, to a relative: "Your 'hay' don't look so dim as it did at one time. I hayed a little for the horse two Sundays ago" (L, 2:360). Such an activity does not conform to the typical views of the poet.

We know there is some "homely" verse such as that in which she remarks "I'm sorry for the Dead—Today— / It's such congenial times / Old Neighbors have at fences— / It's time o' year for Hay" (#529, c. 1862), or describes "A Field of Stubble, lying sere / Beneath the second Sun— / It's Toils to Brindled People thrust—" (#1407, c. 1877).[2] Still, Dickinson could have written that verse without ever having pitched a forkful of hay. It is not, then, the transcription of workaday experiences that determine the character of the poetry and perhaps account for the fact that the record of those experiences receives little emphasis in characterizations of the poet.

There have been studies of the domestic imagery that runs throughout the verse, but we cannot determine precisely the effect that the feel of thread in a needle or the aroma of the famous bread in the oven had on Dickinson's sensibility. Nonetheless, whether working or thinking between the writing of poems, she could never be quite detached from what she was doing. The kinetic response, the kinesthesis, alert attention required in household chores that allow one at the same time to go on thinking or dreaming—all carry over into the poetry. She does not separate herself from what she *writes* any more than she can entirely separate herself from the act of making a garment or a loaf of bread. So readers often assume that she is her own subject.

In the verse narrative based on a passage in Genesis, she depicts "A Gymnast and an Angel" who wrestled long and hard "Till morning touching mountain— / And Jacob, waxing strong, / The Angel begged permission / To Breakfast—to return—" (#59, c. 1859). Like Melville, who shared "Jacob's mystic heart," Dickinson may be wrestling "with the angel—Art" or with God. Melville talks about the art of creating "pulsed life" and lending form to "many a brave unbodied scheme";[3] she infuses the event with tension and energy. The details of the morning touching mountain after the nocturnal contest and of the angelic need to break fast, about which the insistent Jacob is less concerned than that he be blessed, give a feeling of immediacy to the struggle, as if Dickinson at least had cheered him on. It is the "pulsed life" in the fusion of "unlike" orders of experience (including the biblical account she knew well, the common meal she might have put on the table, and the word-play she could not forgo) that marks the poem as Dickinson's. Her "angel" and her "Jacob" have different needs of which the teller of the tale gives an account. But "Stranger!" than the struggle itself, Jacob is blessed and finds that he "had worsted," not bested, God. We want to say that Dickinson is Jacob.

In the poem, "The Bustle in a House / The Morning after Death / . . . The Sweeping up the Heart / And putting Love away / We shall not want to use again / Until Eternity" (#1078, c. 1864–66), the simple language and quiet emotion amid the bustle take their character from a woman's duties. Since the poet relies on housekeeping imagery for the tropes, we might think that they came to her while she was making order after a death in the Dickinson home and wrote the verse down when she had a minute to spare. If we accept the approximate date of composition as 1866, the provenance of the poem is verifiable. She reported in early May 1866 to a friend: "A woman died last week, young and in hope but a little while—at the end of our garden. I thought since of the power of death, not upon affection, but its mortal signal" (L, 2:453). Indebted to a woman's busy work of "cleaning house," the poem is a poignant personal response in women's words, as if the poet both witnessed and experienced what the neighbors had experienced. Can we not conclude, then, that she writes the elegy for them and for us?

A persona in one of her poems engages in unsuccessful bargaining with "The Mighty Merchant" (God?) who "sneered" and "twirled a Button— / Without a glance" her way (#621, c. 1861). Addressing God as "Father," another persona "observed to Heaven— / You are punctual" when he lit "All of Evening . . . / As an Astral Hall" (#1672, n.d.). These tropes are not essentially different from the mortal signals in the poet's prose: "I open my window, and it fills the chamber with white dirt. I think God must be dusting" (L, 2:504). Whether she is fanciful or witty, Dickinson seems to participate in what she is saying about both emotional states and objective phenomena.

When biographical readings take precedence over the poems, however, one's focus blurs. Dickinson wonders "What is—'Paradise'—" and asks "Who live there— / Are they 'Farmers'— / Do they 'hoe'—" (#215, c. 1860). Then there is the famous quatrain with a confident persona's argument, by analogy, for a knowledge of a heaven she has never visited: "I never saw a Moor— / I never saw the Sea— / Yet know I how the Heather looks / And what a Billow be" (#1052, c. 1863). The contradictions between the questioning and the certitude can be and have been resolved by critics interested in Dickinson's religious views, but both of the poems are also exercises similar to her affirmation of the pleasures of imaginative travel when she writes as a host: "Many cross the Rhine / In this cup of mine. / Sip old Frankfort air / From my brown Cigar" (#123, c. 1859).

The literal-minded remember that Dickinson "hayed a little"; even the skeptic agrees that she probably wrestled with necessary angels, bustled about the house, went shopping, et cetera. It is, furthermore, certain that she mourned for neighbors and friends who died and that she complained about God's ways. Finally, she had never seen a moor, but she had seen the sea and probably did not smoke cigars. She had, of course, a poet's mind capable of bringing together disparate experience, observations, and fictions so that she lives in her words. Cognizant that the words are not always records of the poet's actual experience, we continue to search for new methods of approaching Dickinson.

For instance, a poem about an imaginative child is generally thought to be in the personal register: "They shut me up in Prose— / As when a little Girl / They put me in the Closet— / Because they liked me 'still'—" (#613, c. 1862). Since there is no record of Dickinson's ever having been "put in a closet," perhaps the phrase in the figure is to be read figuratively, but who knows? There is the fact that as a young woman the poet wrote to her brother Austin, with whom she shared laughter before he left home: "We don't have *many* jokes tho' now, it is pretty much all sobriety, and we do not have much poetry, father having made up his mind its pretty much all *real life.*" Yet, having said that, she hardly sounds confined: "Fathers real life and *mine* sometimes come into collision, but as yet escape unhurt!" (L, 1:161). Perhaps it is relevant that she commented on George Sand as a "poor child [who] must make no noise in her grandmother's bedroom" (L, 2:376). Was the verse suggested by Sand's experience? Or, was Dickinson's sympathy based on her having had, in all likelihood, to be quiet sometimes? The poem continues:

> Still! Could themself have peeped—
> And seen my Brain—go round—
> They might as wise have lodged a Bird
> For Treason—in the Pound—
>
> Himself has but to will
> And easy as a Star
> Look down upon Captivity—
> And laugh—No more have I—

One can guess that Dickinson was such a child. Her brain went round.

But, to be more far-fetched, was the poem triggered by her having read that Maria Brontë, at the age of seven, "would shut herself up" with the newspaper in the children's study (during their mother's fatal illness) "only to be able to tell everything when she came out"?[4] To put a fine point upon it, a poet's empathy with another child is not quite the same as having been that child. Is the poem merely a depiction of a resourceful child's way of reacting to restrictions? If one has doubts, as I have, that the persona is Dickinson in "They shut me up in Prose," the memorable opening line encourages the reader to think so. Furthermore, did she not write of poets as birds and compare birds to poets?

She was able to rescue the trope from convention, for example, in another memorable line: "the eggs fly off in Music"; the image of fledglings in summertime, however, is perceived by a person whose unhappiness "'Twouldn't afflict a Robin— / All His Goods have Wings—," but "I—do not fly" (#956, c. 1864). Now the poet's persona is lodged in a Pound.

Writing to a friend on a December night in 1859, Dickinson says, "I cannot walk to distant friends on nights piercing as these, so I put both hands on the window-pane, and try to think how birds fly, and imitate, and fail, like Mr. 'Rasselas'!" (L, 2:357). No matter, there were always creative acts of which she was capable: "I could," she continues, "make a balloon of a Dandelion."

Because of the kaleidoscopic quality of the poet's mind, her images change into innumerable patterns and combinations of values from which we can construct more "stories" than the data, the facts we have about her life, warrant. I want, therefore, to look first without benefit of the poems at the character of the historical Emily Dickinson in "real life" when she was not transforming dandelions into balloons but occupied at home.

II

The poet's childhood seems, on the basis of scant evidence, to have been sometimes happy and sometimes unhappy, but not traumatic and not without advantages or reasonable care. The first glimpse of her is at the age of two and a half when she was sent to the farm of her maternal grandfather, Joel Norcross, for a month's stay at the time of Mrs. Dickinson's illness following the birth of Lavinia. Letters from Aunt Lavinia Norcross, who cared for her, noted that she was contented, very affectionate, and did not "moan"—"There never was a better child."[5] The next reports of her—at the age of seven—are in letters from Mrs. Dickinson to her husband, who was attending the assembly of the Massachusetts General Court in January 1838. She wrote: "Emily sais [sic] she wishes I would write you that she should be glad to see you but she hope [sic] it is all for the best that you are away"; two weeks later, the mother again wrote that Emily "speaks of her father with much affection. She said she is tired of living without a father." And since she sent him a request for "a little Emery to clean her needles with,"[6] she must already have learned to sew. The regard for her views as well as her wishes suggests that she was encouraged to speak for herself and perhaps for her maligned mother.

Other glimpses of the poet's childhood, years later in her letters, include occasional reminiscences of her mother such as that when she journeyed she always brought presents (L, 3:755); or the poet recalls "Two things I have lost with Childhood—the rapture of losing my shoe in the Mud and going Home barefoot, wading for Cardinal flowers, and the mothers reproof which was more for my sake than her weary own for she frowned with a smile . . ." (L, 3:928–29). The mother must often have been tried by the exceptional child—eager, inquisitive, questioning.

Speaking of "the cordiality of the Sacrament," Dickinson said it interested her "extremely": "when the Clergyman invited 'all who loved the Lord Jesus Christ, to remain,' I [as a child] could scarcely refrain from rising and thanking him for the to me unexpected courtesy . . ." (L, 3:835). Or when she asked "the early question, 'Who made the Bible,' " she thought the reply, "Holy Men Moved by the Holy Ghost," was insufficient (L, 3:756). And "No Verse in the Bible has frightened me so much from a Child as 'from him that hath not, shall be taken even that he hath.' Was it because it's dark menace deepened our own Door?" (L, 3:751).

She began primary school at the age of five and was enrolled in Amherst Academy when she was ten. In a letter written two years later, she reported studying Latin, history, and botany, said she "liked the school very much indeed," and made fun of "two young men" who had read silly compositions (L, 1:7). Writing to a friend three years later, the fifteen-year-old girl mentioned that she had four studies: mental philosophy, geology, Latin, and botany. "How large they sound dont they?" She said that she wrote a composition once a fortnight but selected a piece to read from "some interesting book" the alternate week, and referred for the first time to Shakespeare (L, 1:14).

The subjects she studied had for her a reality that must have pleased the teachers. She wrote years later: "When Flowers annually died and I was a child, I used to read Dr Hitchcock's Books on the Flowers of North America. This comforted their Absence— assuring me they lived" (L, 2:573). She was also the kind of pupil who was devoted to her teachers. But she advised an overly serious friend that she should not let her "free spirit be chained" by prim, starched-up young ladies who "are perfect models of propriety and good behavior" (L, 1:13). On the other hand, she wrote, "I have some patience with these—School Marms. They have so many trials" (L, 1:17).

As she was growing up, she was in and out of school. At some undetermined time during early childhood, she was "in consumption" (L, 2:515). When she was morose, she was sent in 1844 for visits with Aunt Lavinia Norcross in Boston and Uncle William Dickinson in Worcester. She wrote in the fall of 1845 that she had been "very unwell" and her mother thought her not able "to confine" herself to school. Again, in the fall of 1846, she wrote that her health "demanded a release from all care," so she had left school the previous term and done "nothing" except "ride and roam the fields." She had been, she said, "quite down spirited" but had "regained" her health and "usual flow of spirits." She was, nevertheless, not enrolled in the academy for the fall session. She went again for another visit with the Norcross relatives in Boston, about which she wrote enthusiastically. She was even more enthusiastic when her father bought her a piano of her own. She learned to make bread, "got plenty of exercise by staying at home," attended singing school on Sunday evenings, took music lessons, and practiced the piano (L, 1:20, 36). When she was seventeen, she finished the seventh year at the Academy and went to Mount Holyoke Seminary, where she did well but declined to take part in the religious revivalism with which the faculty and students were almost as preoccupied as they were with academics. She was "not very well all winter" but protested being withdrawn in spring. She said she "could not bear to leave teachers and companions before the close of term," went on with her studies at home, and returned to the seminary for completion of the summer classes; she was, nevertheless, quite pleased when "father decided not to send" her to Holyoke for another year. He wished, she said, to have her at home (L, 1:65–67).

Amherst was to her "a fair place."[7] As a young woman in a college town, she associated with two or three generations of students and tutors, some of whom she came to know well. The most frolicsome years began when she returned from Holyoke in 1848 and continued at least through 1852. During Valentine's season, comic and sentimental notes flew, she said, like snowflakes. "The last week," she wrote in February 1849, "has been a merry one in Amherst." The next winter was even merrier. "Amherst," she said, "is alive with fun this winter." Sleigh rides were "as plenty as people. . . . Parties cant find fun enough—because all the best ones are engaged to attend balls a week beforehand—beaus can be had for the taking—maids smile like the mornings in June—Oh what a very great town is this!" Two weeks later, she wrote: "There is a good deal going on just now . . . a general uproar." She described "a sleigh ride on a very magnificent plan [:] a party of ten from here met a party of the same number from Greenfield—at South-Deerfield the evening next New Year's—and had a frolic, comprising charades—walking around *indefinitely*—music—conversation—and supper—set in most modern style; got home at two o'clock—and felt no worse for it the next morning." This grand outing was followed by evenings that included "Tableaux at the President's," a sliding party, several "cozy sociables," a "party *universale*," and "one *confidentiale*" (L, 1:76, 80, 83–85).

Although she did not always let herself go in such flourishes of description, she spoke of "good times" during the summer of 1851 or "pleasure parties of which I was a member," rambles in the woods, and "sugaring with a large company" during spring. There were rides through the country in all seasons. If there was a beautiful day in February, "everybody was out." If it were fall, a party ascended Mount Holyoke. And Lavinia, who kept a diary during the year 1851, entered for June 24: "rode with Father & Emilie." Then Lavinia wrote to Austin: "Father took Emilie & me to ride Wednesday morning & we climbed a mountain & had quite a romantic time, picked flowers, talked sentiment, etcetera."[8] In her diary, Lavinia mentions the names of more than forty young men, as well as a number of young women, with whom the Dickinson sisters were friends during that year. On an evening in July, when "Father" was out of town, there were six young men who "called." One of them wrote to his sister: "I go to see Vinnie & Emily often— have good times with them."[9] Emily gave Austin an amusing account of a winter evening when three young men came to see her. One retreated, but she tried to make conversation on dull topics with the others while her father sat in the parlor; mother and sister giggled in the kitchen until Squire Dickinson joined his wife, and Lavinia joined the young folks. The Dickinson sisters even dared to receive callers on Sunday evenings now and again.

There were candy pullings, horticultural shows, cattle shows, and concerts. There was, of course, the church, and there were discussions of the sermons. Emily said of the Reverend Edward Strong Dwight, "I never heard a minister I loved half so well"; he and his wife became friends with whom she read Tennyson during frequent visits to their house on winter evenings (L, 1:250; 2:384). Or if there was a preacher who did not please the Dickinsons, the family enjoyed father's mimicking him (L, 1:251). When Squire Dickinson had business in Northampton, his wife and daughters sometimes went with him, met "distinguished" people, and dined at the hotel. In Amherst, there were student "exhibitions" (skits or orations), at one of which a friend of Emily played the role of "Slum," candidate for Congress in a colloquy on "The Politician"; at others, Austin and his classmates discussed "Longinus on the Sublime," "What Is Life?" or "The Infidel Spirit of the Times." There were public lectures by professors, on Adam Smith, for example, and by visiting luminaries on "Saints and Heroes" or Shakespeare. Emily joked that she was preparing a lyceum lecture; and Shakespeare was not considered sufficiently moral to be taught at the college, so almost everyone was eager to read the plays. Edward Dickinson asked his son to buy them in Boston. The young people organized a reading club that both Emily and Lavinia attended in the years 1850–52. When a tutor proposed that "the questionable passages" be marked out, the women held that the men could do what they liked but "We shall read everything"; Emily Dickinson declared that there was "nothing wicked" in Shakespeare and if there was she did not want to know it.[10] She wrote to Austin: "When we had finished reading, we broke up with a *dance*"; the tutors, she added, "come after us and walk home with us—we *enjoy that!*" (L, 1:116). She obviously preferred those evenings to what she considered "old-fashioned" senior levees, at one of which "Vinnie and dodging *Chapin* [a tutor] was the only fun," but "Vinnie played pretty well!" Emily, however, refused to join the sewing club that the young women formed to make clothes for the poor and said she was "set down as a brand consumed" (L, 1:84).

The sisters rebelled in different ways during those lively years. Lavinia Dickinson, who was described by Joseph Lyman, one of her suitors, as "very pious and very pretty,"[11] noted more than once in the diary that when she had been out with or visited by William Howland, her mother disapproved. The young woman was most defiant on a lovely September 26, 1851, when she rode with "Mr. Howland" to Ware, about sixteen miles from Amherst, and was gone all day. They exchanged rings and had "nice time!" but, she recorded, the parents were displeased.[12] Emily told Austin that Lavinia's going to Ware "made a hubbub in the domestic circle" (L, 1:139). Howland, who was a tutor at the college and a law student in Squire Dickinson's office, continued to call and once barely escaped before his employer arrived at the house. Although Lavinia never indicated why she did not accept Howland's marriage proposal subsequent to the trip to Ware, she noted within ten weeks another young man, "Twombly supped & spent evening. Father displeased highly."[13] Howland took his "last farewell" on February 6, 1852 (L, 1:174). Some years later, when the Dickinson girls had grown too old for escapades with students, tutors, and law clerks, Emily wrote that Lavinia "lives much of the time in the State of Regret."[14] One of the last entries in Lavinia's diary read: "Emilie is pensive just now[,] recollections of 'by gones' you know, 'Old un' [Chapin] etcetera."[15] The younger sister also wrote to Austin the next summer that Emily's hair was cut off and she was "very pretty."[16] Lavinia could as well have made the comments about herself, but she was very supportive of her older sister, and the bonds between them were strong, whatever happened.

There is no record, during those well-documented years, of the poet's having any radical conflicts with her parents over young men. Her conflicts seem to have been most frequently within herself. As early as the autumn of 1846, she wrote of "assisting mother in household affairs" and "a quantity of sewing." "I could hardly give myself up to 'Nature's sweet restorer,' for the ghosts of out-of-order garments crying for vengeance upon my defenceless head" (L, 1:40). During her twentieth year, in January 1850, when Lavinia was attending Wheaton Female Seminary at Ipswich, Emily complained to a friend: "Vinnie away—and my two hands but *two*—not four, or five as they ought to be—and so *many* wants— and me so *very* handy—and my time of so *little* account—and my writing so *very* needless—" (L, 1:82). She may have had only the writing of a letter in mind. Yet in 1850 Emily Dickinson permitted the printing of her satirical valentine, "a gew-gaw," in the Amherst College *Indicator*, and wrote a long jesting valentine in rhymed couplets ("Awake ye muses nine, sing me a strain divine") for a young bachelor in her father's law firm; in 1852, furthermore, she sent another bantering, if bombastic, valentine ("Sic transit gloria mundi") to William Howland just after he took final leave of Lavinia.[17] By the spring of 1853, she was chiding Austin, who was also versifying: "Raised a living muse ourselves, worth the whole nine of them. Up, off, tramp! Now Brother Pegasus, . . . I've been in the habit *myself* of writing some few things, and it rather appears to me that you're getting away my patent, so you'd better be careful" (L, 1:235).

She continued the complaint to the friend in 1850 by bringing charges against herself:

> and really I came to the conclusion that I should be a villain unparalleled if I took but an inch of time for so unholy a purpose as writing a friendly letter—for what need had *I* of sympathy—or very much less of affection—or less than they all—of friends—

She then parodied the parental voices:

> mind the house—and the food—*sweep* if the spirits were low—nothing like exercise to strengthen—and invigorate—and help away such foolishnesses—work makes one strong, and cheerful—and as for society what neighborhood so full as my own?

The voices, and perhaps her own was among them, reminded her of opportunities "for cultivating meekness—and patience—and submission—and for turning" her back "to this very sinful, and wicked world." She inclined, she said, "to other things—and Satan covers them up with flowers, and I reach out to pick them." The tirade concluded: "The path of duty looks very ugly indeed—and the place where *I* want to go more amiable—a great deal—it is so much easier to do wrong than right—so much pleasanter to be evil than good, I dont wonder that good angels weep—and bad ones sing songs" (L, 1:82).

It was in this letter that she also mentioned having received a "beautiful" copy of Emerson's *Poems* from Ben Newton, who had been a student in Dickinson's law office and had left Amherst to become an attorney in Worcester, where he would die within three years. Within a year, Abbie Ann Haskell and John Spencer, two of the members of the party with whom the Dickinson girls had climbed Mount Holyoke, were dead. The frivolous years were not only quickly over: they were never, for a young woman who wanted to be a poet, quite carefree.

She would, she said, make a little destiny for herself. Emerson's program of intellectual independence, liberation from the restraints of mundane values, and reliance on one's own creative energy encouraged her youthful nonconformities. She might have said, as Whitman did, "I was simmering and Emerson brought me to a boil." Even the inconsistencies that have troubled readers interested in the mind of Emily Dickinson were sanctioned by transcendental doctrine: "with consistency the great soul has nothing to do." The Emersonian corollary, "whoso would be a man must be a nonconformist," required only a change of one word: whoso would be a poet must be a nonconformist. It was, accordingly, her thoughts that were rebellious, but they were rebellious in relation to her sense of duty contrasted with the place she wanted to go.

There was, for instance, another episode, in May 1850, that reveals Dickinson's conflict over her woman's work, including care for her mother, who was then briefly ill, and an invitation to ride in "the sweet-still woods" with a friend she loved "*so* dearly." She told him she could not go; he said she "*could*, and *should*," and the choices seemed to her unjust. Having described her struggle "with great temptation," she finally belittled herself for *seeming* to think that she "was much abused," but came to her "various senses in great dudgeon at life, and time, and love for affliction, and anguish." She went on, in the personal debate, by saying she had been at work "providing the 'food that perisheth,' scaring the timorous dust, and being obedient, and kind. *I* call it kind obedience," but "in the books the Shadows write in, it may have another name. . . . God keep me from what they call *households*." Then she made a characteristic comment: "Dont be afraid of my imprecations, they never did anyone any harm, and they make me feel so cool, and so very much more comfortable!" (L, 1:98–99).

She had many tests of her fortitude. Writing to Austin on a Sabbath evening, June 8 of the next year, 1851, when there was a "northeast storm" outside, she was preoccupied by a more serious storm within the house and within herself. She reported that after tea she had visited two friends (young women) and arrived home at 9 o'clock to find her father "in great agitation" over her "protracted stay." Her mother and sister were in tears "for fear he would kill me." Perhaps she exaggerated to her brother; their father had a fierce temper and was given to inconsistencies himself—two and a half weeks later he would take the daughters on the trip to the mountains where they would talk "sentiment." And his high-spirited daughter pitted herself against him and his unreasonable severities. They both had self-discipline, passion, and a flair for the dramatic. So, telling Austin that she missed him very much, Emily recounted her behavior in the storm: "I put on my bonnet tonight, opened the gate very desperately, and for a little while, the suspense was terrible—I think I was held in check by some invisible agent, for I returned to the house without having done any harm!" If, she said, she had not been afraid Austin would "poke fun" at her, she would write a "*sincere* letter" (L, 1:111–12). She returned to the house because there was no other place to go, not even to an older brother teaching school in Boston.[18] Virginia Woolf's imaginary Judith Shakespeare—the playwright's wonderfully talented sister who ran away to London because she wanted to act, had a genius for fiction, and the heat and violence of a poet's heart—"killed herself one winter's night and lies buried at a crossroads where the omnibuses now stop outside the Elephant and Castle." She never wrote a word.[19]

Home, no matter how much Emily Dickinson groused about it, was a blessed state and very dear to her. She and Lavinia had visited their brother in Boston for three weeks in September 1851, but returned to Amherst rich in conversation as well as disdain for Boston and Bostonians. One got, the poet said, "a *brimfull* feeling—when *away*," but "*we* meet our friends, and a constant interchange *wastes tho't* and feeling, and we are obliged to *repair* and *renew*" (L, 1:141). She worried humorously that Austin "would turn into a bank, or a Pearl Street counting room," if he had not already "assumed some monstrous shape living in such a place" as Boston (L, 1:187). She observed that her more "mature" friends were "nipping in the bud" fancies which she let blossom, even though she told one young woman who also became a writer that "*me* and *my spirit* were fighting this morning" (L, 1:104, 90). To her future sister-in-law, whom the poet fancied "descending to the schoolroom with a plump Binomial Theorem" down in Baltimore, she wrote that "the dishes may wait dear Susie—and the uncleared table stand, *them* I have always with me." Lavinia was sewing away: "I half expect," Emily said, "some knight will arrive at the door, confess himself a *nothing* in the presence of her loveliness, and present his heart and hand." Lavinia was twenty and Emily was twenty-two; they had been talking about growing old. "I tell her I dont care if I am young or not, had as lief be thirty. . . . I do feel gray and grim, this morning, and I feel it would be a comfort to have a piping voice, and broken back, and scare little children." Then she hastened to add, "Dont *you* run, Susie dear, for I wont do any harm" (L, 1:144, 175). By the spring of 1853, however, writing to Austin, she longed for the "far off times" and confessed honestly, "how to grow up I don't know" (L, 1:241). It was out of such contrary feelings that the poems would come. The mundane life incited Emily Dickinson's imagination. She did not remain forever young.

With the exception of the gaieties, the continuing friendships, and the pleasure excursions—the last of which was the trip to Washington and Philadelphia in February and March 1855—or two extended periods in Boston for the treatment of her eyes during 1864 and 1865, the poet was usually at home. And at work.

III

It has been assumed that Emily Dickinson's was "a long leisurely life,"[20] or, from an opposite perspective, that the "routine of household chores" was sustaining when she was in crisis and needed relief from emotional turmoil;[21] but, year in and year out, the sisters shared in the household responsibilities. Although Edward Dickinson, soon after his elder daughter's first tirade on duty in 1850, placed a "Wanted" advertisement in the local *Express* for "a girl or woman capable of doing the entire work of a small family,"[22] it was not until after the "small" family moved back to the Homestead that there was any but occasional help by the day. Beginning probably in 1856, Margaret O'Brien worked at the Dickinsons until 1865, but left at the time the poet returned from a second stay in Boston for treatment of her eyes. Maggie Maher replaced O'Brien in 1869 and remained with the family until after the poet's death in 1886. There was, even with help, always much for the Dickinson women to do.

When one of them was away from home or not well, the others' work increased. Writing to Susan, who was vacationing in Geneva, New York, during the autumn of 1860, the poet reported: "Vinnie is still on her 'Coast Survey' [a visit to Boston] and I am so hurried with Parents that I run all Day with my tongue abroad, like a Summer Dog" (L, 2:464). She signed a letter to Samuel Bowles in October 1861 "Marchioness," the drudge in Dickens's *The Old Curiosity Shop* (L, 2:382). Or when Maggie Maher contracted typhoid fever, the poet wrote teasingly to her: "The missing Maggie is much mourned, and I am going out for 'black' to the nearest store" (L, 3:741). At another time, in December 1877, Dickinson wrote to a friend: "Wrenched from my usual Route by Vinnie's singular illness—and Mother's additional despair—I felt like a troubled Top, that spun without reprieve" (L, 2:595–96). In later years, after the early sixties, the poet was ill infrequently. "I am in bed today—a curious place for me," she comments in a letter written probably during the winter of 1868 (L, 2:459). She seems often to have taken the nursing duties in the family.

Guests also made for extra work, sometimes grudgingly, sometimes willingly done. Anticipating a visit from a relative she did not like, the poet wrote in the summer of 1869 to the Norcross cousins: "I hoped she'd come while you were here, to help me with the starch, but Satan's ways are not as our ways. I'm straightening all the property and making things erect and smart." Lavinia was "all disgust, and I shall have to smirk for two to make the manners even" (L, 2:462). It was approximately at this time that the poet herself declined an invitation from Thomas Wentworth Higginson to come to Boston for his paper on the Greek goddesses, or a music festival in June, or sea air (L, 2:462). Lavinia probably would have gone; she thought housekeeping was a weariness; her sister thought it a prickly art. Both of them earned their keep. During the financial crisis of September 1873, the poet offered to lay her "net" on the national altar. "I am not yet 'thrown out of employment,' nor ever receiving 'wages' find them materially 'reduced,' " though when daily bread would become a "tradition" was, she said, the exclusive knowledge of the Dickinsons' handyman and gardener (L, 2:515). A paper on Greek goddesses would have been academic. Describing bluebirds, in the spring of 1870, she said they "do their work exactly like me. They dart around just so, with little dodging feet, and look so agitated. I really feel for them, they seem to be so tired" (L, 2:469–70).

There are many instances of letters in which she comments that she hasn't had time to write. Two examples, picked at random, are in letters to Austin during March 1854: "so very hard at work that we havnt so much time to think, as you have. . . . I have more to say, but am too tired to now"; and three days later, "the work goes briskly on—we are almost beside ourselves with business, and company" (L, 1:288–89, 290). It is understandable that a biographer is occasionally surprised by "the range of Emily Dickinson's awareness of her times, their idiom and chief concerns," or the social criticism of Emerson and Thoreau.[23] But she knew more about "economy" than the famous Henry David, whose experiment in self-reliance at Walden Pond is justly celebrated. She was no pioneer woman, and she never hewed logs or built a cabin in the woods. She would have appreciated that Thoreau grew and cooked the food he ate or lived off berries and savored a woodchuck raw; she would also have enjoyed the ironies in the fact that he mentioned not having received a bill "for washing and mending, which for the most part were done out of the house," but failed to think it of literary interest to say whether mother or sister performed the tasks for him.[24]

Lavinia Dickinson's 1851 diary included such entries as "Washing day. Worked hard." Or: "Sewed and ironed all day." When one young man called, she noted that "he assisted in weeding."[25] Emily's letters to Austin spoke of washing his clothes as well as mending his shirts, gloves, and stockings. She wrote to him, in the fall of 1851, that she had been "too tired" to go to the lecture at chapel "last evening" (L, 1:134).

She reported that the vegetables were not gathered, but she "got" her plants in, or it was so cold "last night that the squashes all had to be moved," or it snowed and "we gathered all the quinces" (L, 1:137, 268, 152). Lavinia once picked currants at four o'clock in the morning and made wine. Someone made cider. There might be a boy to help harvest the homegrown apples, cherries, figs, and grapes; Austin noted in his diary, when he was over fifty years old, that he picked the peaches for his sisters. The women, then, had to prepare and cook or preserve all that food. Even spices had to be ground. In addition to making the family's bread, the poet also made confections, jelly, jams, cakes, pies, ice cream, and puddings.[26]

In the early years, water had to be drawn from a well for all uses. There were neither faucets nor automatic heaters. Father saw to it that the town got waterworks. The poet was grateful for a load of shavings. She described her father's stepping like Cromwell to bring in kindling.

There were usually men at the barn to take care of the cow and horses, but Austin also helped out there. As a boy, his main chore was apparently the chickens, and the first letters the poet, at the age of twelve, wrote to him when he was away at school were attentive to news of the rooster and gathering of the eggs. Chickens, of course, had to be dressed for table. "Old Amos" did the hoeing and had "oversight of the thoughtless vegetables" in the kitchen garden. Mrs.

Dickinson, when she was well, cleaned the gutter spouts and tended the lettuce that the poet admitted neglecting. She spoke of Lavinia's "abetting the Farm." There were also flower gardens to tend. The women gathered, dried, stored, and planted seeds in both gardens. Lavinia wrote of improving the grounds, which were ample, especially at the Homestead, and in hot weather moaned that God was no help. Dickinson gives the impression that it was also Lavinia who did most of the cleaning and dusting in the house, but "we shall move the table [or the stove] into the sitting room" for winter, and it was Emily who was first up in the morning to build the fires and cook the breakfast while the others bathed and dressed. She sometimes read novels as she waited for time to serve the meal of meat, potatoes, and brown bread, for instance. Or she might apologize that an untimely knock necessitated her "flight from the Kettle" so that the berries she was cooking to send next door were "overdone." Even though she was particularly expert in culinary matters, she must often have had to do the washing up because Austin's purchase of a dish drainer was a welcome present which she said worked "admirably."

The Dickinsons ate well. There is no suggestion that any of them ever denied themselves either a substantial diet or delicacies. The poet enjoyed writing about food: "the little luxuries you always get at home" (L, 1:240). If it were summer, she would exclaim about the overabundance: "amazing . . . beets and beans and *splendid* potatoes" (L, 1:127). She described "Sugar pears with hips like hams, and the flesh of bonbons" (L, 2:476). She wrote of peaches: "very large—one side a *rosy* cheek, and the other a *golden*, and that peculiar coat of velvet and of down, which makes a peach so beautiful" (L, 1:137). She said of one of her recipes, "I am pleased the Gingerbread triumped" (L, 2:492). Sending roasting chickens to Austin's family, she once wrote: "Enclosed please find the Birds which do not go South"; and again, "To broil our Benefits, perhaps, is not the highest way" (L, 3:879). She called her sister-in-law's kitchen "Mrs. Delmonico's." She noted having champagne for dinner and a fine time when friends, such as Elizabeth and Josiah Holland, were guests.

Having become acknowledged leaders in the town of Amherst when Emily Dickinson was growing up, the family entertained at teas, dinners, and receptions. The great and the near-great called at the Dickinsons. Their guests included newspaper editors, bishops, distinguished preachers, judges, lawyers, politicians, academic and literary people, relatives, generations of students, and an occasional general or senator. "Our house," the young poet wrote in the summer of 1853, "is crowded daily with the members of this world, the high and the low, the bond and the free, the 'poor in this world's goods,' and the 'almighty dollar' " (L, 1:257). Writing in June 1877 to a friend who had moved away from Amherst, she reported: "There is a circus here, and Farmers' Commencement, and Boys and Girls from Tripoli, and Governors and swords, parade the Summer Streets. They lean upon the Fence that guards the quiet Church Ground, and jar the Grass, now warm and soft as a Tropic Nest." Then she said that many people call and her sister, Lavinia, "beats her wings like a maddened Bird, whose Home has been invaded" (L, 2:585). When even the gregarious Lavinia Dickinson was bothered by visitors to the house, it is perhaps reasonable that anyone who wanted peace to read or write would withdraw from the crowd.

The Dickinsons, however, were adept at strategies for being themselves. The Honorable Edward Dickinson, for instance, was the kind of man who replied, when asked what he thought about the wish of two young nieces to go to a circus that was not considered respectable entertainment for ladies: "Go and make it respectable."[27] He was forty-seven years old before he joined the First Congregational Church by profession of faith. The pastor said to him at the time: "You want to come to Christ as a lawyer—but you must come to him as a *poor* sinner—get down on your knees."[28] The year before he died he wrote, "I hereby give myself to God."[29] The daughter was never willing to give up "the world" for the church.[30] When she was young, she attended religious services frequently. She counted among her friends more than one minister as well as at least three women (Lucy Elizabeth Dwight, Eliza Coleman Dudley, and Sarah Maria Jenkins) who were married to clergymen. But the letters show that she also stayed home frequently and used the quiet time for correspondence before she ceased going out altogether. One could say of her that she wanted to come to God as a poet. "Let Emily sing for you," she wrote to the Norcross cousins in 1863 when their father died, "because she cannot pray" (L, 2:421).

In later years, the children next door were her charge on Sunday mornings and remembered the joy of being with her at the Homestead. The work changed with the years and the seasons, so there were quiet times for dashing off poems or revising them. She was often up late at night to work on them as others slept. Inclement weather provided days for reading also, and Emily Dickinson never found them dull. She liked to describe the house when it was "snug and warm," "faithful," and "whole." She was sincere in the note she sent to Higginson when he asked if he might call on August 16, 1870: "I will be at Home and glad" (L, 2:472). She had earned that place in history. The poet's occupations were at home.

The legends have failed to acknowledge the equilibrium required in her competent performance of family *service* at the same time that she persevered in her life as a writer. Martha Dickinson Bianchi, her niece who was born in 1866, remembered that "Aunt Emily was busy, always busy." While the niece tended to idealize the hurried life and the renunciations of a relative whose fame enhanced memories of her, one cannot discount altogether the observations about the poet's "rigor of personality" and the family's respect for what were to Bianchi "the sacred centers" the poet claimed as her own. "I," the niece also recalled, "have seen her face stern, as if in judgment of her own soul or fate. She looked like my grandfather then—trying the Providence above her, perhaps, before her own tribunal."[31]

Although Bianchi's reminiscences included an account of a life which sounded genteel, they were not without a recognition of its pressures for the poet. "She was always sweetly welcoming, though any interruption must have cut in on that time she wanted." Bianchi described a typical evening in the house long after the "far off" years when dalliance was in flower: "Downstairs with the family it was oftenest a Boston paper or the *Springfield Republican* she glanced over until the rest were happily employed, when she would sit straight under the big reading lamp on the table and be lost to them in the book before her." The niece, perhaps more bothered than the poet about opinions of other people, wrote her defense to temper the charge of eccentricity: "Once in that happy place I repeated to Aunt Emily what a neighbor had said—that time must pass very slowly to her, who never went anywhere—and she flashed back Browning's line: 'Time, why, Time was all I wanted!' " There is also a glimpse of one of the ways she coped with the terms of existence when all was not happy in the house. "Another exciting line" from Browning quoted "with her pet gesture of bravado," according to the niece, "in the face of domestic complications," was " 'who knows but the world may end tonight?'—as if for her part she wished it would—dared it to—and would like to see it do it!"[32]

The poet's letters frequently rival her verse both because of the interest with which they describe the life she observed—the caprices of weather, the people she knew, the household, and her own emotional states—and because of the revelation of her changes of style according to the topic as well as her ability to make much out of little or little out of much. Lavinia said that "Emily had to think" for them,[33] but it is possible the sister, with the Dickinson humor, meant to acknowledge appreciation of the poet's willingness to write for them. She handled most of the correspondence for the women in the family. She wrote letters of solace and comfort to friends or relatives at the time of the death of people they loved; she sent congratulations upon the occasion of a marriage, the birth or school graduation of a child; she invited guests and cheered the sick; she sent "thank you's" for many kindnesses and courtesies; she wrote witty notes accompanying presents of food such as desserts, wine and honey, or fruit and flowers from the kitchen, garden, or her greenhouse. More than a thousand letters have survived, and they suggest that she could be a proper lady with the most discreet sympathies, an imperious opponent, a teasing rogue, a good neighbor, or a magnanimous and sensitive friend. She considered the writing of the briefest of messages a gracious art. She might be studied and mannered, cryptic and covert, open, intimate, unguarded, and extempore, but she always wrote with an ear for language and the sense that she could do with it as she pleased.

Some of the letters and notes, inevitably, were poems and the source of poems. Some included poems, more than two hundred and fifty of them, sent to both close and distant correspondents. The first recipient of her verse was Austin, for whom she wrote a sonnet, "There is another sky" (#2), disguised as prose, in 1851 (L, 1:149). The last was Higginson, to whom she sent in late April 1886, shortly before she died on May 15, a poem mourning the death of their friend, Helen Hunt Jackson:

> The immortality she gave
> We borrowed at her Grave—
> For just one Plaudit famishing,
> The Might of Human Love—

The sweet Acclamation of Death divulges it—There is no Trumpet like the Tomb—

> Of Glory not a Beam is left
> But her Eternal Home—
> The Asterisk is for the Dead,
> The Living, for the Stars—
>   (L, 3:904)

Dickinson, then, kept watch over both the asterisk, the small star that she chose as a sign for the dead, and those who reached toward the far constellations. Although she never knew the acclaim the poems she wrote would bring to her as well as the attention to the people she loved, she was nonetheless faithful to her duties and her demons. There would not, otherwise, have been any poems at all.

2

Duplicities and Desires

Taking part in the diurnal rounds of life at home for over five decades, Emily Dickinson proved that she was both competent and stable within the restraints of a patriarchial society. At the same time, however, she rebelled against it: she did not marry; she chose the company she kept; she did not fritter time away with nonessentials after she met the obligations to the family and friends with whom she was in close touch; she wrote poetry. She overcame the odds against her.

If she was cognizant of the benefits of being a wife, she was also aware of the sacrifices women made to be married. A neighbor once commented that Emily Norcross Dickinson (Edward Dickinson's wife and Emily Dickinson's mother) was "as usual full of plaintive talk."[1] She was said to have been "a young woman of good acquirements."[2] The daughter spoke of her more than once as "timid."

Men, the poet also knew, had other tensions. Edward Dickinson served for thirty-seven years as treasurer of Amherst College, which his father, Samuel Fowler Dickinson, had sacrificed law practice, health, and the Homestead to help found and secure. Edward followed him as a representative in the General Court of the Commonwealth of Massachusetts, but thereafter became a state senator and a member of the United States Congress. After one term, he lost the seat and did not return to political office until he stood for election to the State House, of which he was a member at the time of his sudden death in 1874.

He had been a major in the militia, moderator of Town Meeting, president of the Amherst Cattle Show, and a leader in the temperance movement. He was instrumental in securing the location of the Massachusetts Agricultural ("the Farmers' ") College at Amherst, the establishment of the local waterworks, and the opening of telegraph service. The achievement he considered of particular importance was the organization of the company that brought the railroad to Amherst. It would be difficult to guess which pleased him more: the fact that he was awarded an honorary degree by Amherst College or that he had a locomotive named for him. He was, according to the *Boston Journal*, "one of the old 'River Gods' " of the Connecticut Valley.[3]

Yet Emily Dickinson wrote of him: "Father says in fugitive moments when he forgets the barrister & lapses into the man . . . that his life has been passed in a wilderness or on an island—of late he says an island."[4] Attentive to tones and fugitive moments when people revealed themselves to her, she made independent judgments that reveal her sensitivity and compassion. She also remembered her father's reading "at Prayers, with a militant Accent that would startle" her, and she spoke, after his death, of passing his "Door—I used to think was safety" (L, 2:537). "His heart," she said, "was pure and terrible and I think no other like it exists" (L, 2:528). A self-willed daughter of a strong-willed man, she loved him, she sometimes stood up to him, she never feared him.

It was, however, her brother, Austin, with whom she was most apt to be in league. A year older, he saved all the letters his devoted sister wrote to him from the time she was twelve and he was a boy at Williston Seminary until he came home from Harvard Law School to join his father's practice in Amherst. Neither as ambitious nor as distinguished as Squire Dickinson, Austin succeeded him as treasurer of the college and carried on the paternal tradition of civic activity. He served as moderator of Town Meeting and president of the Town Improvement Association as well as a member of the board of two banks, the water company, the gas company, and the library. He wrote a history of representative men of the parish, liked to go to the theater in Boston or New York, and collected paintings. He oversaw the building of a new Congrega-

tional Church, founded and laid out the grounds of Wildwood ceme-
tery, had the town swamp drained, and landscaped the common.
He was teasingly called "the indispensable man in Amherst."[5] The
poet followed both his career and his interests.

When he married Susan Gilbert, the wedding was announced in
the *New York Times* and the *Tribune.* An orphaned daughter of a
ne'er-do-well tavern keeper, she was a woman with social ambitions. She liked to entertain at teas, musicals, whist or dancing
parties (oyster stew served at 10 P.M.),[6] and enjoyed what she called
"royal guests."[7] They included Emerson, Henry Ward Beecher,
Wendell Phillips, Samuel Bowles, Frances Hodgson Burnett, Helen
Hunt Jackson, Frederick Law Olmsted, Daniel Chester French, and
perhaps Matthew Arnold. Austin Dickinson spoke of the house as a
tavern. Although the poet described him as "cynical," she wrote in
1877 that he was "overcharged with care, and Sue with scintilla-
tion" (L, 2:575).[8] At the time of his death in 1895, the newspapers
said that he was the town's "most influential citizen."[9] Lavinia
Dickinson wrote as if she might have been another poet in the
family, "There is no landscape since Austin died."[10]

The familial life the poet shared with the Dickinson men and the
milieu that surrounded her explain much about her willingness to
initiate correspondence with prominent public figures. There was
no reason for Emily Dickinson to be in awe of men who interested
her, no matter what romantic episodes went awry. The view of her
as timid, like her mother, is hardly in accord with the assurance
the poet's exchanges with important men show.

II

Although there are difficulties in determining the nature of the
poet's relationships to some of the men she knew, especially those
with whom she corresponded, there have been few quibbles about
most of what the poet said in the bid she made to Thomas Wentworth Higginson for confirmation of the quality of the verse she
was amassing. He was, at the time, not yet the arbiter of literary
taste he was to become in New England but was well known as a
leader in the abolition movement and contributor of editorials to
newspapers or magazines she read. To Higginson's credit, the letters from the unknown young woman with a "good" family name
were not thrown in the wastebasket.

Writing first to him when she was in a period of great creative energy, she followed his career, continued the correspondence throughout her life, and received two condescending visits (the last in 1873) from him; he always seemed more interested in the woman and the personality than the poems. That, I think, was the reason she began to write to him as if she were "a romantic" character; he, in turn, took her ruses seriously and romanticized her. Seeing after her death the letters she wrote to Higginson, Austin Dickinson said she had posed in them.

She initiated the correspondence on April 15, 1862, when she sent four poems to him after reading his "Letter to a Young Contributor," which had just appeared in the *Atlantic Monthly*. The idea of asking a critical opinion from a prominent man who spoke with authority about literature may also have been suggested by the poet's having read Elizabeth C. Gaskell's *Life of Charlotte Brontë*, in which there were letters from Branwell Brontë to Wordsworth and from Charlotte Brontë to Robert Southey.[11] Their letters were, without question, influences on Dickinson's tactful approach to "Mr. Higginson."

There is in her first letter to him only the slightest echo of Branwell Brontë's request to Wordsworth to read and pass judgment upon a "Prefatory Scene" that was enclosed. Branwell says that, as he himself does not know the powers he possesses, "I must ask of others what they are worth. Yet there is not one here to tell me." Dickinson, after asking Higginson "to say if my verse is alive," observes: "The Mind is so near itself—it cannot see, distinctly—and I have none to ask—Should you think it breathed—and had you the leisure to tell me, I should feel quick gratitude" (L, 2:403). It is in her second and third letters to Higginson that echoes of the Brontës resound and confirm the posing.

Branwell Brontë writes, "I have lived among secluded hills where I could neither know what I was, or what I could do." Since he was nineteen at the time, he comments that the verse he has sent "does not even pretend to be more than the description of an imaginative child. But read it, sir; and as you would hold a light to one in utter darkness." And finally he pleads: "I must come before you as some one from whose sentence there is no appeal."

Dickinson takes off from the source: "You ask of my Companions[.] Hills—Sir—and the Sundown—and a Dog—large as myself, that my Father bought me—[,]" at best partial truth. She writes: "You asked how old I was? I made no verse—but one or two—until this winter—Sir—"; and "I would like to learn—Could you tell me how to grow—or is it unconveyed—[?]" She was thirty-one and had already written between three or four hundred poems of which she had made fair copies. Anyone who was not an egomaniac might still say sincerely as she did, "I could not weigh myself—Myself— My size felt small—to me" (L, 2:404–5). She is, however, pretending to be a child, and quite lonely, too. She continues, in the next letter to Higginson: "The 'hand you stretch to me in the Dark,' I put mine in, and turn away—" Dickinson's final rephrasing of Branwell Brontë's epistle is: "I have no Tribunal" (L, 2:409).

Charlotte Brontë's first letter to Southey does not survive, but the response she received from him and her answer provide Dickinson with additional ideas from which to make "an image" that will please her correspondent. Southey advises the hopeful young woman: "Write poetry for its own sake; not in a spirit of emulation, and not with a view to celebrity; the less you aim at that, the more likely you will be to deserve and finally to obtain it." The twenty-one-year-old Charlotte cleverly repeats the advice: "You do not forbid me to write. . . . You only warn me against the folly of writing for the love of fame, for the selfish excitement of emulation. You kindly allow me to write poetry for its own sake." "I smile," Dickinson comments to Higginson, "when you suggest that I delay 'to publish'—that being foreign to my thought, as Firmament to Fin—If fame belonged to me, I could not escape her—if she did not, the longest day would pass me on the chase—" (L, 2:408). At least, she improved on the original.

When Dickinson writes that delaying to publish is as foreign to her thought as firmament to fin, the pronouncement makes good copy. But did she mean that delaying was "foreign" or that publishing was "foreign" to her thought? By the year 1864, eleven of her poems had appeared in print.[12] Among the poems were "Safe in their Alabaster Chambers" (#216, c. 1861) and "Some keep the Sabbath going to Church" (#324, c. 1860), both of which she included in the dozen submitted to Higginson during the first weeks of their correspondence. (Another poem she sent him was "Success is counted sweetest.") When she saw that he did not regard the poetry as publishable, it was necessary to write her own cover story: "I smile," she said imperiously to him. It was also necessary to continue to believe in herself. She had the example of Southey and Charlotte Brontë, and knew, even if Higginson did not recommend publishing, that she was a poet. "I . . . could not," Dickinson said, "drop the Bells whose jingling cooled my Tramp" (L, 2:408).

In the long run, she was right. Higginson had many chances to say so, but he was a little dense.[13] She made him, he would later admit, feel "clumsy" (L, 2:462). He told her that "you shroud yourself in this fiery mist & I cannot reach you, but only rejoice in the rare sparkles of light." Her reply? " 'Seen of Angels,' scarcely my responsibility" (L, 2:460–61). Samuel Bowles, ribbing her, called her "Queen Recluse." There is no sign that Higginson ever appreciated or perceived that she was affecting a character; he saw only that she hid herself.

She sometimes simply lied. When she was a young woman, in the summer of 1854, she wrote to her friend Abiah Root, of West Springfield: "You asked me to come and see you—I must speak of that. . . . I dont go from home, unless emergency leads me by the hand, and then I do it obstinately, and draw back if I can. Should I ever leave home, which is improbable, I will with much delight, accept your invitation" (L, 1:298–99). Dickinson did not want to see her old friend but did not want to say so; the letter is the last of twenty-two Emily had written her since 1845. The classmates were outgrowing one another: Abiah was soon to be married to a minister; Emily was making new friends. She had been, with Lavinia, to visit Dr. and Mrs. Josiah G. Holland in Springfield for a few days during September 1853, and would go again to the Hollands during the autumn of 1854. An extended visit to Washington and Philadelphia was still to come in February and March 1855, as was one to Middletown, Connecticut, in the fall of 1860. None of them was an emergency. The social lie may not be very serious, but it reminds us that we cannot take everything she wrote as gospel truth, which she would sacrifice for a good phrase or a good pose.[14]

Upon Higginson's having invited her in June 1869 to come to Boston either to hear him read the paper on Greek goddesses for a program at the Woman's Club or to meet with him on some other day when he was not so taken up, she politely thanked him, said she should be glad if he came to Amherst, and added, "but I do not cross my Father's ground to any House or town" (L, 2:460). The statement reads well, is especially quotable, and has been often cited to mark the poet's withdrawal into the confines of the Homestead. Yet three months later, she wrote to Susan Gilbert Dickinson, who was vacationing in Geneva, New York: "Come Home and see your Weather. The Hills are full of Shawls, and I am going every Day to buy myself a Sash." The poet also reported: "I humbly try to fill your place at the Minister's, so faint a competition, it only makes them smile" (L, 2:464). She was, the remarks indicate, still crossing the ground to walk in the hills around Amherst and to visit the J. L. Jenkins family who lived in the manse which was not as far away as Boston, but neither the hills nor the manse would have been listed as Edward Dickinson's property. She did not want to go to Boston, even though Higginson told her "all ladies do." She had already, as a matter of record, refused him twice. What was a lady to say when there wasn't a word for *no?* She made up an excuse—since she was clever, it had some truth in it. She did withdraw more and more into the Dickinson house and garden, although the time at which she withdrew is also not what her father would have called a "fixed fact." Writing to a relative in April of the spring that she died, for instance, the poet referred to "a loved paragraph" in *Romeo and Juliet* which she said "has lain open on my Pillow all winter," and observed "but perhaps Shakespeare has been 'up street' oftener than I have, this Winter" (L, 3:902). What, if anything but a desire to read or be up and about, does the lament mean? Or, when she told Higginson that her father read only "serious" books, did they include the novels of Charles Dickens, his favorite author?

One doesn't know, consequently, when to trust her and when not to trust her in the important correspondence with Higginson. Can one believe she meant it when she told him, also in her letter of June c. 1869, that he was not aware of having saved her life.[15] Was she flattering him? What did he do for her? He answered her letters, he paid compliments, he raised questions, he read the poems she sent to him.

Higginson's third invitation to her to come to Boston began: "Sometimes I take out your letters & verses, dear friend, and when I feel their strange power, it is not strange that I find it hard to write." Then he wrote, "I have the greatest desire to see you, always feeling that perhaps if I could take you by the hand I might be something to you." Given to fictionalizing her, he said, "it is hard to understand how you can live" so alone, "with thoughts of such a [quali]ty coming up in you." She clearly commanded his imagination but not his understanding. He concluded: "Yet it isolates one anywhere to think beyond a certain point or have such luminous flashes as come to you—so perhaps the place does not make much difference" (L, 2:461).

Dickinson's responses indicate principles of an aesthetic, the subtlety of her way of writing, and her confidence in the power of her language. "A Letter," she wrote, "always feels like immortality because it is the mind alone without corporeal friend. Indebted in our talk to attitude and accent, there seems a spectral power in thought that walks alone." Having made clear that the ghostly demarcations of words were gloriously sustaining, she told him her life had been "too simple and stern to embarrass any." Ingenuous as the assertion was, she went on to say honestly that it was difficult "not to be fictitious in so fair a place, but test's severe repairs are permitted all." Then she gave Higginson the insight for which he had asked: "When a little Girl I remember hearing that remarkable passage and preferring the 'Power,' not knowing at the time that 'Kingdom' and 'Glory' were included" (L, 2:460).

Perhaps Higginson was someone she could outwit and thereby prove herself; but, more likely, he was someone with whom she could try out ideas about language and literature, as well as a critic by whom she could measure contemporary taste. The people with whom she maintained the most enduring correspondence, in fact, were readers such as Elizabeth Holland, the Norcross cousins, or Higginson, receptive to exchanges about writers or writing. The poet, for instance, craftily asked Higginson as "her safest friend" to disapprove of her accepting Helen Hunt Jackson's request for something to be published in the "No Name Series," which included fiction as well as poetry. He replied: "It is always hard to judge for another of the bent of inclination or range of talent; but I should not have thought of advising you to write stories, as it would not seem to me to be in your line." He added patronizingly: "Perhaps Mrs. Jackson thought the change & variety might be good for you" (L, 2:562–65). He sent her a photograph of himself. She continued to send poems to him as long as she lived.

III

Singular as she was in the work she undertook, it was characteristic of the poet that she enjoyed—to use an old-fashioned word— converse with men like Higginson important in public life. She did not restrict herself entirely to a narrow circle of acquaintances, nor to romantic encounters. She seems to have taken it for granted that, choosing her words, she could say what she wished and get away with it. She once told Higginson that he asked final questions accidentally.

When the first installment of William Dean Howells's novel *A*

Fearful Responsibility (1881) appeared in the summer issue of *Scribner's Monthly*, she wrote telegraphically to Josiah Holland, the editor: "Doctor—How did you snare Howells? Emily—" The response: "Emily—Case of Bribery—Money did it—Holland—" (L, 3:702). There was an exchange of a few notes between Dickinson and Thomas Niles, of Roberts Brothers, who published the "No Name Series." She sent copies of seven poems to him between 1878 and 1885. He sent her an advance copy of Mathilde Blind's *Life of George Eliot* in 1883 (L, 2:626, and 3:725–26, 768–70, and 886).

After the death of her friend Ben Newton at the age of thirty-two, in 1853, she took the liberty of writing about him to the Reverend Edward Everett Hale, who had not yet become famous for *The Man Without a Country* (1863), but was well known regionally as a participant in political causes and an advocate of "the social gospel." Bishop Frederick D. Huntington, who taught at Harvard, spoke on important occasions in Amherst, and shared the platform with Emerson, remembered Emily Dickinson after her death: "It was long ago that she gave me her confidence and made herself my friend, tho' afterward I scarcely saw her."[16]

When James D. Clark, lawyer, schoolmaster, and businessman, who was a friend of the Reverend Charles Wadsworth, sent a copy of the Philadelphia minister's sermons to Dickinson in 1882, a brief correspondence began between Clark and the poet. Since Clark was ill at the time, the correspondence was taken over by his brother, Charles H. Clark, a member of the New York Stock Exchange, and continued until shortly before Dickinson's death in 1886. She shared reminiscences with the Clarks about Wadsworth, whom she called "My Clergyman." He, like Higginson, visited her twice. (The first visit was probably in 1860, after the death of Wadsworth's mother in 1859; the second, on a summer evening two years before his death in 1880.) She had received, as a gift from a maternal cousin, a copy of one of his sermons in January 1858.[17] One undated formal note from him to the poet survives. There was also, apparently, an exchange between Dickinson and him of at least three letters or notes which the Hollands transmitted in 1877–79.[18] And she seems to be referring to him when she writes in 1877 to Elizabeth Holland, who had recently been in Philadelphia: "The Sermon you failed to hear, I can lend you—though Legerdemain is unconveyed—" (L, 2:572–73).[19]

Writing to another eminent minister, Washington Gladden, in 1882, the poet inquired about the question of immortality. Gladden, editor of *The Independent*, held "modern theological views" that would have been closer to those of Higginson and Holland, who were also liberal theologically, than to Huntington and Wadsworth, who were conservative. If she did not limit her interests to men of one religious party, she also did not limit herself to men of the cloth, even though they were apt to be heedful to women.

She shared the Dickinson family friendship with Samuel Bowles, Sr., whose influential newspaper she read every day; and, in her later years, she became intimate with Otis Phillips Lord, justice of the Massachusetts Supreme Court. She did not frequent the salons of Paris or belong to the coterie of writers in Boston; she was derisive about her "Backwoodsman ways"; and it was sometimes "still" in Amherst, where she valued solitary hours. She had, nonetheless, a regard for men of consequence and sought opportunities to know them. She was not lacking in aplomb or the charm to hold her own in exchanges with them. These various exchanges, furthermore, may have given her ideas for poems on religious or other matters, but because of incomplete evidence there are few connections that can be substantiated. She was not, however, so much isolated from "the world" as legend would stress; "nor was her work, in her thought of it, eternally sealed."[20]

IV

The matrix experience of Dickinson's "womanly" life is believed to have been a romantic one, for which readers cite the famous "Master" letters in rough draft detailing disappointment and hurt, emotional turmoil and rejection. The order of their composition has been uncertain until recently, when R. W. Franklin settled on the dates of the spring of 1858, early 1861, and the summer of 1861. Although it is not known to whom—if to anyone—she sent fair copies, the first is addressed "Dear Master," the second is without salutation, and the third begins curtly with "Master." The style is metaphorical and ambiguous. In the first, written in springtime, Dickinson grieves that the man has been ill and says she herself is ill ("this pain denies me"); she talks of her poems as disobedient "flowers," whose meaning he seems not to know how to read; she wishes she were great, "like Mr. Michael Angelo, and could paint" for the correspondent. In the next, three years later, she is anxious to know that she has not offended him, admits a love "so big it scares her," tells him she "never flinched thro' that awful parting—

but held her life so tight he should not see the wound," and begs him to come to her or let her seek him. She repeats, in the last, that she is wounded but knows the Master has altered her, wonders if he could forget her in "fight, or flight—or the foreign land," says she has waited for him a long time, "can wait more," and wants to see him: could he, she asks, "come to New England—(this summer)," "to Amherst," because it "were comfort forever—just to look" in his face.[21]

Judgment varies from the view that she suffered a crisis so grave that she collapsed psychologically to the view that the writing of the letters was the means by which she "came to terms with the turbulent experience." In the opinion of Richard Sewall, "probably no poem she wrote after the experience recorded in the three letters was entirely unrelated to it. After it, she had to go somewhere or perish."[22] She had, simply, to go it alone, but she had abundant resources in the quest for personal and poetic autonomy.

Having "stayed out" during a visit Samuel Bowles made in October 1861 to the Dickinsons, she explained: "something troubled me—and I knew you needed light and air—so I did'nt come"; and, since he had been ill, she wrote again to him in early December, "The hallowing—of pain—makes one afraid to convalesce—because they differ—wide—as Engines—and Madonnas"; then, she added, "The Cages—do not suit the Swiss—well as steeper air," and "I think the Father's Birds do not all carol at a time—to prove the *cost* of *Music*—not doubting at the last each Wren shall bear it's 'Palm' " (L, 2:382–83). The poet's sleight-of-hand in her letters and our sense of her ability to expend herself in words constitute a dilemma which the urge for narratives cannot resolve. We consequently say more than we can prove.

Emily Dickinson's psychological resilience in coping with her own and others' suffering, the work at home, pursuit of varied interests, and quick changes of point of view or mood cast doubt on the importance that has been given to the "Master" letters among hundreds. An unhappy, even a traumatic and educative, experience in love does not necessarily remain a constant in a busy life. The failure of a romance can determine that one does not marry; but spinsterhood—less than marriage itself—does not determine everything that a woman does or all the ways in which she endures and grows into self-possession. The letters, in the perspective of years and the contingencies of being a Dickinson, document an episode that may indeed have altered without disorienting a poet whose character was stronger than memory itself. Writing, probably in the summer of 1883, to a faithful friend, Elizabeth Holland, about a woman who had "been much in our family, assisting in many crises," Dickinson commented "and was it not crisis all the time in our hurrying Home?" (L, 3:782). She was, according to Austin, who saved the drafts of the "Master" letters, in love more than once.[23]

There is no other extant correspondence pointing to romantic love with anyone except Otis Lord, old-fashioned, widowed, eighteen years Emily Dickinson's senior, and eminent jurist of Salem, Massachusetts. He had been her father's closest friend and had become a counselor of the family after the death of Edward Dickinson in 1874. Lord saw to it that Mrs. Dickinson and the daughters drew up a will; he dined at the house of Austin and Susan Dickinson; he visited all of them, especially the poet, with increasing frequency after the death of Mrs. Lord in 1877.

There is a letter in rough draft, written by the poet to Lord about 1878, that states unequivocally: "I confess that I love him—I rejoice that I love him."[24] Although none of Lord's letters to her survives, he was a man of forensic talent and was known for "terse, vigorous expression." Dickinson's letters to him imply that she took his appreciation of "style" for granted and sound as if they anticipate a poet's biography.

She adapted Antony's manner of addressing Cleopatra as "Egypt" in Shakespeare's drama and wrote: "My lovely Salem smiles at me. I seek his Face so often—but I have done with guises." She called herself "his Amherst." Figures of speech using the conventions of adversary proceedings in courtship or the idolatry of love, and even verbs ("curbed" and "crush"), also suggest that she took a correspondence course from the playwright. "I had never tried any case," she wrote to Lord, "in your presence but my own, and . . . with your sweet assistance—I was murmurless." Or "Dont you know you have taken my will away and 'I know not where' you 'have laid' it? Should I have curbed you sooner? . . . Oh, my too beloved, save me from the idolatry which would crush us both—" (L, 2:614 and 616). He gave her the *Complete Concordance of Shakespeare* for Christmas in 1880. She feared, she said in one letter to him, that "Language was done between us" (L, 3:664).

She obviously enjoyed writing to him: "The Air is soft as Italy, but when it touches me, I spurn it with a Sigh, because it is not you" (L, 3:728). As he took on heroic proportions, she matched them: "The trespass of my rustic Love upon your Realms of Ermine, only a Sovereign could forgive—I never knelt to other".[25] She continued: "The Spirit never twice alike, but every time another—that other more divine. Oh, had I found it sooner! Yet Tenderness has not a Date—it comes—and overwhelms" (L, 3:728).

He apparently proposed marriage as early as 1878, but she refused: she was, with her sister, nursing their invalid mother at the time, but she did not give that as a reason. "Dont you know," she told him, "you are happiest while I withold . . . dont you know that 'No' is the wildest word we consign to Language?" (L, 2:617). She teased him; she called him "my blissful Sophist"; she observed that he had "a good deal of glee" in his "nature's corners." She worried that she had been too frank with him; she said she spoke to him as she felt "without the dress of Spirit"; she reported the death of "My Philadelphia" (Wadsworth) along with mention of the death of Emerson, and recollected Ben Newton, who taught her "Emerson's name"; she alluded to Darwin or to legal cases over which Lord presided; and she told him anecdotes. He wrote to Lavinia to express concern over "Emily's health" and her unselfish devotion to duty.[26]

Lord suffered a stroke on May 1, 1882 but recovered remarkably within a few days and completed the work of the court for that year.[27] She broached the question of marriage not long after the death of her mother on November 14, 1882. Writing that "a Night is so long, and it snowing too, another barrier to Hearts that overleap themselves," the poet jumps from the Shakespearean trope to one of the venerable judge's affectionate names for her to a change of name: "Emily 'Jumbo'! Sweetest name, but I know a sweeter— Emily Jumbo Lord. Have I your approval?" (L, 3:747). It was Lord who appears to have warned that time was against him, because she wrote, "You said with loved timidity in asking me to your dear Home, you would 'try not to make it unpleasant,' " and observed, "You even call me to your Breast with apology! Of what must my poor Heart be made?" She knew how to worry about the man she cared for: "I hope you wear your Furs today. Those and the love of me, will keep you sweetly warm, though the Day is bitter. The love I feel for you, I mean, your own for me a treasure I still keep" (L, 3:753).

He made his last visit to see her in September 1883. There are also two fragments of her correspondence that editors date about 1883. One of them is ambiguous in relation to events about which we have to guess; but the imagery is sexual: "The withdrawal of the Fuel of Rapture does not withdraw the Rapture itself. Like Powder in a Drawer, we pass it with a Prayer, it's Thunders only dormant" (L, 3:786). The other is simple and clear: "I feel like wasting my Cheek on your Hand tonight—Will you accept (approve) the squander— Lay up Treasures immediately—that's the best Anodyne for moth and Rust" (L, 3:786).

Writing about 1883 to her niece, Martha Dickinson, and a visiting friend who would have been seventeen, the poet said she hoped they were having superb times and was sure they were, for she heard their voices "mad and sweet—as a Mob of Bobolinks." She sent the girls her light-hearted advice:

> If ever the World should frown on you—he is old you know—give him a Kiss, and that will disarm him—if it dont—tell him from me,
>
>> Who has not found the heaven—below—
>> Will fail of it above—
>> For Angels rent the House next our's,
>> Wherever we remove—
>>
>> (L, 3:787)

That mood was again soon shattered. Emily Dickinson herself was ill from October 1883 to January 1884, following the sudden death from typhoid fever of Austin and Susan's youngest child, Gilbert, a death that devastated the whole family. Lord died on March 13, 1884, after a stroke two days earlier. Writing in February 1885, to Benjamin Kimball, Esquire, a cousin of Lord and executor of his estate, she noted: "On my way to sleep, last night, I paused at the Portrait. Had I not loved it, I had feared it, the Face had such ascension" (L, 3:860). She said (in other words) the same of her father. She was usually at ease with "old River Gods."

The love Emily Dickinson experienced and expressed for Otis Lord, who apparently reciprocated it, is commensurate with her work. Realizing the depths of their feeling for one another, she thought the happiness at first "an improbable." But the allusive and dramatic language which may seem almost affectation is characteristic of Dickinson's way of living through literature, while the genuine experience denies that she was fearful of her own emotions or incapable of mature friendship and passion. Whatever the vicissitudes of the poet's adult life, few men that she met were her equal. The correspondence with Lord is a coherent passage for measuring the development of a nineteenth-century scribbling woman who was able to hold together the strains of a "hurrying" existence at home and the freedom of a literary imagination.

She was aware of the discrepancies between the public and private lives of the Dickinson men in whose pride and pain she took a sympathetic part. She matched the courage of the men she sustained; she kept herself intact, relatively undiminished and generous, at considerable cost. It was no small achievement. The events of the poet's "private" life are otherwise less sensational and more commonplace than her guises and fictions, initiated in the letters to Higginson but perpetuated by the continuing interest in the biography because of the imaginative work.[28]

3

The Prickly Art of Reading Emily Dickinson: The Terror Since September

I

When Emily Dickinson wrote on April 25, 1862, "I had a terror since September—I could tell to none—and so I sing as the Boy does by the Burying Ground—because I am afraid" (L, 2:404), she could not have known the speculation that the word *terror* would provoke. She was replying to questions from Thomas Wentworth Higginson, to whom she had sent four poems for criticism ten days earlier. Having succeeded in piquing his curiosity, she not only pretended that she had written very little before the winter of 1861–62 but implied that she found her voice after she began to be afraid and sent four additional poems. Although she was thirty-two at the time, she refused to tell him her age and posed as a naïf: she had gone to school but had no education; her mother did not care for thought; her father bought her books but begged her not read them for fear they joggled the mind; she wanted instruction and encouragement. Calculated as it was to interest Higginson in the poetry, the cryptic advertisement for herself became the stuff of legend. And while we can discount as hyperbole what she said, for example, about having written little before the winter and having no education, almost no one doubts that there was a crisis—a terror we cannot forget in our readings of Dickinson the poet.

The terror, if we follow one reading of the life and work, is expressed in anxieties about madness, a tendency toward madness, or actual madness. Important critics, studying relationships between the biography, selected poems, and the historical situation of woman as writer in the nineteenth century, have often been susceptible to the image of Emily Dickinson as a heroine in a Gothic house of fiction.[1] There is an immoderate irony in the predisposition that depicts the first woman to become a great American poet as half-cracked, a mad woman in a bedroom, or a reclusive spider sewing flimsy webs of verse in which readers are all entangled.

An oversimplified outline of Emily Dickinson's life begins with an image of a high-spirited and lively young girl who enjoyed "giving three cheers for American Independence!" when her friend Susan Gilbert outwitted relatives in order to do as she pleased (L, 1:233). Young womanhood, it is said, ended for the poet in the "violent and turbulent emotion of the year of 'terror,' " beginning in the fall of 1861. The most common explanation of the terror is that she was disappointed in love.

The story is familiar. She put on white, renounced "life," and wrote her heart out. The drafts of the love letters to an unidentified "Master" reveal that she was rejected and indicate clearly that she was hurt. She writes, in early 1861, that she suffers from "a Tomahawk" in her side but "that dont hurt" her "much"; "Her Master stabs her more." Then, in the summer of 1861, she compares herself to a "Bird" hit by a bullet, tells the "Master" "I used to think when I died—I could see you—so I died as fast as I could," and asks "What would you do with me if I came 'in white'? Have you a little chest—to put the alive—in?"[2] Whether the poet was dead or alive, she had not yet put on "white." And the identity of the man is still uncertain.

The most frequently accepted nominee is the scholarly Reverend Charles Wadsworth, whose work as pastor of Presbyterian churches in Philadelphia and San Francisco has been surpassed by his part in the poet's life.[3] "It is," Dickinson wrote to Wadsworth's friends after his death in 1882, "almost an apparitional joy to hear him cherished now. . . . The Griefs of which you speak were unknown to me, though I knew him [to be] a 'Man of sorrow.' " She must have thought he knew her better than she knew him; she volunteered, "with the exception of my Sister," he was "my dearest earthly friend, though the great confidences of Life are first disclosed by their departure—" (L, 3:744, 764). Further comments in her letters verify that the minister came to comfort rather than to hurt or betray, came to counsel rather than to wound. The poet remembered him as "a Balm," and although she speaks of an "intimacy of many years with the beloved Clergyman" (L, 3:737), there is no indication that he was other than an understanding friend. The story of Wadsworth as "that man" is attributed to Susan Gilbert Dickinson.[4]

Lavinia Dickinson is said to have told a different story, in which George Gould is the man who didn't marry the young poet because her father disapproved.[5] Gould was among her friends with literary ambitions during student days at Amherst College, is known to have spoken critically of Squire Dickinson, became a Presbyterian minister, was not married until October 15, 1862, and said after the poet's death that he "had quite a cherished batch" of her letters "kept sacredly in a small trunk" which had been lost.[6]

There are, however, several other persons who have been seriously proposed for the honor of spurning Emily Dickinson, or being unavailable to her. Among them are: Major Edward B. Hunt,[7] who was married to Helen Fiske (later Jackson), was a scientist and engineer killed in an explosion preceding the test of a rocket he had designed in 1863, and who, the poet once said, had interested her more than any man she ever saw (L, 2:475); Samuel Bowles, Sr.,[8] frequent guest of all the Dickinsons, and the recipient—along with his wife—of nearly fifty poems and many letters from the poet, for whom he transmitted letters to someone confusingly identified as "Austin" in the winter of 1861 and spring of 1862; and Otis Lord,[9] whom she had known since childhood as her father's friend, and with whom it is argued she was in love long before the death of his wife in 1877 and his later romantic interest in the poet. Since, like Wadsworth, these men were married, it is taken for granted that it would have been a "terror" for a young woman to have fallen in love with any one of them.

An alternate theory is that Emily was a lesbian, suffering intense attachments to women, and painful rejections by the two she most loved: Susan Gilbert Dickinson and Sue's friend Kate Scott Turner (later Anthon), a widow, who paid a long visit to Amherst in 1859.[10] At least one psychoanalytic study argues that Austin Dickinson was the poet's "love object," constituting "a means" whereby she was "allowed . . . a vicarious and innocent outlet for her desire that young women be her own sexual objects."[11] It remains for scholars to argue that she was in love with her sister, Lavinia, and her sister's fiancé, Joseph Lyman, who went South and married neither of them.

Emily Dickinson, in fact, was the idealized subject of a Gothic sketch that Lyman left among papers which also included a few passages he had copied from what he described as her "long and beautiful letters." The undated sketch is titled "EMILY," with the subtitle "Things are not what they seem" and "Night in Midsummer":

> A library dimly lighted, three mignonettes on a little stand. Enter a spirit so draped as to be misty[,] face moist, translucent alabaster, forehead firmer as of statuary marble. Eyes once bright hazel now melted & fused so as to be two dreamy, wondering wells of expression, eyes that see no forms but gla[n]ce swiftly to the core of all thi[n]gs—hands small, firm, deft but utterly emancipated from all claspings of perishable things, very firm strong little hands absolutely under control of the brain, types of quite rugged health[,] mouth made for nothing & used for nothing but uttering choice speech, rare thoughts, glittering, starry misty figures, winged words.[12]

Lyman, writing under the influence of Edgar Allan Poe's story "Ligeia," with a heroine who is the embodiment of will and intellectual prowess, may tell us more about himself and the nineteenth-century imagination than about Emily Dickinson; but whatever the limitations of Lyman's sketch, the phrases describing her "very firm strong little hands absolutely under control of the brain, types of rugged health" are useful counters to the images of a woman who was mentally ill and those from Poe's fiction that Higginson conjures up when he writes of her. Following her death, he noted in his diary: "To Amherst to the funeral of that rare & strange creature Emily Dickinson. The country exquisite, day perfect, & an atmosphere of its own, fine and strange about the whole house & grounds—a more saintly & elevated 'House of Usher.' "[13] And there are what Poe would have called emanations from "The House of Usher" in Higginson's private view of "my partially cracked poetess." After his visit to Amherst in 1873, he wrote on December 9 to his sisters:

> I saw my eccentric poetess Miss Emily Dickinson who *never* goes outside her father's grounds & sees only me & a few others. She says, "there is always one thing to be grateful for—that one is oneself & not somebody else["] but Mary

[Mrs. Higginson] thinks this is singularly out of place in E. D.'s case. She (E. D.) glided in, in white, bearing a Daphne odora for me, & said under her breath "How long are you going to stay." I am afraid Mary's other remark "Oh why do the insane so cling to you?" still holds. I will read you some of her poems when you come.[14]

II

In addition to the character sketches and post-Gothic theories, there are the poems. One of them, "I felt a Funeral, in my Brain," has been especially important—crucial—in the psychobiography of the poet. Because the poem is in a dramatic voice identified only as "I" who recounts an experience that is emotionally overwhelming, it is cited as indisputable proof of the poet's psychosis.[15] In view of the use of the poem as a document in a case history, it is tempting to believe Dickinson anticipated that fashion in criticism. She recognized, at least, the common desire to read works of the imagination, especially those written in first-person singular, as if they were an account of the author's life. Having assumed the personal voice in tones that are assured and conclusive, she warned Higginson in July 1862: "When I state myself, as the Representative of the Verse—it does not mean—me—but a supposed person" (L, 2:412). It is easy, when there are questions about the reliability of the poet's statements to him, to ignore the caveat. Isn't the syntax unclear? Does Dickinson mean that the "I" of the poem is "a supposed person" or that she is stating herself as "a supposed person"?

The possibility that she depicts the impact of an actual funeral on a "supposed person," any grief-stricken person, is almost too simple, even when the grammatical order of the first line of the poem encourages one to consider a movement from the world out there to the images within the mind that responds to it. We should not raise routine epistemological questions; the poem is a metaphysical conceit, isn't it? Or is it?

> I felt a Funeral, in my Brain,
> And Mourners to and fro
> Kept treading—treading—till it seemed
> That Sense was breaking through—

And when they were all seated,
A Service, like a Drum—
Kept beating—beating—till I thought
My Mind was going numb—

And then I heard them lift a Box
And creak against my Soul
With those same Boots of Lead, again,
Then Space—began to toll,

As all the Heavens were a Bell,
And Being, but an Ear,
And I, and Silence, some strange Race
Wrecked, solitary, here—

And then a Plank in Reason, broke
And I dropped down, and down—
And hit a World, at every *plunge,
And †Finished knowing—then—
                              (#280, c. 1862)[16]

*Crash
†Got through

   Assuming that the poem is autobiographical, for instance, Theodora Ward comments that "at the climax of a desperate condition, it seemed to her [the poet] she had actually died. With the horror of finding that her last hold on reality had given way, she was plunged into the merciful void of unconsciousness, where contact with the roots of being might once more be found."[17] Reading a letter written by Emily Dickinson in early August 1884, twenty-three years after the year 1861, which is the approximate date assigned by Johnson for "I felt a Funeral, in my Brain," we may be surprised to find the following:

Dear Cousins [Louise and Frances Norcross]. . . .

Eight Saturday noons ago, I was making a loaf cake . . . when I saw a great darkness coming and knew no more until late at night. I woke to find Austin and Vinnie and a strange physician bending over me, and supposed I was dying or had died, all was so kind and hallowed. I had fainted and lain unconscious for the first time in my life. Then I grew very sick and gave the others much alarm, but am now staying.

> The doctor calls it "revenge of the nerves"; but who but
> Death has wronged them? (L, 3:826–27)

One letter does not make a thesis; nor does one poem. But the letter opens a window in that house of Gothic fiction where the ghost of Emily Dickinson lives. Whatever terror she suffered during the autumn of 1861, the "plank" in consciousness did not break. And perhaps Johnson's error in dating the poem, "I felt a Funeral, in my Brain," c. 1861 is an honest one, since the more accurate date, c. 1862, determined by R. W. Franklin, would make little difference in consideration of the poem as a record of collapse, had one occurred the year before. The revised date is, nonetheless, apposite in reconsidering the likely genesis of the poem and for relocating it in relation to events she shared with close friends, relatives, and the people of Amherst during the American Civil War.

The change in the dating of the poem not only enables us to explore these connections but also the view that its source is the poet's "mental abberation" and "gradual conquest by madness."[18] The connections, moreover, cast doubt on a reading of "I felt a Funeral, in my Brain" as an example of her "withdrawal into language." Extending the view that Dickinson was reclusive and "divorced from society," one critic holds that she was also estranged from outer reality and wrote in a "void of solipsism"; words became, consequently, "more important to her than social experience." In "I felt a Funeral," then, he sees "language in the act of displacing reality" along with "the subject matter of instability and disintegration." The poem's surreal images ("Then Space— began to toll," et cetera) stand as hermetic or enclosed discourse that is said to be typical of most of Dickinson's poetry, which is both "pathogenic" and "autogenic."[19]

It is unusual—because there are almost no breaks in the continuity of documents—that there is sufficient evidence for ascertaining probable sources of the imagery and affective power of a poem given as much weight as "I felt a Funeral" in Dickinson studies. It is, in part, because the poem may be a response to the realities of the Civil War that we can recover the surroundings in which I think the poem belongs. There are a few "war" poems that have been long recognized, particularly by Thomas W. Ford, although the view that Dickinson remained "aloof" from the stirring events of her time, especially the war, prevailed until Shira Wolosky's recent examination of the impact of the crisis on the work of the poet.[20]

When Dickinson wrote to Higginson in 1863 that war felt to her "an oblique place" (L, 2:423), she was accurately situating herself in relation to soldiers in battle. Or asking, in the spring of 1861, "When did the war really begin?" (L, 2:376), she had been discussing experiences of young women, particularly George Sand and Elizabeth Barrett, as victims of tyrannies and restraints that she associated with the issues of the national conflict over the enslavement of Blacks. Among the excerpts that her cousins Louise and Frances Norcross copied from her letters of the same spring or summer, we find: ". . . Think Emily lost her wits—but she found em, likely. Don't part with wits long at a time in this neighborhood" (L, 2:376). The humor directed against herself and the rapier remarks about the war show the same discernment and characteristic Dickinsonian refusal to accept cant or superficial explanations of actualities. She might, because she knew also that humankind cannot bear too much reality, tell the truth "slant," as she advised in one of her poems (#1129, c. 1868); she might pose, as her brother testified; but she found her style in the search for language that expressed a sense of actualities. She did not dodge them. "When she asserts that she 'sang off charnel steps,' " as Wolosky says, Dickinson "is only being literal."[21]

On December 31, 1861, she reported to Louise Norcross that "Frazer [sic] Stearns is just leaving Annapolis. His father has gone to see him today." (Young Stearns was the son of the president of the college at which the poet's father was treasurer.) Her letter concluded: "I hope that ruddy face won't be brought home frozen" (L, 2:386). Frazar Stearns, a lieutenant in the Pittsfield company of the Twenty-first Massachusetts regiment, and the first Amherst man to lose his life in combat, died March 14, 1862. The event was especially shocking to all who knew him (L, 2:400).

Writing in late March to the Norcross cousins, the poet tells them of "brave Frazer—'killed at Newbern,' . . . his big heart shot away by a 'minie ball.' " She reports, almost objectively, "Just as he fell, in his soldier's cap, with his sword at the side, Frazer rode through Amherst. Classmates to the right of him, and classmates to the left of him, to guard his narrow face!" She abandons the martial rhythms as she recounts the circumstances of Stearns's death and its impact on those who knew him:

> He fell by the side of Professor Clark, his superior officer—
> lived ten minutes in a soldier's arms, asked twice for water—
> murmured just, "My God!" and passed! Sanderson, his class-
> mate, made a box of boards in the night, put the brave boy
> in, covered with a blanket, rowed six miles to reach the
> boat,—so poor Frazer came.... He went to sleep from the
> village church. Crowds came to tell him goodnight, choirs
> sang to him, pastors told how brave he was—early soldier
> heart. And the family bowed their heads, as the reeds the
> wind shakes.

She even explains, without giving a reason, that the doctor
would not allow anyone, including the soldier's father, to look on
him. "So our part in Frazer is done."[22] The restraint with which she
conveys the details of the news is matched by her understanding
that the cousins will mourn the death of their friend: "you must
come next summer, and we will mind ourselves of this young
crusader—too brave that he could fear to die. We will play his
tunes...; we will try to comfort his broken-hearted Ella, who, as
the clergyman said, 'gave him peculiar confidence.' " There is then
a break in the letter, and Dickinson says of her brother in one lone
sentence: "Austin is stunned completely" (L, 2:397–98).
She also writes in late March to their friend Samuel Bowles that

> Austin is chilled—by Frazer's murder—He says—his Brain
> keeps saying over "Frazer is killed"—"Frazer is killed," just
> as Father told it—to Him. Two or three words of lead—that
> dropped so deep, they keep weighing—
> Tell Austin—how to get over them!
>
> (L, 2:399)

Bowles, who had not been well for the past year, wrote to Austin
and Susan: "and then the news from Newbern took all the remaining life. I did not care for victory, for anything now" (L, 2:400).[23]
"I felt a Funeral, in my Brain" probably has its origins, then, not
in the poet's personal collapse but in her sympathetic and imaginative participation with those she loved in the rites for the ruddy-
faced boy they had all finished knowing. Its "words of lead" belong,
I suggest, to a sequence of four poems that culminate in an elegy
expressing gratitude for the sacrifice he embodied.
On the basis of the letters just cited, another poem, "It dont

sound so terrible—quite as it did" (#426, written about 1862), seems also to have been prompted by the death of Lieutenant Stearns;[24] and while the poem depicts with stringent honesty the ways by which one tries to accustom oneself to "a Funeral in the brain," the poet is also writing out of the sorrow over the death of the young man. She begins the second line by echoing her brother's words, "killed," "killed":

> I run it over—"Dead," Brain, "Dead."
> Put it in Latin—left of my School—
> Seems it dont shriek so—under rule.
>
> Turn it, a little—full in the face
> A Trouble looks bitterest—
> Shift it—just—
> Say "When Tomorrow comes this way—
> I shall have waded down one Day."
>
> I suppose it will interrupt me some
> Till I get accustomed—but then the Tomb
> Like other new Things—shows largest—then—
> And smaller, by Habit—
>
> It's shrewder then
> [to] Put the Thought in advance—a Year—
> How like "a fit"—then—
> Murder—wear!

The soliloquy of a person in the act of mentally distancing oneself from the sudden news of death—"that bleeding beginning that every mourner knows" (L, 3:678)—is in contrast to the dramatic narration by a disturbed witness of a funeral service both without (in the sense of outside) and *within* the brain. Had Emily Dickinson not shared in the community of grief, had she not sympathetically perceived the anguish of those she loved, she might still have written the poems. She was, after all, expert in pain and sorrow. Would the successful poem be any more meaningful if there were a footnote explaining its connection to a war? Furthermore, how can we know if she does not tell us that the poems are "war" poems? Reading "I felt a Funeral, in my Brain" as "a unique and daring statement of a condition of mind near to madness"[25] is in fact an acknowledgment of the power of the poem's disquieting images to convey the magnitude of experience when reason is useless and human knowledge inconsequent. The critics who assume that the origins of the poem's images and events are only in the poet's preoccupation with the self deny the efficacy of imaginative intelligence in transfiguring perceptions of the experiences of others as well as oneself into evocative language. But those critics also deny Emily Dickinson a measure of her humanity. When Whitman, in "Song of Myself," writes "Agonies are one of my changes of garments. / I do not ask the wounded person how he feels, I myself become the wounded person" (11, 844–45), he is stating both a spiritual ideal and a creative principle which Emily Dickinson exemplifies as well as he.

There are at least two other poems that are responses to the "murder" of Frazar Stearns. One of them derives from the account of the young man's "having lived ten minutes in a soldier's arms, asked twice for water—murmured just 'My God!' and passed!" The poem (#566, dated c. 1862 by both Johnson and Franklin) is told from the point of view of a person asked for the water:

> A Dying Tiger—moaned for Drink—
> I *hunted all the Sand—
> I caught the Dripping of a Rock
> And bore it in my Hand—
>
> His Mighty Balls—in death were thick—
> But Searching—I could see
> A Vision on the Retina
> Of Water—and of me—
>
> 'Twas not my blame—who sped too slow
> 'Twas not his blame—who died
> While I was reaching him—
> But 'twas—the fact that He was dead—
> *worried

Since the poem does not describe the tiger as young, fierce, or aggressive, it would be impossible without the poet's letter to know that Emily Dickinson has chosen the tiger with "Mighty" eyes as emblem for the heroic figure of the wounded and dying soldier.[26] At the same time, the poem does not altogether depend on the epistolary account for the meaning with which she invests it. It depends, rather, on the vision of water as a necessity for sustaining life, juxtaposed to the frustration, and the sense of "pure contingency" when the effort to save the life of one dying for water is futile. A glimpse at the beginnings of the poem and an awareness of what she made of the traumas of war are indicative of one of the important entities of Dickinson's verse. She was not—and she said that she was not—always writing primarily about herself.[27] The poem, however, has been read predictably as an allegory of "one of Emily's lovers,"[28] or as the poet's autobiographical recognition of herself "in the dying eyes of the tiger" and her awareness that her life "had passed beyond the point where the power of great instinctual forces could be realized."[29] One of course sees oneself, has a vision "of me," in the death of another, but Dickinson had not passed beyond the point that she was unable to realize with imaginative force the experience of a soldier helpless in easing the death of a comrade. The soldier's words are "supposed."

"He gave away his life" (#567, c. 1862) is, I believe, also inspired by the death of young Stearns. In Dickinson's own arrangement of the poems, it immediately follows "A Dying Tiger—moaned for Drink—" (Franklin, 1:645). It seems therefore to have been completed later than "I felt a Funeral, in my Brain" or "It dont sound so terrible—quite—as it did—," and may well have been written after Otis Lord's Amherst commencement address of July 9, 1862, when he "spoke most feelingly of the death of Frazar Stearns":[30]

> He gave away his Life—
> To Us—Gigantic Sum—
> A trifle—in his own *esteem—
> But magnified—by Fame—
>
> Until it burst the Hearts
> That fancied they could hold—
> When †swift it slipped its limit—
> And on the Heavens—unrolled—
>
> 'Tis Ours—to wince—and weep—
> And wonder—and decay
> By Blossoms ‡gradual process—
> He Chose—Maturity
>
> And §quickening—as we sowed—
> Just obviated Bud—

And when We turned to note the Growth—
Broke—perfect—from the Pod—

*estimate
†quick
‡common
§ripening

Although the poet personally elegizes a "brave boy" who "Chose—
Maturity," the tribute is from the point of view of the common-
weal. The casual phrasing of the opening lines so ironically appropriate to the "valueless" life and the explosive images by which she
expresses the quickening break of that life into perfection finally
resolve "the fact that He was dead." Intimating the Christ-like quality of the sacrifice, the "Gigantic Sum— / A trifle—in his own
esteem— / But magnified—by Fame," the poet nonetheless anticipated the elegiac resolution when she first wrote of him as "this
young crusader—too brave that he could fear to die." And the
poem, giving as it does attention to *us*, unequivocally opens up the
range of Dickinson's intelligence, her regard for others' gallantries,
and her sense of common causes.

Not only do the four poems compose a thematically coherent
group that has not been recognized; but, in contrast to "I felt a
Funeral, in my Brain," about which at least fifty critics have commented, "He gave away his Life—" has been ignored. The reason
for the oversight must be related to the entrenched view that Dickinson, primarily concerned with herself, remained "aloof" from the
war.[31]

Among other responses to the war, I think, there are also "Super-
fluous were the Sun / When Excellence be dead' (#999, c. 1864–66),
an expression of disbelief and loss; and "The first We knew of Him
was Death— / The Second—was—Renown" (#1006, c. 1864–66), an
ironic commentary on the honor that death confers upon one previously unknown. The astute social criticism in "A Sickness of this
World it most occasions / When Best Men die" (#1044, c. 1864–66)
may refer to the death of good soldiers or of Lincoln. Another poem
is clearly a meditation on the president's martyrdom and a tribute
to his greatness: "We learn in the Retreating / How vast an one /
Was recently among us— / A Perished Sun / / Endear in the departure / How doubly more / Than all the Golden presence / It was—
before—" (#1083, c. 1864–66).

There are several poems bearing directly on different aspects of
the war and large issues related to it. In the set of work dated about

1864–66, for instance, poem #1082 immediately preceding the tribute to Lincoln as "A Perished Sun" is on the themes of revolution and liberty, for which the poet tries out metaphors of a common garden variety. "Revolution," she writes, "is the Pod / Systems rattle from / When the Winds of Will are stirred / Excellent is Bloom." Who would expect such a pronouncement from Emily Dickinson?[32] The slant rhyme of the first stanza, the tense phrasing, and the break in the poem's continuity when she introduces the question of liberty, confirm that the verse is hers: "But except its Russet Base / Every summer be / The Entomber of itself, / So of Liberty—" After the break, one sees that the figure of pod for revolution—even with the "Russet Base"—was not completely adequate. There is, the poem indicates, a chance that the seed pod will be "Left inactive on the Stalk / All its Purple Fled." And so, the equation changes to one that stipulates the need for revolutionary movement: "Revolution," she concludes, shakes the pod for "Test if it be dead."

In an earlier poem, Dickinson considers whether or not it is appropriate for a mother to feel pride ("Imperial Conduct") in Paradise, but concludes that she may legitimately be proud of an "only Boy" killed in the action at Balls Bluff on the Potomac in October 1861: "even in the sky . . . Bravoes— / Perpetual go abroad / For Braveries . . . in Scarlet Maryland—" (#596, c. 1862). Another poem, "My Portion is Defeat—today" (#639, c. 1862), takes the point of view of a survivor of an unspecified battle that has been lost and speaks for any soldier who believes in the cause for which he "would have been content to die."[33]

The poet also writes a hauntingly beautiful tribute (#409, c. 1862) to the soldiers who "dropped like Flakes— / . . . like Stars— / Like Petals from a Rose— / When suddenly across the June / A wind with fingers—goes— / / They perished in the Seamless Grass— / No Eye could find the place."[34] Since she does not name the battle from which she is by necessity distanced, we must surmise that she is responding to the reports of heavy loss of life in the first battle near Manassas junction (July 1861), or the indecisive second major engagement of the war at bloody Shiloh (April 1862), or the thousands killed in the Battle of Malvern Hill, which marked the end of General George B. McClellan's unsuccessful peninsula campaign (July 1862).[35] Although the poet does not cite the specific battle or the death count, she has seen bulletins from the war and the inevitable casualty list, as the language of the closing lines makes clear: "But God can summon Every face / On his Repealless—List." The finality of the "Repealless List" that only God has the legal power to summon—"such the law," in Melville's ironic phrase—is both disquieting and assuasive.[36] The lack of geographical or historical references in "They dropped like Flakes," by comparison with mention of the Potomac or "Scarlet Maryland," however, does not justify the conclusion that there is no history in the poem. It is a history of any war.

If Dickinson gave voice to those who survived, paid tribute to the victims, and clearly remembered a mother whose only son was killed in action (". . . proud in Apparition— / That Woman and her Boy / Pass back and forth, before My Brain / As even in the sky— / . . . Bravoes— / Perpetual go abroad / For Braveries"), did the poet forget the young woman, Stearns's "broken-hearted Ella, who 'gave him peculiar confidence' "?

The records are blank with regard to her, as they often are for women whose men are killed in wars. Yet we know that one of Dickinson's Norcross cousins came for a month's visit from June 10 to shortly after July 10, 1862, and the other cousin was there also for commencement on the latter date. The poet had written to them in May that she was still "hopeless and scared," and regarded commencement "as some vast anthropic bear, ordained to eat me up" (L, 2:410–11 and 407). She had reported to Higginson that she was ill in late April, but wrote to Samuel Bowles, who was abroad, in early summer that "we did not die—here—We did not change. We have the Guests we did, except for yourself" (L, 2:404 and 410). She joked, in an August letter to Bowles, that when he got home "next Winter," he would find both "Vinnie and Sue, have gone to the War," but, observing seriously that "It is easier to look behind at pain, than to see it coming," she then ridiculed the women of the household, including herself, by reporting that "A Soldier called— a Morning ago, and asked for a Nosegay, to take to Battle. I suppose he thought we kept an Aquarium" (L, 2:416). Men fought, women wept. When husbands and fiancés were killed, women endured the casualities and, like Ella, whom "we will try to comfort," had scant memorial. Is it possible, with almost no evidence but the poem, that "I tie my Hat—I crease my Shawl— / Life's little duties do— precisely— / As the very least / Were infinite to me—" (#443, c. 1862) expresses the reaction of the woman bereft?

The poem is among those in Dickinson's fascicle 24 that includes "When I was small, a Woman died—" as well as "It feels a shame to be Alive— / When Men so brave are Dead" and "Unto my Books—so good to turn— / Far ends of Homely Days" with the lines "It may be Wilderness—without— / Far feet of failing Men—" (#604, c. 1862).

The woman who does life's little duties is aware of the ironies she faces:

> I put new Blossoms in the Glass—
> And throw the old—away—
> I push a petal from my Gown
> That anchored there—I weigh
> The time 'twill be till six o'clock
> So much I have to do—

Fragile flowers are little comfort. The deliberately slow action, the heaviness, and the weariness belong to the burden of mourning; the void after great loss leaves one still with "much to do."

> And yet—Existence—some way back—
> Stopped—Struck—my ticking—through—
> We cannot put Ourself away
> As Completed Man
> Or Woman—When the Errand's done
> We came to Flesh—upon—
> There may be—Miles on Miles of Nought—
> Of Action—sicker far—

If she thinks the reason for living is "finished," she can only anticipate a meaningless existence, but she must pretend, she must think of others, she must continue:

> To simulate—is stinging work—
> To Cover what we are
> From Science—and from Surgery—
> Too Telescopic Eyes
> To bear on us unshaded—
> For their—sake—not for Ours—

It is from a stoic selflessness that she draws the strength and resolve to go on:

> Therefore—we do life's labor—
> Though life's Reward—be done—

> With Scrupulous Exactness—
> To hold our Senses—on—

It has been inevitable that readers would interpret the monologue as another item in the poet's autobiography following her report of a terror in the fall of 1861 that she said, in the letter to Higginson, she could tell to none. During 1862, however, she did not keep from those close to her that she could not carry on with "stinging work." She was, for instance, ill again in November of that year, wrote to Samuel Bowles that she lacked the art of "recovering our Health," said "Do not yet work," and did not see him later in the month when he visited Amherst (L, 2:418–19).

In February 1863, having read in the newspaper that Higginson had joined the army, she wrote to him: "I trust you may pass the limit of War, and though not reared to prayer—when service is had in Church, for Our Arms, I include yourself." She could not avoid anxieties about the risk he was taking and said awkwardly: "Should you, before this reaches you, experience immortality, who will inform me of the Exchange? Could you, with honor, avoid Death, I entreat you—Sir—It would bereave." When he wrote in early summer of 1864 that he had been wounded, she sent a moving and beautiful verse (#829): "The only News I know / Is Bulletins all day / From Immortality" (L, 2:423–24 and 431). There were, it is safe to say, funerals in many brains, even those for whom war was "an oblique place."

A less familiar poem (#582, c. 1862) recalls "I felt a Funeral, in my Brain," not because the mood or the point of view is similar but because the observant author mediates between the external events and their impact on the perceiver of them. The lyric poem's theme, the awareness of the solemnity, the piercing quality of "Things too gay," also evokes the sense of foreboding in the pageantry and fanfare with which soldiers went off to war once upon a time.

> Inconceivably solemn!
> Things *so gay
> Pierce—by the very Press
> Of Imagery—
>
> Their far Parades—†order on the eye
> With a mute Pomp—
> A Pleading Pageantry—

Flags are a brave sight—
But no true Eye
Ever went by One—
Steadily.

Music's triumphant—
But ‡the fine Ear
§Winces with delight
The Drums ‖too near

*too
†halt
‡a
§aches
‖to hear

Like many of Dickinson's poems, those that record her responses to the Civil War cannot always be identified in relation to the sources which moved her to write them. She was no Melville composing *Battle-Pieces* primarily from printed accounts which he "unified more by determination than by art,"[37] although she followed the course of the war in the newspapers. Nor was she a wound-dresser like Whitman, bemoaning in the voice of experience "the real war that never gets in books," although she writes in another verse that takes its figure from a battle in the American Revolution: "But that solemn War / Could you comprehend it / You would chastened stare—" (#1174, c. 1870).

Stating herself as the representative of her verse, she frequently heard with a fine ear the drum-taps "too near" and gave voice to the woes they signified. When she did not state herself as the representative of the verse but mediated between "Time's Affairs" and their implications, she was at her best equally powerful. Among the poems assuming the perspective of the observant author is one pertinent to the cause for which many of the victims of the war died.[38] It does not have to be read in its historical context since it is primarily "a last judgment" and carries the authority of profound belief in concepts about which revolutions are fought. But, dated about 1864, it is in fact Emily Dickinson's ironic emanicipation proclamation consonant with the ideal of equity, for which she well understood people give away their lives. It is one of her great poems.

Color—Caste—Denomination—
These—are Time's Affair—

Death's diviner Classifying
Does not know they are—

As in sleep—All Hue forgotten—
Tenets—put behind—
Death's Large—Democratic fingers
Rub away the Brand—

If Circassian—He is careless—
If He put away
Chrysalis of Blonde—or Umber—
Equal Butterfly—

They emerge from his Obscuring—
What Death—knows so well—
Our minuter intuitions—
Deem *implausible—

                              (#970, c. 1864)

*incredible

III

If an approach to Emily Dickinson's own terror by way of her war
poems and her declaration of belief in the radical democracy of
death is circuitous, the purpose has been to substantiate that even
when she experienced personal crises during the years of violent
military struggle the poet neither withdrew into a self-enclosed life
nor protected herself from what she called "the very press of imagery." In a fragment from an undated letter, written probably during late December 1862 to the Norcross cousins, the poet brings
together the public and private worlds to which she is faithfully
attentive. "Sorrow," she comments, "seems more general than it
did, and not the estate of a few persons, since the war began; and if
the anguish of others helped one's own, now would be many medi-
cines." Continuing with a typical Dickinsonian aphorism, " 'Tis
dangerous to value, for only the precious can alarm," she then
observes, "I noticed that Robert Browning had made another
poem, and was astonished—till I remembered that I, myself, in a
smaller way, sang off charnel steps. Every day life feels mightier,
and what we have the power to be, more stupendous" (L, 2:436).[39]
There is no dissociation of the words from the historical moment

here, nor is there any denial of the challenge of living within that moment.

Writing to Mary Bowles in early April 1862, while Samuel Bowles was on an European tour, Dickinson testifies for herself without realizing she is on trial: "when your life gets faint for it's other life—you can lean on us—We wont break. We look very small—but the Reed can carry weight." She then goes on to comment: "Not to see what we love, is very terrible—and talking—does'nt ease it—and nothing does—but just itself" (L, 2:406). After Bowles returned in November, Dickinson asked him whether "The loss by Sickness—was it loss— / Or that Etherial Gain— / You earned by measuring the Grave— / Then—measuring the Sun." The lines are the last stanza of poem 574 (c. 1862) that begins:

> My first well Day—since many ill—
> I asked to go abroad,
> And take the Sunshine in my hands,
> And see the things in Pod—

She wrote again in late November to him and said: "We used to tell each other, when you were from America—how failure in a Battle—were easier—and you here" (L, 2:418 and 420).

She was, without question, vulnerable to mental as well as physical anguish, but, as Richard Sewall points out, it did not prostrate her.[40] In addition to the ordinary allotment of suffering that comes in the course of measuring the grave, Emily Dickinson feared that she was going blind. The fear was not imagined. In September 1863 (L, 2:431), two years after the terror of which she first wrote to Higginson, she again became ill; the problem must have been primarily with her eyes, and it was determined that she would seek medical help. In February 1864, she went to Boston for a preliminary examination by Dr. Henry W. Williams, an ophthalmic surgeon at City Hospital, author of *A Practical Guide to the Study of Diseases of the Eye: Their Medical and Surgical Treatment* (published in 1862), and later professor of ophthalmology at Harvard. On Williams's advice, Dickinson returned to Boston in late April and remained under his care for seven months, until November 28, 1864; after four months at home, it was necessary for her to go back to Boston, where she stayed almost six months for continued treatment: from early April 1865 until October of that year.

During both periods, the Norcross cousins took "sweet care" of her and let her want for nothing. The doctor was not willing that she should read or write, even letters, and "took away" her pen. Yet she circumvented him by using a pencil, worked in her "Prison," made "Guests" for herself, and wrote some poetry, as well as at least a dozen short letters or notes during the first seven months she was away from home. In May 1864, she told her sister, Lavinia, that "the calls at the Doctor's are painful, and . . . I have not looked at Spring." In July she reported, again to Lavinia, that her cousins mend her stockings, she has had a visit and "beautiful flowers" from relatives, but also has "found friends in the Wilderness." Observing that the letter is the longest that she has written since she was sick and that the doctor is enthusiastic about her getting "well," she added "I feel no gayness yet. I suppose I had been discouraged so long." To her sister-in-law, Susan Dickinson, she wrote in September that "The Doctor is very kind—" and spoke of her "long night." And in November there was a note for Lavinia Dickinson, to whom she said, "I have been sick so long I do not know the Sun . . ." (L, 2:430–31 and 433–35).

Allowed after the first seven months in Boston to go home for Thanksgiving, however, she had improved considerably from the time when she reported to Lavinia that "the Doctor says I must tell you . . . I 'cannot yet walk alone.' " At home, she nevertheless wrote in early 1865 to Louise Norcross:

> The eyes are as [when I was?] with you, sometimes easy, sometimes sad. I think they are not worse, nor do I think them better than when I came home.
>
> The snow-light offends them, and the house is bright; not withstanding, they hope some.

She added:

> Mother and Margaret are so kind, father as gentle as he knows how, and Vinnie good to me, but "cannot see why I don't get well." This makes me think I am long sick, and this takes the ache to my eyes. I shall try to stay with them a few weeks more before going to Boston, though what it would be to see you and have the doctor's care—that cannot be told. (L, 2:439)

The poet's resumption of domestic duties following the return home was gradual. For the first few weeks, she said, she "did nothing but comfort" her plants. Then she was able to "chop the chicken livers," "make the yellow [a mix of egg yolks and butter] to the pies," "bang the spices for cake, and knit the soles to the stockings" that she had knitted "the bodies to last June." If she sounds "childlike," as it has been assumed, it is only that she had been reduced to an unusual dependency. She added, with full awareness of how she seemed, "They say I am a 'help' " (L, 2:439).

There is also other significant evidence for the seriousness of the visual difficulty. For instance, she wrote at an unspecified date to Louise Norcross: "This is my letter—an ill and peevish thing, but when my eyes get well I'll send you thoughts like daisies, and sentences could hold the bees . . ." (The rest of the manuscript is destroyed [L, 2:438]). Or, there was an undated note from "Emily" in reply, one can safely guess, to an invitation from her sister-in-law: "Thanks Sue, but not tonight. Further Nights" (L, 2:440). There was a letter to Joseph Lyman, who copied from it the following:

> Some years ago I had a woe, the only one that ever made me tremble. It was a shutting out of all the dearest ones of time, the strongest friends of the soul—BOOKS[.] The medical man said avaunt ye tormentors, he also said, "down, thought, & plunge into her soul." He might as well have said, "Eyes be blind, heart be still." So I had eight months of Siberia.[41]

The poet's confidant, Samuel Bowles, wrote on August 2, 1865, to Austin and Susan Dickinson, "I beg all sweet things for you all, health & happiness for Sue; eyes for Emily." In late September, near the close of the poet's second stay in Boston, Mrs. Charlotte Sewall Eastman presented her with a copy of *Jane Eyre*, perhaps because of Brontë's depiction of the hero's blindness and his eventual recovery of the sight of one eye after receiving the advice of an "eminent oculist in London." And, finally, Mrs. Eastman, writing from Venice, October 21, 1872, asked, "How are your eyes my dear Emily—Your Dr. Williams will soon have his sisters from Rome to visit him."[42] Among the friends of "Dear Emily," then, there was concern for the problem with her "eyes."

In spite of the irrefutable evidence that Dickinson suffered prolonged visual difficulties, there has been more interest in the search for a missing figure in an unhappy love story than inquiry into the relationship between the terror she experienced during September 1861, the only woe that ever made her tremble, the confinement for treatment of her eyes in Boston, and her subsequent behavior. Yet the poet's letters to her sister during the illness appeared in 1894.

When Sewall published the Lyman papers in 1965, however, he observed that the trouble with Dickinson's eyes "provides a more plausible explanation" than earlier speculation about "an old crux."[43] But after the discovery of the letter to Lyman, John Cody's psychiatric analysis of the poet appeared. Hypothesizing that she "had a nervous breakdown" and that she "actually underwent catatonic agonies of psychological disorganization," Cody "attempts to establish the proposition that Emily Dickinson's eye disorder was a psychosomatic affliction," which succeeded "her renounced love affair," although "a grave psychological upheaval was in progress in the poet many years before her eyes began to give her trouble." Stating that we do not know the degree to which the eye affliction had an organic basis, he believes it was "slight," but "whatever physical pathology was present" would have been intensified by "the emotional investment the poet had in her eyes and by her irrational expectation of blindness." Dr. Williams, it is argued then, served primarily as a counselor. While Cody acknowledges that "the evidence for psychogenic disturbance is circumstantial," he concludes that there was no impairment of visual acuity and that "after a period of approximately two years" Dickinson "never had any recurrence of the trouble."[44] The strongest support for Cody's conclusion is from her letter describing a great fire in the early hours of July 4, 1879: "And so much lighter than day was it," she wrote, "that I saw a caterpillar measure a leaf far down the orchard" (L, 2:644).

Cautioning that a retrospective study of a person's medical problems is difficult, Richard Sewall and Martin Wand, an ophthalmologist, undertook an investigation of "the eye problem" They found that Dickinson suffered from "divergent strabismus" or *exotropia*, the medical term for being walleyed. The opinion is based on Dr. Wand's measurement of Dickinson's features in the only known photograph of her, the frequently reprinted daguerreotype taken in 1847 or 1848 when she was seventeen or eighteen years old. The outward sign of the disease is a deviation in the alignment of the

eyes, resulting in an inability of one to attain binocular vision because of an imbalance of the muscle of the eyeball. In the photograph, Dickinson has "a prominent right exotropia of at least 15°, a
high degree of deviation." For most patients with exotropia, according to Wand and Sewall, the onset is close to birth, but "this deviation is often intermittent at the beginning. . . . With time, the deviation becomes more constant, usually first for distant vision, and
later for near vision as well. This progression may be slow; a person
may reach age thirty or later before developing a constant *exotropia*." If the eye disorder was *exotropia*, a "genetic inheritance factor
is involved," and there is evidence, in a family portrait, that there
was a deviation in the alignment of the eyes of Mrs. Dickinson; there
is further evidence in photographs of Lavinia that she also had "a
right exotropia." Giving primary attention to Emily Dickinson, however, Wand and Sewall review the symptoms they think revelant to
the problem: "eye strain, blurring of vision, difficulties with prolonged periods of reading, headaches, and diplopia," as well as in-
variable complaints of photophobia. "It now seems clear" that the
poet's "eye trouble, at least, was physiological."[45]

The analysis, nevertheless, raises some questions, one of which
they point out. Citing the fact that Dr. Williams, in both *A Practical
Guide to the Study of the Diseases of the Eye* and *Recent Advances in
Ophthalmic Surgery* (1866), not only discussed surgery as a benign
treatment for *exotropia* but also warned of the risk in rare excep-
tions of serious injury to the eyeball by inflammation arising subsequent to an operation, they speculate that he might have operated
and imply that there were complications. Such an outcome would
explain "the chronic and debilitating nature" of her problem; but,
they also say, "the only conclusion [they] cannot make with certainty is that Dr. Williams did indeed operate."[46]

Wand and Sewall, moreover, find no evidence that, although
Emily Dickinson often experienced great discomfort from light
(photophobia) and probably strained her eyes, she suffered from
either blurred vision or double vision (diplopia). With regard to
other members of the family, there is nothing but an occasional
report of a "headache" to suggest that Lavinia Dickinson had a
visual handicap. Austin Dickinson, on the other hand, had trouble
with his eyes and saw an oculist in his early twenties (L, 2:150 and
257); their father wore glasses,[47] and Mrs. Dickinson is known to
have had an eye problem that concerned her family. The daughter

wrote in mid-May of 1865 from Boston: "I hope Mother is better, and will be careful of her Eye. The Doctor says it must heal while Warm Weather lasts, or it will be troublesome" (L, 2:442).

Because of the lack of medical records, as well as differences between nineteenth- and twentieth-century knowledge of ocular, muscular, or nervous disorders from which Dickinson may have suffered, it is impossible to reconstruct in contemporary terms the exact nature of the malady or maladies for which she was treated. Matching data from the poet's correspondence with the diagnosis and methods of treatment by Williams in *A Practical Guide to the Study of the Diseases of the Eye*, however, Gerald W. Jackson has explored the likelihood that she suffered from acute iritis (inflammation of the iris).[48] The patient usually experiences "great intolerance to light," and "the pain of iritis," as Dr. Williams notes, "is deep-seated and circumorbital." Often severe, sometimes agonizing, it is "described by the patient as if tension of the eye even to bursting were taking place." The danger of the disease, if it goes untreated, is blindness. Dr. Williams recommends treatment with a solution of atropia (a compound derived from belladonna) to dilate the pupil for relief of spasms, and restriction of the patient's use of the eyes in order to keep the pupils dilated. Although alleviation of the distress is difficult, according to the ophthalmologist, "very severe pain and tension may sometimes be relieved by puncturing the cornea and letting the aqueous humor escape."[49]

In addition to the indications of photophobia and bilateral pain which Dickinson experienced, Jackson also finds other salient details in her letters to support the view that Williams treated his patient for iritis. For instance, she told her sister-in-law in June 1864 that "For caution of my Hat, He says, the Doctor wipes my cheeks," which suggests that "hat in lap" Dickinson had received a dosage of atropia.[50] A month earlier, she had written to Lavinia: "the calls at the Doctor's are painful, and . . . I have not looked at Spring" (L, 2:432 and 430). The treatments were clearly not benign—perhaps the cornea was punctured; they were repeated; and the use of the eyes was also restricted.

The cause of iritis is undetermined. The prognosis, according to Williams, was also guarded:

> The severe symptoms yield, the pain and the infection gradually subside, the photophobia disappears, and the normal movements of the pupil are restored. The dimness of

vision, however, often continues for several weeks after the infection has vanished; but if the physician detects no traces of organic change in the iris or pupil, he may confidently assure his patient that vision will be completely restored. . . .

If reasonably prudent, the patient may enjoy immunity from a second attack; but he should be cautious, at least for some months in regard to the exposure to glare of light from snow or from light surfaces, or to cold or damp winds. If residing at a distance, it is well that he should be provided with a solution by means of which he can secure prompt dilation of the pupil at the outset of any fresh attack.[51]

If this restriction is not adhered to, future attacks are likely and are more common when an individual has been seriously affected.

The question of whether or not Emily Dickinson had further difficulties with her eyes remains to be considered. Dickinson wrote, for instance, to Louise Norcross in late 1869: "Thank you for recollecting my weakness. I am not so well as to forget I was ever ill, but better and working. I suppose we must all 'ail till evening' " (L, 2:466). Since the poet did not return to Boston after the second period for additional treatments, however, Jackson agrees with Cody that Dr. Williams must have completely arrested the disease. Both of them cite the letter she wrote to Higginson in early 1866. "I am uncertain of Boston," she said. "I had promised to visit my Physician for a few days in May, but Father objects because he is in habit of me." Asking then "Is it more far to Amherst?" she offers "a spacious Welcome—" (L, 2:450).

The letter is one of three on the subject of further sojourns in Boston, to which she apparently never returned. In June 1866, she again wrote to Higginson, "I must omit Boston. Father prefers so. He likes me to travel with him but objects that I visit." She then extended a second invitation to the man who, she later said, saved her life: "Might I entrust you, as my Guest[,] to the Amherst Inn? When I have seen you, to improve will be better pleasure because I shall know which are the mistakes" (L, 2:453). If there were no other evidence, it is reasonable to say that her concern with improvement indicates she was still writing poetry; and, although she may be prevaricating, "travel" suggests that she was not yet willing to say that she had withdrawn into her own domain. Then, once again, three years later, she refused Higginson's invitation to come to Boston: "You speak kindly of seeing me. Could it please your convenience to come so far as Amherst I should be very glad, but I do not cross my father's ground to any House or town" (L, 2:460). The felicitous statement, although not quite reliable at the time she wrote the letter, is equal in significance with "I had terror in September"; together with "I felt a Funeral, in my Brain," they are pivotal points by which the stories about weird Emily Dickinson are plotted.

Having leaned on her father as an excuse each time she refused the overtures from Higginson, she was inevitably seen as a victim of the tyrannies of a man about whom she confided to her Norcross cousins that he was "as gentle as he knows how" to be (L, 2:439). And even though she had the requisite room of her own in "his" house, as well as a garden that she always spoke of as hers, it was from her father's house, her garden, and her room that she haunted the good people of Amherst. Not one of the reminiscences of her during her later years tells us that she withdrew because she suffered from sensitivity to the glare of light, snow, and bright surfaces, or from exposure to damp winds and cold, but there is evidence that she found it necessary to be cautious in the use of her eyes, especially since it was her intention to keep writing.

There was, during her later years, an intermittent but a continued problem with her eyes, whatever the disease may have been. Among the variations in the accounts of the poet's behavior from 1865 until her final illness and death, there are details which indicate a pattern of frequent avoidance of strong light. For instance, Annie Holland Howe, daughter of Dickinson's friends, the Hollands, recalled a commencement reception in 1866 when the poet was so surrounded by people that the young woman had no chance to talk with her, but was asked to call the next morning, and was received "in a little back hall . . . that was dimly lighted."[52] Mabel Loomis Todd noted, from conversations with Lavinia, that Emily Dickinson "had crept out one evening with her brother . . . in order to see the new [Congregational] church" which had been completed in the fall of 1868.[53] This was to Mrs. Todd "legend," and in another version "one evening" had become "in the moonlight." Higginson, after having been received by Emily Dickinson in August 1870, wrote that the parlor "was dark and cool and stiffish" (L, 2:472–73).[54]

Following a visit to her on October 10, 1876, Helen Hunt Jackson wrote a letter of apology:

I feel as if I had been very impertinent that day in speaking to you as I did—accusing you of living away from sunlight,—and told you that you looked ill, which is a mortal piece of ill-being, at all times, but truly you seemed so white and moth-like. Your hand felt like such a wisp in mine that you frightened me. I felt like a great ox, talking to a white moth and begging it to come and eat grass with me to see if it could not turn itself into beef! How stupid.[55]

Clara Bellinger Green remembered the evening in June 1877 when she, her sister and brother as "the choir invisible" sang for the Dickinson women listening upstairs.

At the close of the singing a light clapping of hands, like a flutter of wings, floated down the staircase, and Miss Lavinia came to tell us that Emily would see us . . . in the library . . . dimly lit from the hall. . . . As she stood before us in the vague light of the library we were chiefly aware of a pair of great dark eyes set in a small, pale delicately chiseled face.[56]

Martha Dickinson Bianchi said of her aunt that "the last time she ever came across the lawn to our house was in the night—long past midnight. My brother Ned was ill,"[57] during September 1883; but a neighbor wrote that "Miss Emily Dickinson" went over to Austin's house the night the youngest of the children, Gilbert, died, October 5, 1883.[58] The constant is the fact that she went at night. A final, grudging account by Mrs. Annie Currier Brown, stepdaughter of Mrs. Elizabeth Dickinson Currier, of a visit to Emily Dickinson in mid-January 1885 is especially telling:

Her last interview with certain near relatives was very peculiar. They had come from a distance [Worcester] and at first she declined a meeting, but later she consented to five minutes conversation each with uncle and aunt in a dark hallway. It was a visit of words only, for vision was impossible.[59]

Perhaps Emily Dickinson was overly cautious: perhaps she became her own physician, withdrawing to prevent or protect herself from the menace of strong light and following Dr. Williams's regimen when attacks periodically occurred. She kept no log of the weather that would have provoked them, but in letters to Elizabeth Holland, it is obvious that the poet continued to find New England winter an excruciating time; there is, for instance, comment in early 1883 on "the glazed Light which the Snows make, with us they are falling always now, and the last is faithful for three Days, an inclement constancy—" (L, 3:759–60). Someone in the Dickinson household had bought Williams's *Recent Advances in Ophthalmic Science* (1866). But as late as 1885, Emily Dickinson was still receiving belladonna,[60] which was probably for the control of the symptoms of an eye disease. There is no record of the systemic effects of the belladonna upon her during those years. (It leaves one temporarily lethargic.)

Other indications that the poet's problem with her eyes persisted for at least twenty-five years come from disparate sources. Bianchi mentions casually that her brother Ned, during a period she does not specify, "carried the illustrated foreign reviews" to their aunt "when her eyes forbad her the strain of constant reading and writing, filling a place in her rapidly emptying life that no one else did."[61] Ned, who was born in 1861, could have begun the custom within a few years after Emily Dickinson's long stays in Boston for eye treatment, but the reference to "her rapidly emptying life" seems to be to the last few years or the last decade of her life (1876–86). Describing the manuscripts for poems written in the period "subsequent to Edward Dickinson's death in 1874," Millicent Todd Bingham says that "the strokes of the pencil are often faint and confused, the letters half-formed as if jotted down in the dark."[62]

R. W. Franklin points out that when the poet stopped binding fascicle or "book" sheets of fair copies of her poems about 1864, "it was a conscious change rather than an action deferred and then forgotten." The fact that "she continued to copy fascicle sheets without binding them suggests," he says, "that she found the bound books difficult to use.... By 1864 unbound sheets may have been easier for her to use—connected perhaps to the eye trouble of 1864 and 1865." Franklin, concluding that the poetic drive was "somewhat spent" in the later 1860s, notes that Emily Dickinson stopped copying fascicle sheets; then "for a time in the 1870's she revived such copying," but "attempts at bookmaking appear to have ended with the 1870's." The last of the dates he gives for the unbound sets of transcribed poems is about 1873–77.[63] He does not speculate further about a connection between the eye strain and the work of copying the poems. The handwriting for sets 8–15 (from 1870 to the mid-1870s) tends to be noticeably larger and more sprawling than it was in the manuscripts from the early years.

It is even possible that Dickinson shared with James Joyce a reason for wearing white. Suffering for years from iritis, as well as other nearly blinding diseases of the eyes, Joyce worked tenaciously and resorted to many ingenious devices in order to continue writing. Among them was the habit of wearing a white coat that reflected a bearable light on the paper and enabled him to see a little better as he wrote.[64] It is not known when Dickinson began dressing in white. But writing to Louise Norcross, in a letter for which the date is likely to have been December 1860, the poet thanked her for a cape: "My sphere is doubtless calicoes, nevertheless I thought it meet to sport a little wool. The mirth it has occasioned will deter me from further exhibitions! Won't you tell 'the public' that at present I wear a brown dress with a cape if possible browner, and carry a parasol of the same!" (L, 2:370). She mentioned, in a letter of early March 1866, that her sister-in-law has just given her "a Cashmere print" (L, 2:449). The first description of "the white election" that can be accurately dated is Higginson's after his visit of August 16, 1870, when she was "in a very plain & exquisitely clean white pique & a blue net worsted shawl" (L, 2:473). "During my memory of her," Bianchi, who was born in 1866, writes, "she wore white exclusively."[65]

Joseph Lyman's fictional sketch of "EMILY" was not, then, altogether without a basis in fact: "a spirit clad in white. . . . Eyes bright hazel now melted & fused so as to be two dreamy, wondering wells of expression, eyes that see no forms but glance swiftly to the core of all things." Lyman, who probably did not see the poet from the spring of 1851, when he went south, until the fall of 1863, when he returned to Cambridge, and who died on January 28, 1872, in New York City, might have visited her in Amherst between 1863 and 1872. The details of the white dress and unusual eyes (from the use of belladonna?) suggest that he saw her sometime during the years 1866–72. It is, significantly, the eyes he chooses to indicate the change in the appearance and character of the young woman with whom he had once walked on a March day[66] when she was not yet twenty-one and uncertain of her future.

So it is that the author of more than seventeen hundred poems, as many as fourteen hundred of them presumably written in the years after 1861, when she experienced what was to be "the only woe" that ever made her tremble,[67] became an apparition in virginal white or the odd woman in American literature.

IV

There are at least two poems that are pertinent to a discussion of Dickinson's personal crisis: "Don't put up my Thread and Needle" (#617, c. 1862) and "Before I got my eye put out" (#327, c. 1862). By contrast with "I felt a Funeral, in my Brain," which has been analyzed as a document in the records of a mental patient, "Don't put up my Thread and Needle" has received little attention and, then, not with regard to her visual impairment. It has been read as a metaphor about writing poetry,[68] although it is first of all a poem literally about sewing, an art Dickinson learned in childhood. The images and themes belong to period before she received the care of the eye specialist. Having reported to Lavinia in July 1864 from Boston that their cousins even mended her stockings, she wrote to her sister in mid-May of the next year that "The Hood is far underway and the Girls think it a Beauty. I am so glad to make it for you, who made so much for me" (L, 2:442). The vision had improved sufficiently for the poet to resume sewing. If one reads the verse with a knowledge of its biographical content, it is not necessarily more poignant or better than many of the poems, but there is good reason to say that the voice of the poem is her own:

> Dont put up my Thread and Needle—
> I'll begin to Sew
> When the Birds begin to whistle—
> Better Stitches—so—
>
> These were bent—my Sight got crooked—
> When my mind—is plain
> I'll do seams—a Queen's endeavor
> Would not blush to own—
>
> Hems—too fine for Lady's tracing
> To the sightless Knot—
> Tucks—of dainty interspersion—
> Like a dotted Dot—[69]
>
> Leave my Needle in the furrow—
> Where I put it down—

I can make the zigzag stitches
Straight—when I am strong—

Till then—*dreaming I am sewing
Fetch the seam I missed—
Closer—so I—at my †sleeping—
Still surmise I stitch—
*deeming
†sighing

"Before I got my eye put out," the other poem it seems pertinent to consider in relation to Dickinson's visual disorder, has been read as a trope for permanent deprivation, or the experience of being blinded by beauty and life, or a narrowing of focus and vision. Since Emily Dickinson did not go blind, the poem is also said to be "a pose"; or it is said to confirm that her reaction to the eye problem "was unrealistic and . . . consequently exaggerated by emotional determinants."[70] She did pose, she did exaggerate; there are emotional determinants at work in the making of powerful poems, and reading them is a prickly art. Does the authority of a writer's voice depend on her actual experience, whether the response is reasonable or histrionic, and is "experience" particularly illuminating in judging the effectiveness of the voice? Are the personae of "Don't put up my Thread and Needle" and "Before I had my eye put out," for instance, the same? It can as well be the consciousness of an *other* which gravely informs the experience of being blinded:

Before I got my eye put out
I liked as well to see—
As other Creatures, that have Eyes
And know no other way—

But were it told to me—Today—
That I might have the sky
For mine—I tell you that my Heart
Would split, for size of me—

The Meadows—mine—
The Mountains—mine—
All Forest—Stintless Stars—
As much of noon as I could take
Between my finite Eyes—

The Motions of the Dipping Birds—
The *Morning's Amber Road—
For Mine—to look at when I liked—
The News would strike me dead—

So safer—guess—with just my soul
Upon the window pane—
Where other Creatures put their Eyes—
Incautious—of the Sun—
*Lightning's jointed Road

Even though the poem was one of four she sent in a letter to Higginson during August 1862, and even though she told him at the time of the first visit he made to Amherst in 1870 about the "long disuse of her eyes" (L, 2:476), there is no evidence that he saw any relationship between either of these matters and the terror which she mentioned when she wrote to him in late April 1862 or that he showed any serious interest in what was obviously an ordeal for her. He can in fairness be partly excused by the fact that having been, in December 1862, commissioned as a colonel of the First South Carolina Volunteers, a regiment of black soldiers fighting in the Union Army, he was wounded in July 1863 and left the service in May 1864. Dickinson, writing from Boston in early June to ask about him, also reported that she had been ill, and under "A Physician's care," but was able to work:

Can you render my Pencil?
The Physician has taken away my Pen.
I enclose the address from a letter, lest my figures fail—
Knowledge of your recovery—would excel my own—
                                        (L, 2:430)

If Higginson, for all his curiosity about the poet, paid scant attention to Dickinson's eyes and failed to comprehend much else that she told him, was it because he saw her as "partially cracked," "eccentric," "strange," and "rare"—clinging to him?[71] For her part, grateful but courageous, she dared to write to him after he sent his photograph to her in late October 1876: "Dear Friend. . . . Your Face is more joyful, when you speak—and I miss an almost arrogant look that at times haunts you—but with that exception, it is so real I could think it you" (L, 2:566). She was, I think, too smart for him, and for us. Granted, she had neither the preternatural intelligence nor supernatural will of Poe's Ligeia; granted, too, no one went blind in the House of Usher, and no one got an eye put out in the Dickinson house.

The poem "Before I got my eye put out," moreover, belongs to that category of fictions Dickinson herself designated at the time she wrote to Higginson: "When I state myself, as the Representative of the Verse—it does not mean—me—but a supposed person." While there is no question that the poem is an imagined experience, perhaps strengthened by fear of a possible loss of sight, there are equally effective poems, such as "Dont put up my Thread and Needle," based on the pressure of personal experience which she has also imaginatively rendered, but such a simple distinction is not always easily made, as the example of "I felt a Funeral, in my Brain" shows. There are far too many lacunae in the biographical data, and there are also many poems in which she expertly transformed a mix of personal factors, observations, and imagined experience into dramatic modes for which she assumed "other" voices. It is the work of the critical reader to perceive them as a play of voices without becoming oneself a writer of Gothic romances.

The burden of "Before I got my eye put out" is not just that it began in the anxieties of the poet, or that she knew there was more than one way to see. It is also that she used the resources of language to transcend the limits and terrors of finite eyes.[72]

4

"I wish I were a Hay": The Histrionic Imagination

The drama of mere being is especially congenial to Emily Dickinson. A sense of both the tragic and comic in life quickens the ways that she perceived the world and the language she found for expressing the vision.

Painful realities, requiring stamina and sacrifice, came to rest in metaphors that confirm a predilection basic to the poems. She wrote, for instance, on December 3, 1882, to Otis Lord: "The month in which our Mother died, closed it's Drama Thursday, and I cannot conjecture a form of space without her timid face" (L, 3:753). The death of a parent, without fanfare, was a tragic event. Or over two decades before, in November 1858, during the time that the timid mother was suffering a protracted illness, the young poet had written to the Hollands, with whom she had been friends at least five years:

> I shall not tell how short time is, for I was told by lips which sealed as soon as it was said. . . . You were not here in summer. *Summer?* My memory flutters—had I—was there a summer? You should have seen the fields go—gay little entomology! Swift little ornithology! Dancer, and floor, and cadence quite gathered away, and I, a phantom, to you a phantom,

76

rehearse the story! An orator of feather unto an audience of fuzz,—and pantomime plaudits. "Quite as good as a play," indeed! (L, 2:341).

The images and rhythms of the prose, veering toward lyric poetry, as well as the illusion of existence as a great outdoor theater where a *deus ex machina* dispatches the troupe's principals (lips sealed) and the young poet herself (surviving only as a stage ghost or a plume from an actor's hat), are for her friends' and her own entertainment. She brings the curtain down quickly, before logic or analysis destroys the illusion, but not before she has shown that gaiety transfigured all the dread inherent in the mortal scene: "*Summer?* My memory flutters—had I—was there a summer?" The final throwaway line, " 'Quite as good as a play,' indeed!" amusingly sums up the word-play which she has been practicing for the poems she would soon write in gracious plenty.

"Drama's Vitallest Expression," a poem begins, "is the Common Day / That arise and set about us—" (#741, c. 1863). Here the poet is no longer fanciful, no longer enjoying the art of illusion; she simply contrasts the reciting of tragedy on the stage and acting it out in reality:

> "Hamlet" to Himself were Hamlet—
> Had not Shakespeare wrote—
> Though the "Romeo" *left no Record
> Of his Juliet,
>
> It were †infinite enacted
> In the Human Heart—
> Only Theatre recorded
> ‡Owner cannot shut—[1]
>
> *leave
> †tenderer
> ‡never yet was

In another poem, the action shifts rapidly from the harmless bravado of children playing in "dreams" to a sudden realization of the less prudent "fact" or "truth—of Blood": "But we—are dying in Drama—/ And Drama—is never dead—" (#531, c. 1862). Or, a whirling dervish with words, the poet is capable of imagining that if she had only "A Diagram—of Rapture! / A Sixpence at a Show— / With Holy Ghosts in Cages! / The *Universe* would go!" (#184, c. 1860).

Dickinson herself could be histrionic. After T. W. Higginson, with whom she had been corresponding for eight years, made the first visit to see her in 1870, he wrote: "She came to me with two day lilies which she put in a sort of childlike way into my hand & said: 'These are my introduction' " (L, 2:473). Childlike or not, she began the interview as a good actress begins by saying that she was frightened, and she had his sympathy; she whispered, she talked breathlessly, she soliloquized, she pontificated, she entertained. He listened, believed her to be ingenuous, and thought what she said was wise. She had probably rehearsed before he arrived, and she did not forget her lines. The performance was a success.

Does Dickinson's sense of the histrionic offer an approach for resolving the ambiguities in her rather clumsy explanation of the use of "myself" or "a supposed person" in the poems? The verse, which states an "I" as the Representative, may include narration or salient description but frequently takes a dramatic form. The speech is often colloquial but also personal, inviting the unwary reader to believe in what James Merrill has called "the illusion of True Confession."[2] Even the wariest of critics customarily reads Dickinson as a lyric poet who presents the images in direct relation to the self and thereby creates herself.[3]

Since it is fashionable, among various schools of criticism, to take for granted that poets write about themselves, if not consciously, at least unconsciously, it is difficult to prove otherwise. If Dickinson imagines in verses that the "I," the "supposed person," is a wife, the bride of Christ, a fallen woman, a bereaved husband, someone dead or alive, girl or boy, a bird, a rose, a fly, what stronger confirmation of a life in which something was amiss? Or, perhaps, she did not know who she was, and the various personae indicate that she was uncertain of her identity, her maturity, her sexual nature? She did not, after all, marry, or did she?[4]

There are so many performances in the poems that Dickinson may elude us. Adopting provisional attitudes and myriad voices, she changes point of view, role, situation, genre, language, and style with remarkable speed and adroitness; we, expecting continuities, hardly know where to have her. Three examples suggest the range, if not the variety, of tones and perspectives in the work. Each of them, however, is dramatic.

A child plays out a scene with God:

Papa above!
Regard a mouse
O'erpowered by a Cat!
Reserve within thy kingdom
A "Mansion" for the Rat!

Snug in seraphic Cupboards
To nibble all the day,
While unsuspecting Cycles
Wheel solemnly away!
(#61, c. 1859)

A young woman, acting all the while, holds a mirror up to herself in a reverie that mocks her insignificance:

I'm saying every day
"If I should be a Queen, tomorrow"—
I'd do this way—
And so I deck, a little,

If it be, I wake a Bourbon,
None on me, bend supercilious—
With "This was she—
Begged in the Market place—
Yesterday."

Court is a stately place—
I've heard men say—
So I loop my apron, against the Majesty
With bright Pins of Buttercup—
That not too plain—
Rank—overtake me—

And perch my Tongue
On Twigs of singing—rather high—
But this, might be my brief Term
To qualify—

Put from my simple speech all plain word—
Take other accents, as such I heard
Though but for the Cricket—just,
And but for the Bee—

Not in all the Meadow—
One accost me—

Better to be ready—
Than did next morn
Meet me in Aragon—
My old Gown—on—

And the Surprised Air
Rustics—wear—
Summoned—unexpectedly—
To Exeter—

(#373, c. 1862)

Another young woman declares herself to be paradoxically yielded up and emancipated, chosen but choosing as a free and "willing" queen in a state of grace to rule her life:

I'm ceded—I've stopped being Their's—
The name They dropped upon my face
With water, in the country church
Is finished using, now,
And They can put it with my Dolls,
My Childhood, and the String of Spools,
I've finished threading—too—

Baptized, before, without the Choice,
But this time, consciously, of Grace—
Unto supremest *name—
Called to my Full—The Crescent dropped—
Existence's whole †Arc, filled up,
With ‡one small Diadem.

My Second Rank—too small the first—
Crowned—§Crowing—on my Father's breast—
‖A half unconscious Queen—
But this time—Adequate—Erect,
With **Will to choose, or to reject,
And I choose, just a ††Crown—

(#508, c. 1862)

*term
†Eye
‡just one

§whimpering/dangling
‖An insufficient
**power
††throne

By questioning the propensity to read these dramatic monologues as autobiographical guises and listening instead to the different voices within the configuration of the poet's creative work,
we gain a sense of her sense of the world as if, in the words of
another of her poems, "a Kingdom—cared" (#260, c. 1861). While
the "real" Dickinson parodies the vocative, "Our Father who art in
heaven" in "Papa above!" the poet's child takes for granted the
right to express a familial affection for him and for a helpless
creature he may have neglected to notice. Although Dickinson herself argued with God, it has been said that she was given to being
coy and did not want to accept the responsibility for expressing
heretical notions. But it is possible to conceive of children who
have dared confront God, and of a poet who wittily gave them
voice, just as it is possible for her to have read history and put
words in the mouth of a girl whose fantasies of good fortune humorously dramatize the distance between reality and expectation, or
to affirm from observation or experience the power of a woman to
choose to grow as she is destined. The poet can identify at will with
victim or victor, beggar or queen, the brash, the hopeful, the majestic and sovereign. She can play all the parts, even pleading for a
mouse. There is no record that Dickinson was baptized.

She writes "as the Representative" of the verse and the "supposed person" to claim the privilege to draw upon whatever resources are available to her for writing. If "other people are a *problem* for lyric poetry," the dramatic monologue is a genre by which
to move beyond "me, myself" into a relationship with them.[5] The
use of the form obviously enlarges the scope or situation about
which poets can write and allows them ways of saying that there
are more people than themselves in the world, a prerogative that
the tellers of tales and playwrights have long enjoyed. The view
that she wrote almost exclusively about herself, however, pervades
Dickinson studies. Dramatic monologues signal other views.[6]

There are, of course, poems that depend largely upon Dickinson's
own experiences, albeit the poet situates the emotions in dramatic
structures close to but hardly synonymous with the biography.
There is another kind of poem in which she imagines a voice speak-

ing of situations that she also imagines. Other poems bring together emotions through which she has lived and a dramatic moment that she imagines. The critical problem is in distinguishing among them. Since there is much that we do not know about the life, we are always circumscribed in reading from it to the poems; yet they were hardly written without connections to it. On the other hand, the liberties she enjoys in condensing, combining, changing shapes, transposing, inventing, and supposing "lives" for poems are suspect as documents of her life. We can, without being able to resolve these complex issues completely, say that the biography gives us glimpses of the modulations of a few experiences into words that reveal some of the ways Dickinson worked.

II

Dickinson recognized, early in her career, the value of the dramatic monologue and learned to use it with skill. A well-known poem, dated about 1858 or 1859 when the apprenticeship was nearing its end, serves both as an example in which she has not quite mastered the form but is alert to its efficacy and as a work in which she draws on her own experience but changes it in the act of speaking about it.

> I never lost as much but twice,
> And that was in the sod.
> Twice have I stood a beggar
> Before the door of God!
>
> Angels—twice descending
> Reimbursed my store—
> Burglar! Banker—Father!
> I am poor once more!
>
> (#49)

The story line of the verse is addressed to an imagined interlocutor on the subject of the power of God; when the poet allows the speaker to address God directly, however, the break in point of view discloses that Dickinson has not yet learned to integrate narration and drama. The austerely restricted language of the narrative is right for the recollection of painful loss in contrast to the defiant and improvident moment when the persona forgets the unidentified listener and turns in line seven to revile God directly, but an experienced poet does not lose awareness of the audience assumed in a monologue even when the character being depicted rages on.

Despite the violation of point of view, or perhaps because of it, the supplicant's outburst continues to reverberate in our ears as we listen to the falling strain of a voice quickly regaining control and we believe we have overheard Emily Dickinson herself quarreling with God. When we find in a second poem, "Going to Heaven!" (#79, c. 1859), that the persona, a young girl who both hopes to go and is glad she isn't going to heaven, says, "If you sh'd get there first / Save just a little place for me / Close to the two I lost—," we look elsewhere for the experiences about which *she* is talking in the angry indictment of God. Who, among the people she loved, we ask, died during Dickinson's childhood and youth? And what other personal loss is of the enormity of death? Because neither poem gives any clues, we search the biography for them.

There was more anguish in the life of young Emily Dickinson than "I never lost as much but twice" enumerates. She recalled, in a letter of March 28, 1846, to Abiah Root, whose schoolmate had just died, an experience of early sorrow. The opening words of the recollection prefigure the idiomatic cadence in which the poem begins. She wrote: "I have never lost but one friend near my age & with whom my thoughts & her own were the same. It was before you came to Amherst. My friend was Sophia Holland. She was too lovely for earth & she was transplanted from earth to heaven. . . . Then it seemed to me I should die too." Emily, who was fourteen at the time of the death of her friend in the spring of 1844, gave way to "a fixed melancholy," told no one the cause of her grief, and was not well. Her parents sent her to Boston, where she stayed with relatives for a month and her health improved so that her "spirits were better" (L, 1:32). In May 1846, her maternal grandfather, Joel Norcross, died; there is no record of how she felt about him, but she went again in August to Boston for her health. In May 1848, during her seventeenth year, Jacob Holt, a friend about whom she anxiously asked more than once in letters from Holyoke, died at the age of twenty-six; he wrote some rather commonplace poems, one of which she copied in her Bible. There were, also, other persons who are usually suggested as "the two" she lost in death. Since the emotions of loss became more complex as she matured, they well may be fused beyond one's ability to extricate them in the poem.

Leonard Humphrey, who was principal of the Amherst Academy in 1846–47, Emily's last year there, died at the age of twenty-six in

November 1850; reporting the death of her "master" to Abiah, Emily mourned but did not give way to melancholy: "my rebellious thoughts," she asserted, "are many" (L, 1:103). Thereafter, Ben Newton, who introduced her to Emerson's poetry in 1850, left Amherst for Worcester, married in 1851, and died at the age of thirty-two on March 24, 1853. He taught her to read, she said, and was "the first of my own friends" (L, 1:236). Had she forgotten Sophia Holland, who has not counted in explanations of the poet's loss?

Additional comments in the letters seem to lend support to readers who identify "the two she lost" as Humphrey and Newton (Or are they "three": Holt, Humphrey, and Newton?) Writing on April 25, 1862, to Higginson, the poet said: "When a little Girl, I had a friend who taught me Immortality—but venturing too near, himself—he never returned—Soon after, my Tutor, died—and for several years, my Lexicon was my only companion." As if she were explaining "I never lost as much but twice," which Higginson had not seen, she added: "Then I found one more—but he was not contented I be his scholar—so he left the Land" (L, 2:404). This remark causes further speculation about whether the final loss in the poem is a kind different from that "in the sod." Casual readers then want to hear a name such as Charles Wadsworth or Samuel Bowles, neither of whom had "left the land" before or during the year in which Dickinson made a final copy of the verse ending with the dramatic cry: "Burglar! Banker—Father! / I am poor once more!"

There is not only too much evidence but too much uncertainty about what to choose from it for ascertaining the specific provocations of the poem's dramatic script. Nevertheless, if the letters to Abiah Root began the account of the incremental sorrow that is Dickinson's subject, one can say the soliloquy depends on events that are autobiographical but is not a literal recording of any one among them. The poet was rather finding words to make emotions *sound* true.

The recurrent experience of separations and loss may well be the source of another poem, which is more lyrical than dramatic. The emphasis is again on emotions related to a life "closed twice," but beyond the term "parting" there is no evidence that permits one to identify the events to which the persona refers. If the experiences are personal, they have been transmuted into flawless lines:

> My life closed twice before its close—
> It yet remains to see

If Immortality unveil
A third event to me

So huge, so hopeless to conceive
As these that twice befell.
Parting is all we know of heaven,
And all we need of hell.

(#1732, n.d.)[7]

Although there is no autograph copy or date of composition for this justly famous poem, it points up Dickinson's practice of trying out different aspects of a theme in order to realize the perfection of form inherent in it. The poet ceased, moreover, to be an amateur in exploiting the possibilities of the dramatic monologue, which became the genre for a number of equally memorable Dickinson texts.

Continuing to experiment with the dramatic monologue, she used it in other poems that are not self-referential but reveal as they enact in words situations that she thought significant or interesting. The monologues are not necessarily masks for Dickinson herself; they are often performances that reflect the lives of people whose voices she "supposed." Because she lived among them and responded to many events that went unrecorded in any form but the verse, one cannot know without question all of the explicit relationships between the various histories with which she was familiar and the language into which she transposed them. There are, however, relevant sources for exploring some of the arresting performances.

A poem in which Emily Dickinson imagines both the voice and the situation begins:

Because I could not stop for Death—
He kindly stopped for me—
The Carriage held but just Ourselves—
And Immortality.

We slowly drove—He knew no haste
And I had put away
My Labor and my Leisure too,
For His Civility—

The detached tone of "the posthumous speech" is effectively sustained as the soliloquy, following a narrative line, continues with a description of an early evening ride through familiar country to the House of Death, the grave, where the action inevitably stops. Then there is the denoument:

> Since then—'tis Centuries—and yet
> Feels shorter than the Day
> I first Surmised the Horses' Heads
> Were toward Eternity—
>   (#712, c. 1862)

The poem may be indebted to Robert Browning's "The Last Ride Together," with the theme of "the instant made eternity,"[8] or to Elizabeth Barrett Browning's account of "the enforced journey to corruption taken by Marian Erle in Book VI of *Aurora Leigh*,"[9] or to John Keats's famous phrase, "half in love with easeful Death," since they are the poets Dickinson mentions in answer to an inquiry from Higginson about her "Books." It may owe something to the fact that the Dickinson girls often went for carriage rides with their father and their brother or other young men.[10] The idea for the poem must, nevertheless, have originated in an event about which the poet knew: the death of a distant cousin, Olivia Coleman, at the age of twenty, in Princeton, where her family had moved from Amherst a year earlier. Olivia, a beautiful girl who was admired by the youths of Amherst, particularly Leonard Humphrey, was ill with "galloping consumption," but she died without warning when she went for a drive in a carriage on the afternoon of September 28, 1847. "The circumstances of her death are considered 'romantic.' "[11] Eliza, Olivia's younger sister, was a companion of Emily who wrote in November to Abiah: "You probably have heard of the death of *O. Coleman*. How melancholy!! Eliza has written me a long letter giving me an account of her death, which is beautiful & affecting . . ." (L, 1:56). Since Eliza's letter does not survive, there is no way of knowing Dickinson's indebtedness to it, and the use of the journey motif is common enough that Olivia Coleman's death was not needed to suggest it to Dickinson. Still the event seems the natural origin of the "romantic" idea for the poem.

Moreover, the conception of the event of death in the polite language of a young lady recalling the seduction by a courteous gentleman who carried her away never to return creates just that combination of sad thoughtfulness, languor, and repressed terror, that slight shiver, of which there are intimations in the young poet's words "melancholy, beautiful, affecting" when she writes to her friend. The persona's admission in the denoument that, although the evidence was scant, she guessed the horses were bearing her away forever is more quietly dramatic than the memorable statement with which she begins the account of her fate. And while the tone of the admission is muted, in contrast to the outburst we heard from the persona who dares call God "Burglar!" before she regains control of herself in "I never lost as much but twice," the revelation is also powerful, if not shocking. The effectiveness with which Dickinson employed the convention of life as a journey toward eternity, moreover, has caught the interest of a larger number of critics than any single poem she wrote; there is commentary on it by almost a hundred students of her work, and only one of them has called it "fraudulent."[12]

Among several verses that assume the perspectives of the dead, there is another which a critic characterizes as one of Dickinson's "most obviously hostile autobiographical poems, describing herself as a corpse." The image of a father "with a passion for regularity" evokes for the critic "the member of the household" the poet most resented and respected.[13] Yet the poem has the charm of a genre painting and illustrates that for her a change of voice is a change of style:

> 'Twas just this time, Last year, I died.
> I know I heard the Corn,
> When I was Carried by the Farms—
> It had the Tassels on—
>
> I thought how yellow it would look—
> When Richard went to mill—
> And then, I wanted to get out,
> But something held my will.
>
> I thought just how Red—Apples wedged
> The Stubbles' joints between—
> And the Carts went stooping round the fields
> To take the Pumpkins in—
>
> I wondered which would miss me, Least,
> And when Thanksgiving, came,

If Father'd multiply the plates—
To make an Even Sum—

And would it blur the Christmas glee
My Stocking hang too high
For any Santa Claus to reach
The altitude of me—

But this sort, grieved myself,
And so, I thought the other way,
How just this time, some perfect year—
Themself, should come to me—
                              (#445, c. 1862)

The nostalgia for the rural and family life the child no longer shares points up the youth's need to prove that the dead keep time and remember life; yet the wish to escape the separation in death is denied by a failure of the will and an inability to grasp that "something" she—or he—cannot comprehend; the loss and loneliness, however, are matched by familial love on which the child suddenly remembers to count for consolation. The verse is flawed by the awkward phrasing in the description of apples wedged between grass stubble after harvest, but the poem succeeds in its fusion of image and theme. The memories of the colors of fall and the changes of season, culminating in Christmas glee, anticipate the resolution of the conflict in the heart of the child who waits faithfully for the cherished ones to fulfill the Christian promise that the longing for earth had almost obliterated. Perhaps the poem is an elegy for Sophia Holland, the friend whose "thoughts," Dickinson said, were like her own?

The images of the poem begin, I think, in the poet's willingness to lend her thoughts to those mortal children, whose longing for home is similar to emotions she had during the year she was at Mount Holyoke. She wrote on January 17, 1848, to Abiah Root of a joyful first meeting with her family and of her vacation at home for "four short days" at Thanksgiving; then: "amidst tears falling thick & fast away I went again. Slowly & sadly dragged a few of the days after my return to the Seminary and I was very homesick." Her sorrows, she says, were soon lost in study and she again felt happy, "if happiness there can be away from 'home, sweet home' " (L, 1:58–59). There was no Christmas vacation, because it was not a custom among Congregationalists to celebrate the season with festivities, but there was a two-week recess between terms and Emily went home again in late January. Returning to school, she wrote on February 17 to her brother, Austin:

> I have been quite lonely since I came back. . . . Home was always dear to me, . . . but never did it seem so dear as now. All, all are kind to me but their tones fall strangely on my ear & their countenances meet mine not like home faces. . . .

She continued:

> Then when tempted to feel sad, I think of the blazing fire, & the cheerful meal & the chair empty now I am gone. I can hear the cheerful voices & the merry laugh & a desolate feeling comes home to my heart, to think I am alone.

Since the family had decided that she would not return to Holyoke for another year, she concluded: "But my good angel only waits to see the tears coming & then whispers, only this year! . . . and home again you will be to stay" (L, 1:62–63). Since the sentiments are common to homesick youths away at school for the first time, it may have been a simple matter for Dickinson to transpose them in the poem, "'Twas just this time, last year, I died," with its posthumous voice and those bright images of the place and people lovingly recalled "now I am gone." But the transposition testifies to the poet's largesse and mature triumph over sentimentality. It is a poem of earth and can hardly be said to be "self-centered." She might imagine, but could not have experienced, her own death.

From another angle of vision, she finds a voice that is tender but also bitter and ironic to express the emotions felt by the living who mourn the dead:

> How many times these low feet staggered—
> Only the soldered mouth can tell—
> Try—can you stir the awful rivet—
> Try—can you lift the hasp of steel!
>
> Stroke the cool forehead—hot so often—
> Lift—if you care—the listless hair—
> Handle the adamantine fingers
> Never a thimble—more—shall wear—

> Buzz the dull flies—on the chamber window—
> Brave—shines the sun through the freckled pane—
> Fearless—the cobweb swings from the ceiling—
> Indolent Housewife—in Daisies—lain!
>
> (#187, c. 1860)

The poem, which is more descriptive than narrative, is also a dramatic monologue, and is as graphic as anything Dickinson ever wrote. It sounds as if she had witnessed the scene and felt a need to protest the fate of a woman worn out by the cares and burdens from which dying freed her. Speaking for the voiceless housewife, Dickinson's persona also speaks for herself and affirms the ability of the poet to give distinctive dramatic form to the supposition "if you care."

Emily Dickinson would have known of the death of Amherst women in the years since her childhood, but it was the death of her Boston aunt, Lavinia Norcross (the mother of Emily's cousins Louise and Frances, then eighteen and twelve, respectively) on April 17, 1860, that was probably the emotional matrix of the poem. Lavinia, who married her cousin Loring Norcross against their family's wishes, was the poet's favorite aunt. The poet reported in February 1859: "My mother's only sister has had an invalid winter, and Vinnie has gone to enliven the house, and make the days shorter for my sick aunt" (L, 2:346). In September, Dickinson mentioned the aunt again in a letter: "Mother's favorite sister is sick, and mother will have to bid her good-night. . . . the aunt whom Vinnie visits. . . . Does God take care of those at sea? My aunt is such a timid woman!" (L, 2:354). Upon hearing the news of the aunt's death, the poet wrote:

> Blessed Aunt Lavinia now; all the world goes out, and I see nothing but her room, and angels bearing her into those great countries in the blue sky of which we don't know anything. . . . Well, she is safer now than 'we know or even think.' Tired little aunt, sleeping ne'er so peaceful!

Despite the efforts of the niece to accept the death, she floundered as she tried to express the grief she felt. She spoke of sobbing, crying, and weeping bitterly; she exclaimed "to think how still" Aunt Lavinia lay "while I was making the little loaf and fastening . . . flowers" to send her. She was particularly unrestrained as she wrote: "Oh! Vinnie, it is dark and strange to think of summer afterward! How she loved the summer! The birds keep singing just the same. Oh! The thoughtless birds!" (L, 2:361–62). There is no record that either the poet or her parents went to the funeral.

While the sense of domestic Gothicism in "How many times these low feet staggered" may express the grief Emily Dickinson felt upon receiving news of the death of her aunt, the predominant images of the poem chill and horrify in a way that the comments on Aunt Lavinia lying still in death or the angels bearing her to those great countries in the blue sky do not. The most rueful moment in the persona's soliloquy is the charge, at which she does not cringe: "Handle the adamantine fingers / Never a thimble—more—shall wear." The sentiment recalls a romantic poet's fine sympathy when he says: "Never again the nightingale thou shalt hear, / My dear, oh my dear," but the woman's images are more insistent, more grotesque, and more homely. The eerie flies, the unwashed window, the cobweb, are saliently different from Dickinson's "thoughtless birds" that keep singing; and the aunt's house probably would not have been so unkempt when Lavinia Dickinson was there to help out. The dead woman, the corpse, that the persona views and asks us to view, is not necessarily or specifically the poet's aunt; she is any housewife who has been ill a long time and had to neglect the work of the common day, for which the lowly daisies are emblematic. For Dickinson, the poet, "Drama's Vitallest Expression is the Common Day / That rise and set about us," and that drama is "infinite enacted" in the hearts of many women—and men.

"How many times these low feet staggered," dated two years earlier than "Because I could not stop for Death" or "'Twas just this time last year, I died," illustrates also that the poet quickly learned to make the leap from private emotions—confused, undisciplined, inchoate—to poetry divested of the encumbrances of the self.

III

While an interest in the uses Dickinson made of "herself" tends to obscure the importance of the activities of the imagination in which she was engaged, there are actual matters of such obvious relevance to the character of her work as a poet that they are frequently overlooked. There is, for example, another housewife's poem that dramatizes the effect of the relentless, mundane duties to which the grieving persona attends in the tribute she pays to the dead woman of "How many times these low feet staggered." Emily Dickinson was—if not a housewife—a housekeeper, a fact as significant as any in her life for confirming the strategies she used in her poetry.[14]

Dickinson not only supposes what it is like to be someone else, a young friend or a child who has died in "Because I could not stop for Death" and "'Twas this time last year, I died," but she also appropriates for "The Grass so Little has to do" the situation of a woman, with too much to do, in the act of imagining an existence different from her own. Although the poem shares some of the ironies of "How many times these low feet staggered," the tone is light, and the persona enjoys the activity to which she "confesses": daydreaming. She is, in fact, completely carried away:

> The Grass so Little has to do,
> A Sphere of Simple Green—
> With only Butterflies to brood,
> And Bees, to entertain—
>
> And stir all day to pretty tunes
> The Breezes fetch along,
> And hold the Sunshine, in it's Lap
> And bow to Everything,
>
> And thread the Dews, all night, Like Pearl,
> And make itself so fine
> A Duchess, were too Common
> For such a noticing,
>
> And even when it die, to pass
> In odors so divine,
> As Lowly spices, laid to sleep—
> Or Spikenards perishing.
>
> And then to dwell in Sovereign Barns,
> And dream the Days away,
> The Grass so little has to do,
> I wish I were a Hay.
>
> (#333, c. 1862)

A corollary to this imaginative moment of leisure—this play—may well be Dickinson's remark in a note: "Let me commend to Baby's attention the only Commandment I ever obeyed—'Consider the lilies' " (L, 3:825); the note, alluding to the lilies of the field that neither toil nor spin but are clothed in glory greater than the array of Solomon himself,[15] was sent to Alice Cooper Tuckerman shortly after the birth of a daughter, Margaret, in June 1884. The wit is a woman's wit. The poem, celebrating the majestic leisure of nature, expresses a feeling common to overworked people, but a primary source of the amusing reverie of a "brood" mother is the poet's imagining an easier life when it was necessary, as it often was for her, to assume responsibilities in the Dickinson household. She addressed a copy of the poem to Austin.

The account of one of the most strenuous periods in Emily Dickinson's "career" begins in 1855 when the family moved from North Pleasant Street back to the Homestead. The poet's description of the return to the big house during November of that year is typical of her humor at its most rollicking. She writes in January 1856 to Elizabeth Holland:

> I cannot tell you how we moved. I had rather not remember. I believe my "effects" were brought in a bandbox, and the "deathless me," on foot, not many moments after. I took at the time a memorandum of my several senses, and also of my hat and coat, and my best shoes—but it was lost in the *mêlée*, and I am out with lanterns, looking for myself.
>
> Such wits as I reserved, are so badly shattered that repair is useless—and still I can't help laughing at my own catastrophe. I supposed we were going to make a "transit," as heavenly bodies did—but we came budget by budget, as our fellows do, till we fulfilled the pantomime contained in the word "moved." It is a kind of *gone-to-Kansas* feeling, and if I sat in a long wagon, with my family tied behind, I should suppose without doubt I was a party of emigrants!

After considering a realistic definition of "home," Dickinson becomes more sober but finally mocks her own situation and expresses the feeling that became "The Grass so Little has to do":

> But . . . I have another story, and lay my laughter all away, so that I can sigh. Mother has been an invalid since we came *home*, and Vinnie and I "regulated," and Vinnie and I "got settled," and still we keep our father's house, and mother lies

upon the lounge, or sits in her easy chair. I don't know what her sickness is, for I am but a simple child, and frightened at myself. I often wish I was a grass, or a toddling daisy, whom all these problems of dust might not terrify— (L, 2:323–24)

Mrs. Dickinson's illness continued over a period of at least four years. From the elder daughter, there are in addition to the account of settling at the Homestead only two extant letters and one note which editors date with certainty as having been written during 1856; there are *none* surviving from the year 1857. A friend wrote in late September 1856 that "Eliza Coleman is visiting Emily & Vinnie at present, while they are housekeepers; for Mrs. D's health is poor & she is at the water-cure" in Northampton.[16] The treatment must not have been successful. In early summer of 1858, Dickinson writes to a Norcross uncle:

Much has occurred . . . so much—that I stagger as I write, in its sharp remembrance. Summers of bloom—and months of frost, and days of jingling bells, yet all the while this hand upon our fireside. Today has been so glad without, and yet so grieved within. . . . I cannot always see the light—please tell me if it shines.

She rushes on toward a description of the beauties of summer: strange blossoms that arise on many stalks, trees that receive their tenants, and the choir that bears the canto of evening. Thereafter she confesses: "I hardly know what I have said—my words put all their feathers on—and fluttered here and there" (L, 2:335–36). Her mother, then, is still a great care; while the daughter, who asked "Was there a summer?" in November of the same year, is letting herself go as she does the home work of a poet. If her memory was to do more than "flutter," she knew she had to gather her forces.

She was, without question, trying to make time so that she could continue the reading on which a poet's education depends. There is, for instance, a note written also in the summer of 1858 to a neighbor from whom she wanted to borrow the work of Thomas DeQuincey:

. . . for tho' the hours are very full, I think I might snatch here and there a moment, if I had the books . . . . I should love to pass an hour with you, and the little girls, could I leave home or mother. I do not go out at all, lest father come and miss me, or miss some little act, which I might forget should I run away—Mother is much as usual. I dont know what to hope of her. . . . we are perplexed often— (L, 2:337)

The poet, however, did her "courtesies," as she called them, to new residents in town; and she spent some happy evenings with friends gathered at the house of her brother and Susan, who had married in the summer of 1856, and often entertained guests at the Evergreens next door. But there is, also, an undated note declining an invitation from Susan: "I," Dickinson writes, "have made calls this afternoon, and accidentally left my mind at Prof. Warner's. Please reserve an Ottoman for my spirit . . ." (L, 2:347). She sent Susan another note, with a poem: "to my Father—to whose untiring efforts in my behalf, I am indebted for my *morning-hours*— viz—3. AM to 12. PM. these grateful lines are inscribed" (L, 2:344). Two stanzas of the pedestrian satire read: "Sleep is supposed to be / By souls of sanity— / The shutting of the eye. // Morn is supposed to be / By people of degree— / The breaking of the Day" (#213, c. 1858–59). Edward Dickinson had, nonetheless, acquired for her during 1857 a set of Shakespeare's work, in eight volumes edited by Charles Knight.[17] Emerson lectured in Amherst and stayed at the Evergreens on December 16, 1857, but there is no evidence that the busy young woman heard or met him. During the next year, she gave her sister-in-law E. C. Gaskell's *Life of Charlotte Brontë*.[18] These scattered details suggest that Dickinson was hardly frolicking away the days and nights.

She was, however, still uncertain about whether she could realize her ambitions to be a poet. She wrote in January 1859 to young Louise Norcross, "You remember, dear, you are one of the ones from whom I do not run away." The remark is in a context of work, if not overwork:

I am sewing for Vinnie, . . . and I often lay down my needle, and "build a castle in the air" which seriously impedes the sewing project. . . . I have known little of you, since the October morning when our families went out driving, and you and I in the dining room decided to be distinguished. It's a great thing to be "great," Loo, and you and I might tug for life, and never accomplish it.

Tugging for life, the young poet then says she has heard the cousin "had many little cares," hopes they do not fatigue her, and adds: "Sometimes *I* get tired, and I would rather none I love would understand the word . . ." (L, 2:345).

It is little wonder that she dramatized the wish to dwell "in Sovereign Barns." She not only sewed for her sister but was without her help when Lavinia Dickinson went first at Christmastime in 1858 to be with the Norcrosses, stayed at least three months during February, March, and April 1859, and was again in Boston for some weeks beginning in March 1860. Mrs. Dickinson seems finally, during the early part of that year, to have recovered from her long illness.[19]

The daughter, however, continued to share the work of the women in the family. There is, for instance, the sarcasm of a note written in August 1860 to thank the sister-in-law for bread the poet borrowed when she served tea or dinner to Governor and Mrs. Nathaniel Banks, guests of her parents: "Great times. . . . Wish Pope to Rome—that's all—" (L, 2:366–67).

Or, having expected a visit from Louise Norcross in December 1861 but learning instead that she was ill, the poet wrote on the 31st, "I brushed away sleet from eyes familiar with it . . . and then took up my work hemming strings for mother's gown. I think I hemmed them faster for knowing you weren't coming, my fingers having nothing else to do." The letter breaks, but an old telling point follows the break: "Odd, that I, who say 'no' so much, cannot bear it from others. Odd, that I, who run from so many, cannot brook that one turn from me. Come when you will, Loo, the hearts are never shut here." Then she notes, "I don't remember 'May.' Is that the one stands next April? And is that the month for the river-pink?" (That was the spring and early summer of the last two "Master" letters, but the remark is a reduction in prose of the histrionic passage in the letter of November 1858 to the Hollands.)

Dickinson thereafter reports to the cousin the news "today" of the war death of a "Poor little widow's boy, riding to-night in the mad wind, back to the village burying-ground where he never dreamed of sleeping! Ah! the dreamless sleep!" Going on to ask further anxious questions about the cousin's health, the poet tells her, "I wanted you very much, and I put you by with sharper tears than I give to many" (L, 2:385–86).

The letter is remarkable for the fusion of inner and outer weather, the observations and criticism of herself and the feeling

with others, as well as for the expressive language by which she
conveys emotion and leans away from it almost simultaneously.
These capacities evident in a quiet moment gave the poet an advantage that enabled her to be convincingly histrionic as occasions
required.

Since she was never absolutely free to indulge all wishes or,
unless she herself was ill, to be excused from chores, she sometimes
resorted to complaining jokingly and enjoyed the complaint. She
wrote to Elizabeth Holland in early May 1866:

> I await Commencement with merry resignation. . . . Mother
> resumes lettuce, involving my transgression—suggestive of
> yourself, however, which endears disgrace. "House" is being
> "cleaned." I prefer pestilence. That is more classic and less
> fell. (L, 2:452–53)

Or, in a letter of August 1884 to the Norcross cousins, she said: "I
am glad the housekeeping is kinder; it is a prickly art" (L, 3:827).
And although such comments have been said to suggest that the
poet passed whatever cleaning she could off on her sister,[20] a "member of the family" when Emily Dickinson was young observed that
she was an excellent housekeeper.[21]

After their mother was first stricken with paralysis on June 15,
1875, the daughters, with the help of Maggie Maher, cared for Mrs.
Dickinson during *seven* years of unrelieved sickness; for four of
those years she was a helpless invalid, and she was, according to
Lavinia Dickinson, primarily the poet's patient.[22] There is, then, no
reason to doubt Otis Lord's concern for Emily Dickinson's health
as early as 1877 or his admiration for her unselfishness. She exaggerated, of course, when she said in 1862 that she never had a
mother; yet the child was often mother to the woman and housemaid to the father.

There are clearly more factors than thwarted love to be considered in the relationship between "real" experience and the poetry.
While Dickinson wrote some important poems, between 1858 and
1861, it is reasonable to conclude that she would not have been
nearly as prolific as she became by 1862 had not life changed for
her.[23] The apprenticeship was over, the mother was well, Lavinia
Dickinson was home, and there was less need to "snatch here and
there a moment" for reading and writing. The poet's energies were
not inexhaustible, yet the poet prevailed.

If we compare her with Whitman, whose quasi-autobiographical persona in "Song of Myself" (1855) said enviably: "I loaf and invite my soul, / I lean and loaf at my ease observing a spear of summer grass," Dickinson—during what have been called "the puzzling years . . . rightly regarded as crucial, a time of extra-ordinary stress and inner turmoil"[24]—had to resort to wishing she were "a Hay." The poem is as close to autobiography as any she ever wrote; there must have been many times, during more than four years that included her mother's illness after the family moved to the Homestead and the seven years when her mother was an invalid, that Dickinson longed to be "a grass," "a Sphere of Simple Green," or "a toddling daisy." The "commandment" to consider the lilies meant for her just that: she *considered* them and eventually arrayed herself in glory.

Despite the fact that she was more modest and circumspect than Whitman in declaring an aesthetic program, she was as astute as he was. She never wrote long poems. There probably was not enough free time for them. She did write poetic sequences that are yet to be fully explored as coherent wholes,[25] and the subtleties of the work will continue to yield confirmation of the extent to which she was, like Whitman, dedicated to experiments with language and the quick changes of the pronomial "I." She was the kind of writer who should have provoked critics long before new feminism to say she had her nerve. Because she was not given to self-aggrandizement, however, she would never have thought at her most histrionic moment to declare that she was "Emily Dickinson, a kosmos," or to suggest "I am large, I contain multitudes." But who else would have written "*a* Hay"? She had her nerve, even in the risks she took with genre, style, and idiom. Because her imagination was more dramatic than Whitman's, she created not one persona but many personae whose voices also enlarge our vision of life—and death.

5

"It's easy to invent a Life": Listening to Literary Voices

I

One of the marks of Dickinson's maturity as a poet is her confidence in relation to other writers whose novels and verse were "raw" materials for her work. Reading a Brontë, George Eliot, Hawthorne, the Brownings, or Shakespeare, the parochial young American did not seem overly anxious about their influence on her imagination. She blithely transposed their language, characters, and plots, as well as their delineations of behavior, attitudes, and moods into poems of her own. Dickinson's investment of energy, new rhythms and emphasis, even arguments in the voices of personae who originated in her reading is, moreover, responsible for some of her most powerful poems. And while they tell us that Dickinson was adroit, they also tell us that she was, as T. S. Eliot said of John Donne, expert beyond experience.[1]

She saw, not long after she learned to bake bread, that one needed more than household chores to grow "wise." Writing to Austin Dickinson when she was at Holyoke in 1847, she remarked:

> You are reading Arabian Nights, according to Vinnie. . . . I hope you have derived much benefit from their perusal & presume your powers of imagining will vastly increase thereby. But I must give you a word of advice too. Cultivate

99

your other powers in proportion as you allow Imagination to captivate you. Am not I a very wise *young lady*? (L, 1:57)

She then mentioned in passing that she was studying chemistry, physiology, and algebra. In a letter written the month before she mentioned reciting a review in ancient history and a lesson which was "merely transposition" of Pope's *Essay on Man*. She also practiced the piano (L, 1:54). She was already, at seventeen, in training to be a writer. She continued to school herself in her own independent way.

During the spring of 1860, she read a "fantastic" story by Harriet Prescott Spofford in the *Atlantic Monthly*, which Susan Dickinson had shown her. "Sue," the poet responded, "it is the only thing I ever read in my life that I didn't think I could have imagined myself!" Later, she said: "You stand nearer the world than I do, Susan. Send me everything she writes."[2] The young Dickinson women, who followed the market, read both popular and important writers in fashion or not.

One of the poet's first enthusiasms was for the fiction of the great women novelists of nineteenth-century England. She spoke of the Brontës as "the Yorkshire girls" and of herself as their friend (L, 2:437); she wrote an elegiac poem for Charlotte Brontë, of whom she says:

> Gathered from many wanderings—
> Gethsemane can tell
> Thro' what transporting anguish
> She reached the Asphodel!
> (#148, c. 1859)[3]

Dickinson had read Brontë's *Jane Eyre* in 1849, and it gave her ideas for a cluster of poems. "Before I got my eye put out—," for example, was suggested by the blinding of Rochester, the man Jane Eyre loves and marries. Rochester, it will be remembered, was blinded in the left eye. The account in the novel reads: "one eye was knocked out." The poet's use of the singular "eye" is both accurate and telling. The other eye was inflamed, and the sight was obscured, but it was not "put out." When Jane describes Rochester's lack of vision, she mentions that "the sky was bland to him—the earth a void." Dickinson, working from those observations, writes a dramatic monologue for him. Given anxieties about her own eyes, she may well have been sympathetic to the hero's handicap as she put words in his mouth. The persona contemplates what it would be like to have once again the sky, the meadows, the mountains, all forests, the stintless stars, moon, the motion of birds, and morning's amber road "to look at when I liked—"; the poem then comes to a startling conclusion:

> The News would strike me dead—
>
> So safer—guess—with just my soul
> Upon the window pane—
> Where other Creatures put their Eyes—
> Incautious—of the Sun—
>   (#327, c. 1862)

In that broken image, Dickinson conveys Rochester's weary resignation to his fate and painful sense of his vision as "seared."[4]

Dickinson uses the image of the windowpane in another poem which is also allusively and substantively related to *Jane Eyre*. Brontë's heroine suffers "semi-starvation," which readers remember long after many of the details of the novel have receded from consciousness. Dickinson speaks for her:

> It would have starved a Gnat—
> To *live so small as I—
> And yet I was a living Child—
> With—Food's necessity
>
> Upon me—like a Claw—
> I could no more remove
> Than I could †coax a Leech away—
> Or make a Dragon—move—
>
> Nor like the Gnat—had I—
> The privilege to fly
> And ‡seek a Dinner for myself—
> How mightier He—than I—
>
> Nor like Himself—the Art
> Upon the Window Pane
> To gad my little Being out—
> And not begin—again—
>   (#612, c. 1862)

*dine
†modify
‡gain

The experience of being hungry was a repeated one for Jane. An orphan, she was sent at the age of ten as a "charity-child" to Lowood Institution. During her first day at the school, the children were served burnt porridge for breakfast, a rancid-smelling mix of "indifferent potatoes and stray shreds of rusty meat" for dinner, a supper consisting of a small mug of coffee and a half-slice of brown bread ("I should have been glad of much more—I was still hungry"), and finally a glass of water and a piece of oatcake at bedtime. When such "everyday fare" was edible, it was skimpy: "how small my portion seemed!" she said. "I wished it had been doubled." The meager fare was "scarcely sufficient to keep alive a delicate invalid." "And yet," Dickinson's Jane reminds us, "I was a living Child— / With Food's necessity / Upon me."

If the word "necessity" seems to violate a schoolgirl's point of view, the poem's past tense suggests a remembered experience, and the choice of the word confirms the poet's debt to the novel. Jane, earning her way as a governess years later, recalls "what it was to come back from church to Lowood—to long for a plenteous meal and a good fire, to be unable to get either." The memory is reinforced still later when Jane leaves a situation as governess of Rochester's ward at Thornfield. Without money, friends, or place, she wanders the Yorkshire moor:

> Everywhere sunshine. I wished I could live in it and on it. . . .
> I would fain have become a bee or lizard, that I might have
> found fitting nutriment, permanent shelter here. But I was a
> human being, and had a human being's wants. . . . I was
> brought face to face with necessity.[5]

Dickinson, preempting Jane's experiences, gives her a more dramatic voice than Charlotte Brontë was able to do with copious description, an extended narrative, and melodramatic incident, as strong as their hold is on a reader's memory. Claw, leech, dragon, and gnat are the poet's. Experiences of hunger and the inability to escape it, however, would not have been likely in her household, and there is no biographical evidence to support the theory that the poet's imagery of starvation points to anorexia nervosa, which has been said to be one of her psychological "problems." She liked to write about food and appreciated it.

If one wishes, furthermore, to interpret the subject of a child's actual hunger as a trope for a want of human affection, it is well to suspend that reading until the relationship between another of Dickinson's poems and the novel is considered. Brontë clearly contrasts Jane's experiences at school with her earlier history, from which Dickinson derives metaphors for the following monologue:

> Deprived of Other Banquet,
> I entertained Myself—
> At first—a *scant nutrition—
> †An insufficient Loaf—
>
> But grown by slender addings
> To so esteemed a size
> 'Tis sumptous enough for me—
> And almost to suffice
>
> A Robin's ‡famine able—
> Red Pilgrim, He and I—
> A Berry from Our table
> Reserve—for Charity—
> (#773, c. 1863)

*plain Regaling
†An innutritious Loaf
‡palate/hunger

As an object of charity for years before being sent to Lowood, Jane stayed at Gateshead Hall, the house of Mrs. Reed, widow of Jane's uncle who had adopted her upon the death of her parents and had subsequently died also. Poorer than Mrs. Reed's servants, Jane was an outcast in the house. Excluded from "every enjoyment," dinners and evening parties, festive occasions and the exchange of presents, she "contrived to find a pleasure in loving and cherishing" a ragged doll and "was comparatively happy." She once occupied herself by looking through a window at "the spectacle of a little hungry robin." Opening the window to scatter crumbs from a breakfast of bread and milk on the sill and the cherry-tree bough, she was seen by a housemaid, who observed: "You look quite red as if you had been about some mischief: what were you opening the window for?"

But Jane did not have the privilege to fly. Cruelly punished for fighting to defend herself from a cousin who attacked her while she was reading one of his books, she resolved upon "some strange expedient to . . . escape from insupportable oppression—as run-ning away, or, if that could not be effected, never eating or drinking more, and letting myself die." She came to the conclusion, however, that "I can never get away . . . until I am a woman." Thereafter, confronting Mrs. Reed, Jane charged: "You think I have no feelings, and that I can do without one bit of love or kindness; but I cannot live so." When she was befriended by an understanding teacher at school, Jane remarked, "I would not have exchanged Lowood with all its privations, for Gateshead and its daily luxuries."[6] Dickinson, who once observed that "Affection is like bread, unnoticed till we starve" (L, 2:499), may have integrated the two orders of deprivation in "It would have starved a Gnat," but in "Deprived of other Banquet, / I entertained myself—" she emphasizes the resourcefulness of the lonely child, whose experience the poet assumes in both poems.

Influenced by the novel which Brontë calls an "autobiography" because she uses the narrative "I" for the account of Jane's life, Dickinson nevertheless did not have to plot a continuous story but could draw at will from evocative scenes and motifs in the novel for several of her fictions. There is, in fascicle 21 which includes "It would have starved a Gnat," yet another "Jane" poem. It is based on the heroine's love for Rochester. And while the poet had depicted Rochester's physical and psychological state in "Before I got my eye put out," she adopts the heroine's point of view for an account of her actions in effecting a change in the life of a man whose willful deceptions and self-confidence had been destroyed by events over which he was no longer in control. The poet's mature Jane, faithful to Brontë's story, soliloquizes:

> I rose—because He sank—
> I thought it would be opposite—
> But when his power *dropped—
> My Soul †grew straight.
>
> I cheered my fainting Prince—
> I sang ‡firm—even—Chants—
> I §helped his Film—with Hymn—
>
> And when the Dews drew off
> That held his Forehead stiff—
> I ‖met him—
> Balm **to Balm—

I told him Best—must pass
Through this low Arch of Flesh—
No Casque so brave
It spurn the Grave—

I told him ††Worlds I knew
Where ‡‡Emperors grew—
Who recollect
If we were true—

And so with Thews of Hymn—
And Sinew from within—
And ways I knew not that I knew—till then—
I lifted Him—

                        (#616, c. 1862)

*bent
†felt/bent/stood
‡straight—steady Chants
§stayed
‖gave
**for
††a World
‡‡Monarchs

In six brief stanzas, Dickinson condenses more than two chapters that the novelist required for narrating the reunion between Rochester and Jane. Having learned that she has inherited money and is free to follow the well-remembered but sorrowful voice of Rochester, whom she imagines calling her for help, Jane goes back to Thornfield Hall (from which she had fled upon being informed—on the day she was to be married to him—that he had kept secret a wife, a madwoman in the attic). Jane finds the mansion in charred ruins, hears that he was blinded in an unsuccessful effort to save the woman from fire, and goes in penetrating rain at dusk to a distant manor house on a desolate farm where he is living under the care of servants.

Dickinson's Jane "thought it would be opposite." Rochester, as Jane describes him in the novel, is "a sightless Samson," "a royal eagle, chained to a perch, forced to entreat a sparrow to become a purveyor." He is in a state of "sullen woe," "brooding," and "melancholy." "I have," he says, "little left in myself."[7] Although evening's darkness changes to "a bright, sunny morning," and "there is a tender shining in it," Rochester is not easily consoled. Although he calls Jane "my skylark" or tells her that her "animating voice . . . cheers" his "withered heart" and that "all melody on earth" is concentrated in her tongue, he "relapsed again into gloom." Jane, speaking for herself, recounts that she, "on the contrary, became more cheerful and took fresh courage." Soothing him, she once saw him turn aside as a tear slid "from under the sealed eyelid." She would not be lachrymose. She teased him to make him "less sad"; she reminded him that he could be "stiff about urging his point." Knowing that she suited him, that she could comfort him and that she could revive him, "brought to light and life" her whole nature: "in his presence," she says, "I thoroughly lived; and he in mine. Blind as he was, smiles played over his face, joy dawned on his forehead."[8] Or as Dickinson writes: "I stayed his Film . . . / And when the Dews drew off / That held his Forehead stiff— / I gave him Balm for Balm." Like the novelist's heroine, the poet's persona is a woman capable of grace in adversity. She rose to the occasion.

When Rochester asks the good Jane to marry him, she cannot resist exclaiming self-righteously that virtue is rewarded; he fears that she delights in sacrifice. She is undaunted: "I love you better now, when I can really be useful to you, than I did in your state of proud independence, when you disdained every part but that of giver and protector." They should, he decides, be married instantly. She replies that the "sun has dried up all the rain-drops."[9] When the poet writes "the dews drew off that held his forehead stiff," she encapsulates weather, emotions, and plot in nine words.

Although the summary of events in the novel is a prosaic gloss of "I rose—because He sank," it elucidates what happens in the poem. Its subtleties and ambiguities have been interpreted, for instance, by one critic in relation to other pre-texts. Dickinson, it is said, "inverts the fairytale situation of Sleeping Beauty or Snow White by having the 'fainting Prince' die instead of her. . . . The lack of any felt sorrow and the growing sense of vigor and assurance . . . enact her absorption of the animus in her psyche." The poem, then, is a dream in which the man "died into her, . . . investing her with a strength both 'phallic' and spiritual."[10] If Dickinson's soliloquy is for Jane Eyre, Rochester (whose "Film" is helped "with Hymn") did not in fact die. Having suffered disaster and despondency, he told Jane that he "was forced to pass through the valley of the shadow of death." Once proud of his strength, he experienced remorse and repentance as well as a desire for reconciliation with God, and began to pray to die. Dickinson imagines the woman's response to that acknowledgment: "I told him Best—must pass / Through this low Arch of Flesh— / No Casque so brave / It spurn the Grave." The life of Brontë's Jane had prepared her for comprehending Rochester's mortal trials. She says, "I served as both his prop and guide," and concludes the story of their reunion by the affirmation of their triumph over misfortunes: "All my confidence is bestowed on him; all his confidence is devoted to me; we are precisely suited in character; perfect accord is the result." Rochester found Jane's "benefits no burden."[11] Dickinson liked a woman who knows her own strength, so her Jane concludes: "I lifted Him—"

Still, other critics troubled that "we have no knowledge of events to which the poet refers" in "I rose" as well as many of the love poems, have repeatedly analyzed the biographical data—no matter how recalcitrant or disputed it is—in hopes of identifying the interlocutor and explaining the phenomenon that Jay Leyda called the "omitted center."[12] If, as William Shurr points out, "the reader feels that some essential information is missing," the presumed "lack of 'referentiality' " warrants the search for it. But the references to fictional characters with whom Dickinson was familiar provide centers that have been overlooked in more than a few of the soliloquies.

One of the most light-hearted and amusing of the courtship verses in the canon has origins in Jane Eyre's story of her devotion to Rochester and the efforts she made to cheer, to tease, and to "suit" him:

> You said that I "was Great"—one Day—
> Then "Great" it be—if that please Thee—
> Or Small—or any Size at all—
> Nay—I'm the Size suit Thee—
>
> Tall—like the Stag—would that?
> Or lower—like the Wren—
> Or other heights of Other Ones
> I've seen?
>
> Tell which—it's dull to guess—
> And I must be Rhinoceros
> Or Mouse
> At Once—for Thee—
>
> So say—if Queen it be—
> Or Page—please Thee—

I'm that—or nought—
Or other thing—if other thing there be—
With just this *Stipulus—
I suit thee—

(#738, c. 1863)

*Reservation

In Brontë's novel, Rochester responds: "Jane's soft ministry will be a perpetual joy. Jane suits me; do I suit her?"[13] It is possible, of course, that the poet's own experiences contribute to the brio of the moment, which she finds apt for her skill in changing shapes and images as well as rhyming playfully, but her use of the fictive voice is undeniable.

Attempts to establish a provenance for the love poetry in the life of Dickinson, on the other hand, assume the poems themselves as proof that they were all addressed to a single historical figure, whose identity is the subject of speculation. The serious disagreements among scholars who fasten on one or another person for whom there is no more than questionable evidence beyond the poems is, in turn, the stuff of parody. At least one "detective" fiction solves the mystery by imagining an affair between the poet and Henry David Thoreau at Walden Pond.[14]

Dickinson herself writes:

It's easy to invent a Life—
God does it—every Day—
Creation—but the Gambol
Of His Authority—

It's easy to efface it—
The thrifty Deity
Could scarce afford Eternity
To Spontaneity—

The Perished Patterns murmur—
But His Perturbless Plan
Proceed—inserting Here—a Sun—
There—leaving out a Man—

(#724, c. 1863)

The view of God is caustic. The metaphor of the writer at work, which is the basis of the view of God, is, however, lively and authoritative. The thrifty Dickinson, inserting here a sun, a rhinoceros or a mouse, there leaving out a sun, knows whereof she writes. It was easy for her to invent a scene, a conversation, or "stipulus." With a little help from literary friends, she must have been doing it almost every day by 1863. As she proceeded on her perturbless plan, she must also have enjoyed the gambol.

II

If Charlotte Brontë provided Dickinson with stimuli for poems, so did George Eliot—"*my* George Eliot," the poet called her (L, 3:700). There are, beginning with references in 1862 to *The Mill on the Floss* and continuing off and on until 1886, many evidences of the impact of the English author on Dickinson. They shared a similar sense of satire and social criticism, as well as a talent for characterizing people. Eliot, for instance, writes in *The Mill* (1860) of two condescending young women (given to holding the chin too high or acting with a view to effect) that they were "too well-bred to have any of the grimaces and affected tones that belong to pretentious vulgarity."[15] Dickinson, describing a woman who "dealt with her pretty words like Blades," writes: "She never deemed—she hurt— / That—is not Steel's Affair— / A vulgar grimace in the Flesh— / How ill the Creatures bear—" (479, c. 1862). Then the novelist compares a joyful young woman, who is unmistakably gentle, kind, and generous, to one of "Correggio's cherubs," but thereafter contrasts her with "the world's wife," "the charitable ladies" whose "celestial breasts" and "refined instincts" are easily outraged by the efforts of a good parish priest to aid the repentant Maggie Tulliver when she is "disgraced" and misjudged because she has acted rashly.[16] Combining Eliot's imagery for the two sorts of gentlewomen, Dickinson writes her own satire to ridicule the lack of Christian charity toward what she pleasantly called "freckled Human Nature":

> What Soft—Cherubic Creatures—
> These Gentlewomen are—
> One would as soon assault a Plush—
> Or violate a Star—
>
> Such Dimity Convictions—
> A Horror so refined

Of freckled Human Nature—
Of Deity—ashamed—

It's such a common—Glory—
A Fisherman's—Degree—
Redemption—Brittle Lady—
Be so—ashamed of Thee—

(#401, c. 1862)

Even this poem, with its omniscient eye, its humorous joining of "celestial-sexual" images, its quick tonal changes from mock admiration to mimickry, from gentle chiding to serious wit, has been said to express Dickinson's "gigantic self-hatred."

Dickinson's vindication of Maggie, whose "many imperfections" are measured against the choices she made to "convince" the young people she loves that she is sorry for having wronged them,[17] is dramatically expressed in the troubled rhythms of a death scene more appropriate than that of Eliot's own tragic but flawed ending to the novel. The poet's depiction of death by drowning begins in the middle of a sentence and suggests a gasping for breath:

Me prove it now—*Whoever doubt
Me stop to prove it—now—
†Make haste—the Scruple! Death be scant
For Opportunity—

The River reaches to my feet—
As yet—My Heart be dry—
Oh Lover—Life could not convince—
Might Death—enable Thee—

The River reaches to my Breast—
Still—still—My Hands above
Proclaim with their remaining Might—
Dost recognize the Love?

The River reaches to my Mouth—
Remember—when the Sea
Swept by my searching Eyes—the last—
Themselves were quick—with Thee!

(#537, c. 1862)

*Whatever
†Come near

Eliot's heroine, braving tidal currents and swift flooding of the river Floss, had taken a boat to rescue her brother Tom, who was stranded at the mill. No matter that he had been priggish and mean-spirited about Maggie's conduct. "What quarrel, what harshness, what unbelief in each other," Eliot writes, "can subsist in the presence of a great calamity when all the artificial vesture of our life is gone, and we are all one with each other in primitive mortal needs?" Maggie felt "the strong resurgent love towards her brother that swept away all the later impressions of hard, cruel offence and misunderstanding"; but it was not until Tom, in the boat with her, had pushed off and they were on the wide water that "the full meaning of what had happened" came with overpowering force to him and he was able to comprehend the "revelation . . . of the depths of life that had lain beyond his vision, which he had fancied so keen and clear." Eliot describes them as they sat mutely gazing at each other: "Maggie with eyes of intense life looking out from a weary, beaten face—Tom pale with a certain awe and humiliation." Their boat, however, overturned, and death rushed on them. Brother and sister went down "in an embrace never to be parted."[18] In that death, Maggie not only proved that she loved Tom; she also proved that she has conquered the tumult and anguish of her love for Stephen, the man who, despite his having been affianced to her cousin and having "been tortured by scruples," found renunciation of his passionate love for Maggie impossible.[19] Eliot, concentrating in the final episodes on Maggie's loyalty to her brother, neglects any mention of Stephen, whom the girl loved, or of the cousin she had wronged in spite of herself. It is as if the dutiful Maggie had forgotten them, and the author, preoccupied with a single theme, had forgotten her story. George Eliot's "reiteration of duty," according to the poet's niece, "depressed" Dickinson, "while she admitted its infallibility."[20] The poet, attending to the significance of the internal strife that passion had engendered in Maggie's heart, takes the liberty of dramatizing the resolution of the conflict and infallibly surpasses the novelist's discursive prose in the depiction of the heroine's "supreme moment."

The affinities the poet felt with Eliot, however, were strong; reservation about too much sermonizing in a literary work was tempered in Dickinson's personal regard for the woman, a regard that is pertinent to the poet's response to the work of Nathaniel Hawthorne who was for her also "a living presence."[21] When Dickinson observed that "Hawthorne appalls, entices" (L, 2:649), she must have chosen the words carefully, but one can only guess which of the qualities of the fiction she had in mind. Having read *The House of the Seven Gables* in 1851, the year it was published, she wrote to Austin Dickinson that the "wearying on" of the heroine Hepzibah "for affection's sake, and for the sake of Clifford," her brother, "seemed almost a lesson for us to learn." The poet added, with a pun, "I don't mean that you are *him*, or that Hepzibah's *me*, except in a relative sense, only I was reminded" (L, 1:155). The tone of the comments hardly suggests that Dickinson was either appalled or enticed by the book. *The Scarlet Letter* (1850), however, is the romance to which she is most likely to have given her passionate attention. Although there is no record of her opinion of it, there is evidence that she would have been dismayed by it for more than one reason. She would not have been as equivocal or at least ambiguous as Hawthorne in his attitude toward Hester Prynne, imprisoned, pilloried, and outcast as an adulterous woman by the Puritan society and with the silent consent of the man she loved.

The poet's "whole career," Sewall has said, "may be regarded as a sustained, if muted, rebellion against" the Puritan inheritance. "Among her several rejections" of the doctrine of innate sin, for example, "was a remark on a typical Amherst sermon: 'While the Clergyman tells Father and Vinnie that "this Corruptible shall put on Incorruption"—it has already done so and they go defrauded.' "[22]

Dickinson's view of adultery is implied in her commendations of George Eliot, who lived openly out of wedlock from 1854 to 1878 with George Henry Lewes (having himself condoned his wife's adultery and been precluded from divorce). Dickinson writes, for example: " 'What do I think of *Middlemarch* [1872]?' What do I think of glory—except that in a few instances this 'mortal has put on immortality.' George Eliot is one. The mysteries of human nature surpass the 'mysteries of redemption' " (L, 2:506). The poet, when she wrote to Higginson, obviously made a point of speaking of Eliot as "Mrs. Lewes,"[23] grieved for her when she died (L, 3:685), and wrote a poem in her memory ("Her Losses make Our Gains ashamed—," #1562, c. 1883). Dickinson's tributes leave no doubt that she judged the novelist—and woman—worthy of redemption: "Perhaps she who Experienced Eternity in Time, may have received Time's omitted Gift as part of the Bounty of Eternity," and "The gift of belief which her greatness denied her, I trust she receives in the childhood of the kingdom of heaven" (L, 3:689 and 700).

There is no comparable praise of *The Scarlet Letter;* nor is there more than a brief comment for the author, whose death in 1864 Dickinson noted in a letter but of whom she said shortly thereafter: "Hawthorne's interruption does not seem as it did—Noon is Morning's memoir . . ." (L, 2:431 and 432). She had spoken, moreover, in another voice than his for Hester Prynne when she wrote the poem:

> Mine—by the Right of the White Election!
> Mine—by the Royal Seal!
> Mine—by the Sign in the Scarlet prison—
> *Bars—cannot conceal!
>
> Mine—here—in Vision—and in Veto!
> Mine—by the Grave's Repeal—
> Titled—Confirmed—
> †Delirious Charter!
> Mine—‡long as Ages steal
>
> (#528, c. 1862)
>
> *Bolts
> †Good affidavit—
> ††while

Dickinson imagines the dramatic moment after the death of the Reverend Arthur Dimmesdale on the scaffold of the pillory where seven years earlier Hester, coming out of prison with their child, Pearl, had been displayed before the multitude. The day of the minister's death had been one of public festival, the occasion of the new governor's receiving his office at the hands of the people of the Massachusetts Bay Colony. Dimmesdale had delivered a triumphant Election Sermon. "He stood," Hawthorne writes, "on the very proudest eminence of superiority, to which the gifts of intellect, rich lore, prevailing eloquence, and a reputation of whitest sanctity, could exalt a clergyman"; Hester and the child waited at the foot of the scaffold in the marketplace for the three of them thereafter to board a ship on which they had secretly planned to flee the Puritan state. As the procession of "majestic and venerable fathers" left the church, Dimmesdale paused and turned toward the scaffold. "Hester," he said, "come hither!" With her support, he mounted the scaffold; then freeing himself, he revealed to the horror-stricken people he had long deceived that he too bore a red stigma, and collapsed. As he said farewell to Hester, she whispered, "Shall we not meet again? Shall we not spend our immortal life

together? Surely, surely, we have ransomed one another." Replying "Hush, Hester, hush!" he lectured her:

> "The law we broke! The sin here so awfully revealed!—let
> these alone be in thy thoughts! I fear! I fear! It may be, that,
> when we forgot our God,—when we violated our reverence
> each for the other's soul—it was thenceforth vain to hope
> that we could meet hereafter, in an everlasting and pure
> reunion."

Declaring that God is merciful, His name to be praised, and His
will to be done, Dimmesdale again bade Hester farewell. "That
final word," Hawthorne writes, "came forth with the minister's
expiring breath."[24] Hester said nothing more. Hawthorne allows
her no last word. Dickinson protests for her.

The poet is clearly mindful of Hawthorne's characterization of the
adulterous woman. Having borne public disgrace and moral solitude without the support of the man she loved, having "never put
forward even the humblest title to share in the world's privileges—
further than to breathe the common air, and earn daily bread,"
Hester Prynne was always imprisoned by the scarlet letter. She had,
nevertheless, "a genuine regard for virtue" and led an exemplary life
of service to those who needed help. Hawthorne writes that individu-
als, at least in private, "had begun to look upon the scarlet letter as
the token . . . of her many good deeds"; "the world's heavy hand" had
ordained her "a sister of Mercy"; and the glittering symbol "had the
effect of the cross on a nun's bosom." But "in her lonesome cottage,"
she assumed "a freedom of speculation, then common enough on the
other side of the Atlantic": "the human intellect, newly emancipated" had "overthrown and rearranged . . . within the sphere of
theory . . . the whole system of ancient prejudice, wherewith was
linked much of the ancient principle." She not only "imbibed this
spirit"; she had done penance, but she was not penitent. "The scarlet
letter had not done its office."[25] For Hawthorne, however, Hester's
"life had turned, in great measure, from passion and feeling, to
thought"; he betrays that thought when he assumed it is divorced
from her emotions.

Dickinson's Hester Prynne, in the language of Puritan theology
and politics,[26] passionately affirms her independence, her rightful
beatitude, "long as Ages steal." *Steal* is the dramatic final word
juxtaposed with the possessive and insistent *Mine*. Having ac-

cepted the consequences of love, the grief, the hardships and injustice she suffered, she refuses to acknowledge guilt but pleads for the trust she has earned and the vision of life denied her. Her rage is hardly muted. The scarlet letter had done its office.

A reading of the fictional sources of these poems does not lessen the sense of deprivation in "Before I got my eye put out" or "It would have starved a Gnat," the happiness of "You said that I 'was Great'—one Day," the urgency of the voice in "Me prove it now," or the insistent rhythms of "Mine—by the Right of White Election!" Whether she exploited or extended, tersely fused or took different perspectives from Brontë, Eliot, and Hawthorne, Dickinson made the poems indebted to them her own and made the fictions new.

The poems themselves are comparable to the raids on earlier literary texts by another original American writer whose work is well known for its dramatic moments. When Ezra Pound, in *Personae* (1909), wrote of Bertran de Born, the loquitur of "Sestina: Altaforte," whom "Dante Alighiere put . . . in hell for that he was a stirrer up of strike: 'Eccovi! Judge ye! Have I dug him up again?' " the author protected the character of the poem from the reader's misapprehension. It was, however, at the time Dickinson sent "Before I got my eye put out" to Higginson that she warned him she was not always her own heroine. The caveat was one of the remarks he ignored. Having realized the limitations of the reader and critic, she wrote not long after to the Hollands: "I found a bird, this morning, down—down—on a little bush at the foot of the garden, and wherefore sing, I said, since nobody *hears?*" Such an expression of disappointment is unusual in the letters, and she quickly recovered: "One sob in the throat, one flutter of bosom—'*My* business is to *sing*'—and away she rose! How do I know but cherubim, once, themselves, as patient, listened, and applauded her unnoticed hymn?" (L, 2:413). Perhaps she was too subtle. Perhaps, unlike Pound, she trusted the reader too much. But like him, and many others before him, she comprehended that the poet's imagination can work equally well from both experience and literary resources. She had, according to her niece, "a way of alluding to and talking about characters in books familiar to us both, as if they were people living right about us."27

And like Pound, she saw in the work of Robert Browning—"the consummate Browning" (L, 3:859)—precedents for the poem as dramatic monologue (*Dramatic Lyrics* in 1842, or *Dramatic Personae* in 1864). There were examples for not giving names of the speakers of poems in Browning's "Any Wife to Any Husband," and "A Woman's Last Word," or "Love in a Life," and "Life in a Love," from *Men and Women* (1855), which Dickinson praised as "a broad Book" (L, 2:491). There were poems for which he too "dug up" persons from literature: "Rudel to the Lady of Tripoli" (1842) or "Caliban Upon Setebos" (1864), for instance.

Since T. S. Eliot noted that it was "Browning's greatest disciple, Mr. Ezra Pound, who adopted the term 'persona' to indicate the several historical characters, through whom he spoke,"[28] the genealogist may add that the twentieth-century poet's term, as it is now used to designate any historical or fictional character who tells a story in the first person, was anticipated by the first of Browning's great disciples when she wrote in her homemade phrase that it was "supposed persons" *for* whom she spoke. An emended history of the term might also mention Brontë's *Jane Eyre, An Autobiography*, which "had put certain basic female experiences into words for the first time"[29] in the imagined voice of a young woman. Dickinson, having read the novel at the age of nineteen, recalled the experience thirty-four years later, when she recommended to a friend a "life" of Emily Brontë as "more electric far than anything since 'Jane Eyre' " (L, 3:775). A novelist who wrote fiction masked as "autobiography"[30] and "the consummate Browning," who took different roles from poem to poem, often without a plot to contain or connect the individual monologues, encouraged Dickinson to develop her own fictions masking as "autobiography" in a profusion of personal voices. Her *Complete Poems* is also a broad book.

III

Dickinson, then, worked in relation to literary currents that do not detract from the daring of what she assayed but clarify what she was doing. She never denied those currents or her enthusiasms. She only hid how much she knew, and that has made all the difference. In the 1862 letter alerting Higginson to her method of "supposing," she almost immediately alluded to Robert Browning: "You spoke of Pippa Passes—I never heard anybody speak of Pippa Passes—before. You see my posture is benighted" (L, 2:412). The word *posture* is telling. Although she did not know everything, she was no ignoramus. She was mischievous, if not roguish, with words.

While there is no evidence that she had heard anyone speak of

"Pippa" (1841), she had friends with whom she shared at least a knowledge of "Rudel to the Lady of Tripoli" in Browning's *Dramatic Lyrics* (1842). The images of the poem are susceptible to different interpretations, but the troubadour's charge to a pilgrim contemplating a journey from Provençal to the distant land of the beautiful and indifferent lady obviously appealed to Dickinson. The emblem for the legendary Rudel's verse is the sunflower, "a foolish mimic sun" in comparison with the *true sun* variously interpreted as a symbol of ideal love, passion, the source of energy and light, or the muse. His longing for the East and his devotion to the orient sun are unequivocal:

> Dear Pilgrim, art thou for the East indeed?
> Go! saying . . .
> That I . . . choose for my device
> A sunflower outspread like a sacrifice
> Before its idol! . . .
>   as the flower's concern is . . .
> But solely for the sun, so men applaud
> In vain this Rudel, he not looking here
> But to the East—the East! go, say this,
>   Pilgrim dear!
>   (part 3, 11.21–6 and 33–37)

Dickinson drew upon the poem in four different letters to friends during the years 1859–61.

Writing in March 1859 to Kate Scott Turner, recently widowed, Dickinson called her one of "my girls" and asked her: "Dare you dwell in the *East* where we dwell? Are you afraid of the Sun?— When you hear new violet sucking her way among the sods, shall you be *resolute?*" The poet's advice, more ambiguous than Rudel's charge to the "Dear Pilgrim," may pertain to her friend's trepidations about following one's desires or ideals. The letter continues: "All *we* are *strangers*—dear—The world is not acquainted with us, because we are not acquainted with her. And Pilgrims!—Do you hesitate?" Enclosing "a small bouquet," which must have been a poem since it was "fadeless," Dickinson added: "And should new flower [Kate] smile at limited associates, pray her remember, were there *many* they were not worn upon the breast—but tilled in the pasture!" (L, 2:349–50).

Then she wrote, probably in 1860, to Samuel Bowles: "You spoke of the 'East.' I have thought about it this winter. Don't you think you and I should be shrewder, to take the *Mountain Road?*" She enclosed a rose for Mary Bowles (L, 2:364). Later, "about August 1861," Dickinson wrote to her: "Austin would send his [love]—but he dont live here—now—He married—and went East" (L, 2:377). Finally, in another letter written during early December 1861 to Samuel Bowles: "To take the pearl—costs Breath—but then a pearl is not impeached—let it strike the East!" (L, 2:383).

Dickinson's remarks in these letters have puzzled readers interested in relating the cryptic language to her life and poetry.[31] The East, the hallowed place where the sun rises and the faraway loved one lives, seems clear enough in Browning's verse. The East is also Dickinson's country, whether it was a state of happiness attained or a blessed condition to be sought. The sun figures in only one of the letters to her friends, and then to suggest there is nothing to fear from following it. And Dickinson's pearl? The prize, something of value bought with great price. On whose part, by whom? Dickinson, with the amusing reference to common pasture flowers, was not likely to consider herself a pearl. She was too given to self-derision. When she wrote that Austin married and went East, she was certainly deriding him; the humor is broad: the marriage had occurred five years earlier, and Mary Bowles knew that. Dickinson enjoyed taking liberties with Browning's symbols and themes; if she changed them according to the persons she addressed, she took for granted their familiarity with his ballad for the noble troubadour. Dickinson—whatever she told Higginson—was not "benighted," although in jousting with her friends or with him, she left so much to be deciphered that she herself easily became a legend.

The modifications in Dickinson's verbal play with regard to "the East" are once again signs of her penchant for making literature "live" from within and for taking part in the life of people to whom she was close. She not only had little inclination to shirk responsibilities and stresses in her relationships with family and friends, but she also seems to have had vitality and valor for occasions that were pertinent to her growth as a poet.

She enjoyed, however briefly, exhilirating times with the friends who gathered at the house of Austin and Susan Dickinson. Bowles, "once at ease" when he visited there, was "said to have remarked, 'This, I guess, is as near heaven as we shall ever get in this life!' "[32] Kate Turner (later Anthon) was a houseguest of the Austin Dickinsons first in February and March 1859, after which she made three or four other visits, the last being in the autumn of 1861; and years later, she wrote of the period as "the golden days." She told Susan Dickinson in 1906: "how vividly I recal [*sic*] them! Those happy visits. . . . Those celestial evenings in the Library—The blazing *wood* fire—*Emily*—*Austin*—The music—The rampant fun—The inextinguishable laughter. The uproarious spirits of our chosen—our most congenial circle." Again, in 1917, she remembered "the old blissful evenings at Austin's! Rare hours, full of merriment, brilliant wit, and inexhaustible laughter. Emily with her dog, & Lantern! often at the piano playing weird & beautiful melodies, all from her own inspiration, oh! she was a choice spirit!"[33] The poet's correspondence confirms the recollection. Writing, perhaps in late 1859, Dickinson said to the new friend: "I remember you as fires begin, and evenings open at Austin's. . . . Those were unnatural evenings—*Bliss* is unnatural." She wondered how many years "will sow the moss upon them, before *we* bind again, a little altered it may be, elder a little it *will* be, and yet the same as suns, which shine, between our lives and loss, and violets, not last years, but having the Mother's eyes." The letter concluded: "inducements to visit Amherst are as they were.—I am pleasantly located in the deep sea, but love will row you out if her hands are strong, and don't wait till I land, for I'm going ashore on the other side—" (L, 2:355–56).

   The prescience of a poet was not required to know that those evenings, those days, would end. The congenial circle was inevitably broken. Emily Dickinson experienced "the terror" of September 1861. Susan and Austin Dickinson had their first child, Edward (Ned), in the summer. The Civil War had begun. Susan Dickinson's Christmas letter of that year to Bowles did not mention the poet but spoke of "Austin with his pale sweet face at the office—rebelling mentally at his drudging life," reported that "the town is quiet very—Now and then women all meet to sew for the soldiers and fight with each other," and noted having read (in the paper Bowles edited) a Browning poem to his wife.[34] Kate Turner married again and was soon widowed again, lived abroad, and did not return for a visit to Amherst until the summer of 1877. Bowles, after the ardors of a trip by sleigh during a heavy snowstorm in the spring of 1861 when he and his wife were driving from Amherst to Springfield, was seriously ill for at least a year. "I dont think," Emily Dickinson told him in January 1862, "we shall ever be merry again—you are ill so long" (L, 2:390). He recovered sufficiently to go to Europe in April 1862. Mary Bowles remained at home with a new son, born in December 1861, and named Charles. The poet had asked her to call him "Robert [Browning] for me" (L, 2:385) and later chided Bowles about it. But amid her own worries, she remained thoughtful of the Bowles family. She wrote to Mary: "When the Best is gone—I know that other things are not of consequence—The Heart wants what it wants" (L, 2:405). Reporting to Bowles that she had received a letter from Mary, Dickinson teased him: "I think she tries to be patient—but you would'nt want her to succeed, would you, Mr. Bowles?" The poet also asked: "Should anybody where you go, talk of Mrs. Browning, you must hear for us—and if you touch her grave, put one hand on the Head, for me—the unmentioned Mourner" (L, 2:410).

The irrevocable course of emotions and events that followed fast upon the time of the Dickinson circle's dwelling in the East, "near to heaven," are points of origin for the theme of remembrance in one of the most hauntingly beautiful lyrics the young American poet ever wrote:

> The lonesome for they know not What—
> The Eastern Exiles—be—
> Who strayed beyond the Amber line
> Some madder Holiday
>
> And ever since—the purple Moat
> They strive to climb—in vain—
> As Birds—that tumble from the clouds
> Do fumble at the strain—
>
> The Blessed Ether—taught them—
> Some Transatlantic Morn—
> When Heaven—was too common—to miss—
> Too sure—to dote upon!
>
> (#262, c. 1861)

The postlapsarian imagery is indebted to the biblical story of the exiled Adam and Eve, a little East of Eden; but the experiences one glimpses in the "Eastern" letters, letters that both seriously and jestingly refer to Browning's "Rudel," linked with nostalgia for the spirited fun of "the golden days" when the poet and her friends strayed beyond the amber line, contributed to the resonant tones of "The lonesome for they know not What." The bizarre music of

Emily Dickinson at the piano is transposed in the fine wariness and wit of the observation that "Heaven—was too common—to miss— / Too sure to dote upon!" She did not fumble at the strain.

IV

Having made no secret of the admiration she felt for the Brownings, Dickinson wrote at least two poems as tributes to Elizabeth Barrett Browning, who had died in June 1861. One of them speaks of the impact of the work on Dickinson and is in her own voice. "I think," she begins, "I was enchanted / When first a sombre Girl / I read that Foreign Lady— / The Dark—felt beautiful . . ." (#593, c. 1862). The other, an elegy, after praising the poetry and lamenting the death of the poet, concludes: "Nought—that We—No Poet's Kinsman— / Suffocate—with easy wo— / What, and if, Ourself a Bridegroom— / Put Her down—in Italy?" (#312, c. 1862).[35] Dickinson had, perhaps a year before, also written out of her "easy wo" and her sense of Browning's difficult loss a poem which she included in the fascicle with that for the Eastern Exiles. The voice of a poet-musician, mourning the death of a person who was beloved and loving, cries out:

> Put up my lute!
> What of—my Music!
> Since the Sole Ear I cared to charm—
> Passive—as Granite—laps My Music—
> Sobbing—will suit—as well as psalm!
>
> Would but the "Memnon" of the Desert—
> Teach me the strain
> That vanquished Him—
> When He—surrendered to the Sunrise—
> Maybe—that—would awaken—them!
>   (#261, c. 1861)

Browning's "One Way of Love," in *Men and Women*, voices the defeat of a frustrated poet speaking of Pauline, who will not turn aside as he strews rose leaves where she may pass, and all to no avail. The persona consequently declares: "How many a month I strove to suit / These stubborn fingers to the lute! / Today I venture all I know. / She will not hear my music? so! / Break the string; fold music's wing. . . ."³⁶ Dickinson's lute comes from that poem, but the emotions of her verse are extrapolated also from Browning's "One Word More," which as his final poem in the volume was dedicated "To E. B. B." There, speaking for himself of his subjects— "fifty men and women / Naming me the fifty poems!"—he says, "Take them, Love, the book and me together; / Where the heart lies, let the brain lie also." The verse is relaxed: "Dante once prepared to paint an angel— / Whom to please? You whisper ' Beatrice.' " Or "no artist lives and loves, that longs not / Once, and only once, for one only, / (Ah, the prize!) to find his love a language, / Fit and fair and simple and sufficient / . . . I shall never . . . / Make you music that should all-express me. . . ." Yet, standing on his attainment, he reiterates the offer of the gift to her—"Verse and nothing else have I to give you":

> Love, you saw me gather men and women,
> Live or dead or fashioned by my fancy,
> Enter each and all, and use their service,
> Speak from every mouth—the speech, a poem.
> . . . .
> Poor the speech; be how I speak, for all things.
> . . . .
> This I say of me, but think of you, Love.³⁷

Trusting the evidence of the relation between Browning's work and his desire to find language to express his love, Dickinson needed no other sanction for writing a soliloquy in which she speaks for him. Learning as much as she did about speaking for "all things" from him, she had cause to imagine his grief when she mourned with him at the time of the death of his muse and her "Foreign Lady." She chooses the colossal statue of "the singing Memnon," among the splendid Theban temples in the abode of the dead kings and queens of Egypt, as the shrine the bereaved poet would seek in the East. If only he might learn the secret of the vanquished Memnon, whose music was heard by the living and the dead at sunrise, the poet could perhaps awaken the silent lute and the stone-like ear of his lady. Knowing the consolation of poetry when one is bereaved, Dickinson writes for him. What more appropriate form than a dramatic monologue for expressing the hope that Browning would write again?

It is ironic that she has been suspected of plagiarism. Edgar

Allan Poe had made it an obsessive subject at the time Dickinson was cultivating other powers in proportion as she allowed her imagination to captivate her. She wrote slyly some years later to Higginson: "I marked a line in One Verse—because I met it after I made it—and never consciously touch a paint, mixed by another person. I do not let go it, because it is mine." And then she asked him: "Have you the portrait of Mrs. Browning? Persons sent me three— If you had none, will you have mine? Your Scholar—" (L, 2:415). It is Mrs. Browning from whom Dickinson is said to have most frequently plagiarized.[38] Two examples will suffice for consideration of the manner in which she consciously "touched" the verse of the woman whose poetry she admired. The first poem pertains to the relationship between a passage in Barrett Browning's *Aurora Leigh* (1856) and the use Dickinson made of the passage. In the long narrative poem, Marian Erle is about to recount her "lurid sexual misadventures" to Aurora as they walk through the open squares of Paris. Marian is, however, hesitant. Aurora describes her:

> Not a word
> She said, but, in a gentle humbled way
> (As one who had forgot herself in grief)
> Turned round and followed closely where I went
> As if I led her by a narrow plank
> Across devouring waters, step by step,
> And so in silence we walked on a mile.[39]

Dickinson's strategy vis-à-vis the source is similar to her use of Rochester's point of view in "Before I got my eye put out." She shifts from the perspective of the narrator in the story to that of the person who was the subject of the narrative passage:

> I stepped from Plank to Plank
> A slow and cautious way
> The Stars above my Head I felt
> About my Feet the Sea.
>
> I knew not but the next
> Would be my final inch.
> This gave me that precarious Gait
> Some called Experience.
>
> (#875, c. 1864–65)

Noting that the poem serves almost as an aria "in rhyme to break up the onrushing blank verse of *Aurora Leigh*," Ellen Moers says, "I rather suspect that Emily Dickinson sometimes wrote a verse or two with just that complementary function in mind—that is, to underline and elaborate the emotional content of something that happened in *Aurora Leigh*, rather than in her own life."[40] The quick dissonants, "Plank," "felt," "next," and "Gait," plus the amusing mismatching of "inch" and "Experience," give the offhand humor of the Dickinson monologue for Marian Erle that combination of tones it needs to keep it from being too sardonic. The image of the "final inch" on a plank suspended between stars and sea—the great cosmos—reinforces the contrast between "that precarious gait" and what "Some called Experience." The influence of the lines of *Aurora Leigh* is hardly negligible, but Dickinson's ability to effect a slight tension that the original lacks and her way of converting an "as if" construction into a memorable conceit are superior to the influence.

Another poem more distantly related to Barrett Browning's *Sonnets from the Portuguese* (1850) dramatizes a state of mind also attributable to "experience":

> I'm "wife"—I've finished that—
> That other state—
> I'm Czar—I'm "Woman" now—
> It's safer so—
>
> How odd the Girl's life looks
> Behind this soft Eclipse—
> I think that Earth feels so
> To folks in Heaven—now—
>
> This being comfort—then
> That other kind—was pain—
> But why compare?
> I'm "Wife"! Stop there!
>
> (#199, c. 1860)

The *Sonnets*, written after Elizabeth Barrett's marriage to Robert Browning and addressed to him, are personal and self-revealing; the poet and what she says are inseparable. The tone is earnest, even when the sense and situation are ironic. Although there are forty-four sonnets in the sequence, she writes in #13: "And wilt thou have me fashion into speech / The love I bear thee, finding words enough . . . ?" (11.1–2). She answers, in the sestet:

> Nay, let the silence of my womanhood
> Commend my woman-love to thy belief—
> Seeing that I stand unwon, however wooed,
> And rend the garment of my life, in brief,
> By a most dauntless, voiceless fortitude
> Lest one touch of this heart convey its grief.
>   (11.9–14)

There may be reverberations of "my womanhood," "my woman-love," and "seeing that I stand unwon, however wooed" in the direct announcement of Dickinson's married woman: "I'm 'wife,' " "I'm Czar—I'm 'Woman' now—"; and the sonnet's reference to the break with a father who opposed the Browning's marriage (a rending of the garment of Elizabeth Barrett's life and her "voiceless fortitude") may have influenced "The other kind—was pain" or even the abrupt "But why compare? . . . Stop there!" of Dickinson's poem.

A second source of "I'm 'wife,' " however, seems to be sonnet #27:

> My own Beloved, who hast lifted me
> From this drear flat earth where I was thrown. . . .
>   (11.1–2)

> My own, my own,
> Who camest to me when the world was gone,
> And I who looked for only God, found *thee!*
> I find thee; I am safe, and strong, and glad.
> As one who stands in dewless asphodel
> Looks backward on the tedious time he had
> In the upper life—so, I with bosom-swell,
> Make witness, here, between the good and bad,
> That Love, as strong as Death, retrieves as well.
>   (11.6–14)

Dickinson foregoes Barrett Browning's allusion to the flowering fields of the classical underworld for the view from "this soft Eclipse" and the plain figure of "folks in Heaven," which are more consistent with the sonnet's opening metaphor of the woman's being "lifted" from the drear earth and therefore more coherent. The phrase "folks in Heaven" seems to be a homely Dickinsonian variation on sonnet #39, in which there is an image of "The patient angel waiting for a place / In the new Heavens" (11.8–9). And, perhaps indebted to the sonnets, Dickinson allows the Girl who has become a " 'Woman,' " the " 'wife' " who has become "Wife," her sense of safety, her strength, and her bosom-swell. I do not think the poem is meant to be in the voice of the "Portuguese."

The tenuous relationships between the sonnets and the woman's voice in the Dickinson poem make clear how little the latter really owed to the poet she esteemed. Behind "I'm 'wife' " is an author and questions about her attitudes toward what the persona says. Is the talk merely rendered by a faithful, detached listener, or is the author jealous, amused, delighted, perhaps ambivalent because of the woman's assertion of her comfort and pride? The range of choices of tone (from jubilation, to relieved anguish, to light irony, to the parodic) in which an actress could read the monologue gives an amplitude to the verse that seems at first look a scant and ordinary script.

Emily Dickinson knew countless wives. She had a goodly share of friends who were women, and like most women she knew them more intimately than she was able to know an equal number of men well. Writing confidentially to Susan Gilbert during early June, the month of brides, in 1852, Dickinson had by then perhaps read the sonnets, and her friend would also have read them. They were both in their twenty-second year and single; so, they thought about marriage. "Those unions," the young poet said to her, "by which two lives are one, this sweet and strange adoption wherein we can look, and are not yet admitted, how it can fill the heart, and make it gang wildly beating, it will take *us* one day, and make us all it's own, and we shall not run away from it, but lie still and be happy!" Then she commented, "How dull our lives must seem to the bride, and the plighted maiden, whose days are fed with gold, and who gathers pearl every morning; but to the *wife*, Susie, sometimes the *wife forgotten*, our lives perhaps seem dearer than all others in the world." Dickinson's discussion of the topic with her future sister-in-law is clearly seminal. The marriage poems, of which there are many in different voices, are sustained by a clear consciousness of the complexities of the emotions of women— betrothed, wedded, single, remembered, forgotten.

She continued, in the letter to Susan Gilbert, the observations about women and marriage:

> ... you have seen the flowers at morning, *satisfied* with the dew, and those sweet same flowers at noon with their head bowed in anguish before the mighty sun; think you these thirsty blossoms will *now* need naught but *dew?* No, they will cry for sunlight, and pine for the burning noon, tho' it scorches them, scathes them; they have gotten through with peace—they know that the man of noon is *mightier* than the morning and their life is henceforth to him.

One understands why she asked Kate Turner, seven years later, "Are you afraid of the Sun?" For young Emily Dickinson, the "sun" (in Browning's poem for Rudel) was at its zenith "the burning noon." One is not surprised to read the poet's confession: "Oh, Susie, it is dangerous, and it is all too dear, these simple trusting spirits, and the spirits mightier, which we cannot resist! It does rend me, Susie, the thought of it when it comes, that I tremble lest at sometime I, too, am yielded up" (L, 1:209–10). The word *rend* is E. B. Browning's. It is Dickinson's, too. It was her sister Lavinia, not the poet, who complained when she was nineteen, also in the summer of 1852, "I am tired of receiving wedding cards, they come from some where every day, that pretty cousin Lizzie sent me hers Monday."[41] Emily Dickinson obviously listened to voices other than her own.

V

Among those Dickinson was confident in responding to as she pleased were the voices in Shakespeare's plays and poetry. She dashed off the obvious generalization that Romeo and Juliet's love story was archetypal, "infinite enacted / In the Human Heart" (#741, c. 1863). She had no hesitancy in saying "Hamlet wavered for all of us" (L, 2:587); she freely quoted or rephrased lines from plays as different as *King Lear* and *The Tempest*, but she referred most frequently to *Antony and Cleopatra*, *Macbeth*, and *Othello*. Assuming that Dickinson's poems are about herself, Rebecca Patterson suggests that one of them is an analogue to the situation of Desdemona, for whom "rank, fortune, home, family, even fate, were all submerged" in Othello's "bolder sea."[42] Shakespeare gives

Desdemona only a few words to argue for herself and her truths, so Dickinson fashions into speech the woman-love that should commend a heroine to a husband—the stranger—who failed to hear what the heart conveyed:

> All forgot for recollecting
> Just a paltry One—
> All forsook, for just a Stranger's
> New Accompanying—
>
> *Grace of Wealth, and Grace of Station
> Less accounted than
> An unknown †Esteem possessing—
> Estimate—Who can—
>
> Home effaced—Her faces dwindled—
> Nature—altered small—
> Sun—if shone—or Storm—if shattered—
> Overlooked I all—
>
> Dropped my fate—a timid Pebble—
> In thy bolder Sea—
> ‡Prove—me—Sweet—if I regret it—
> Prove Myself—of Thee—
>
>   (#966, c. 1864)

*Grace of Rank and Grace of Fortune
†content
‡Ask

It was Othello who insisted on "proof" of his wife's betrayal, not of her love for him; it was he who accepted as incontrovertible evidence "a trifle": the handkerchief he had given her as a love token, of which he saw a copy he thought to be the original in the possession of a courtesan, who had received the favor from a man Desdemona had befriended. It was Othello who blindly refused to believe her when she said she had not given the bridal present away and who jealously assumed that she had deceived him.

Dickinson's poem for her begins with a bitter assertion—a double-edged judgment that the tragedy confirms: "All forgot for recollecting / Just a paltry One." In Dickinson's words, Desdemona reminds Othello that he has "forgot" the evidence of all she had given up for him and, instead, measured her love by a trivial sign; she also accuses herself, since she forgot everything dear to her for a man who has betrayed her trust and become as worthy of contempt as of pity. Yet she pleads for him and for herself: "Nature—altered small— / Sun—if shone—or Storm—if shattered— / Overlooked I all." Dickinson, having written to Susan Gilbert ten years before the date of the poem of the *wife forgotten*, recognizes Desdemona as one of the women who "cry for sunlight, and pine for the burning noon, tho' it scorches them, scathes them; they have got through with peace—they know that the man of noon is *mightier* than morning and their life is henceforth to him." Dickinson imagines that Shakespeare's honest Desdemona, who is denied time for so much as a prayer when she is killed in the playwright's plot against her, is no longer timid; she has got through peace, she boldly sues for herself: "Ask—me—Sweet—if I regret it— / Prove Myself—of Thee."

Dickinson also wrote a dramatic monologue (#400, c. 1862) that, as Henry Wells points out, "derives from a number of Shakespearean speeches wherein a lover sends a message of adulation to the beloved, each image piled upon another in a half-humorous extravaganza."[43] The diction, the imperious tone, the rhythms and phrasing of speech as well as the images, suggest that Dickinson can write in any style that suits her fancy for any voice she cares to suppose:

A Tongue—to tell Him I am true!
It's fee—to be of Gold—
Had Nature—in Her monstrous House
A single Ragged Child—

To earn a Mine—would run
That Interdicted Way,
And tell Him—Charge thee speak it plain—
That so far—Truth is True?

And answer What I do—
Beginning with the Day
That Night—begun—
Nay—Midnight—'twas—
Since Midnight—happened—say—

If once more—Pardon—Boy—
The Magnitude thou may
Enlarge my Message—If too vast
Another Lad—help thee—

Thy Pay—in Diamonds—be
And His—in solid Gold—
Say Rubies—if He hesitate—
My message—must be told—

Say—last I said—was This—

There are two more stanzas.

Dickinson was, after all, a virtuoso. She knew, years before she parodied Shakespeare in verse, that she could imitate his styles. Writing to her brother in the summer of 1851, not long after she was "just a girl at school," she echoed the banter of Prince Hal and Falstaff in *Henry IV, Part I*, for the fun of showing off a little learning. She also schooled herself in the art of impersonation and mimicry for the writing of the dramatic monologues. They are literary performances. If she borrows, paraphrases, adapts, and makes the work of other writers her own, she also talks back to them. Responding to Shakespeare's forty-third sonnet, "When most I wink, then do mine eyes best see," she writes, "What I see not, I better see—" (#939, c. 1864). But undercutting his conventional figure, "And nights bright daies when dreams do shew thee me," Dickinson concludes: "I arise—and in my Dream / Do thee distinguished Grace— / Till jealous Daylight interrupt— And mar thy perfectness."

VI

Dickinson's almost excessive versatility enabled her to gather children, men, and women, alive or dead, to enter their histories, and to use their services in the poems. The act is a measure of her security as a writer and justifies her place in a literary tradition extending beyond the boundaries of her esteem for either the great novelists or the Brownings and Shakespeare. The failure of readers to recognize the feat has not only contributed to their finding a direct rather than an "indirect egoism" in the poetry, but to warring theories about the woman who wrote it. She would have appreciated the critics who hold that the poems are autonomous and are to be read for themselves. She might even have smiled at one who says that a poem in which she takes the point of view of the Phoebe (and puns on *ephebe?*) is meant "literally" to represent herself:

I was a Phebe—nothing more—
A Phebe—nothing less—
The little note that others dropt—
I fitted into place—

I dwelt too low that any seek—
Too shy, that any blame—
A Phebe makes a little print
Upon the Floor of Fame—
                    (#1009, c. 1864–66)

Nevertheless, Dickinson did not commonly think of herself as fitting into place the little notes that others dropped, or when she did it was with tongue-in-cheek. She knew the Phoebe, an essentially unassuming and rather timid little bird, is no musician with its two-syllabled call which becomes a trifle monotonous; to have chosen it as a "devise" for herself would have been only a private joke, a self-mocking, of which she was certainly capable.

Dickinson's poems are often a record of the freedom and cultivation of a literary intelligence. It is fortunately not possible to uncover the diverse sources of all the poems; and in tracing something of the genesis of a small number of them, I do not assume I fully account for that number. Source studies, furthermore, are rarely pertinent to the efficacy of a poem as poem. They are relevant to a legitimate interest in the relationship between the historical person and what T. S. Eliot called the mind that creates. They are also relevant to a sense of the poet as "impersonator," who was not as self-absorbed and confessional as is usually believed.

When she blurs the distinction between the self and the other, the ambiguities that result are perhaps inescapable. A refusal to name the grammatical "I," however, is hardly a failure of form if there is a concentration on substance, movement, and tonalities within it. The strategy allows for the reader's direct participation in the intimate feelings and the lives that Dickinson apprehended. Listening to different views of existence or sharing and re-presenting the destinies of other people has always been the privilege of both omniscient and observant authors who remind us of the consequences of being "one person." The best of them may not be evenhanded, but they know the inadequacies of the writer who gives all the good lines to one character. Dickinson, following the mentors from whom she learned so much, recognized the hazards of personality and the power of words to emancipate the mind from the ego. She also valued, among the pleasures of literature, the momentary experiences in which we are disencumbered of the burdens of the separate, single self.

Lavinia Dickinson, writing in 1895 of the poet's achievement, said "her intense verses were no more personal experience than Shakespeare's tragedies, or Mrs. Browning's minor-key pictures."[44] The comment was not necessarily a ploy of the sister to guard what she called "Emily's peculiar and wonderful genius" from the fabulists who rarely want a poet to be pedestrian; the remark was perhaps made with an understanding of the dramatic modes and fictions for which the poet gave the brief explanation to Higginson in 1862, just at the time that the first of the fabulists—the peculiar genius herself—went to work contriving a "romantic" story for him. One concludes perforce either that the sisters were in collusion or that they both were equally at home with literary conventions which gave the poet authority to write in her own inventive way. If the poems are self-revelatory—and they are, of course—it is because she took thought to explore human sympathies, antipathies, moods, gestures, tastes, manners, and morals. She attended to the elementary passions, the fate of others, the rewards of language, and the timbre of many voices. No one who wrote hundreds of poems depicting lives as heterogeneous as the relatively few I have considered could have done so if there had been only one subject: the single subjective "I."

6

"How lovely are the wiles of Words": Trifles

I

When Dickinson writes

> I found the words to every thought
> I ever had—But one
> And that—defies me—

she immediately implicates us in the words. She provokes us to wonder what the thought might have been, even though it could not be articulated. She sounds as if she is bragging, or conning us. She could not have been so fortunate, or clever. Having strained our credulity, she enlarges upon the questionable assertion, which itself becomes representative of a writer's quandary:

> As a Hand did try to chalk the Sun
> To Races—nurtured in the Dark—

After dismissing our first "thoughts," as if we had been caught by an unbecoming curiosity or haste to conclude that the poet is given to self-conceit, we consider the dilemma of anyone who uses language in a community with no common knowledge and experience to which words can refer. She puts the question to us:

How would your own—begin?
Can Blaze be shown in Cochineal—
Or Noon—in Mazarin?
                              (#581, c. 1862)[1]

Who, without a dictionary, knows those exotic words for color: "cochineal" and "mazarin"? Even with a description of the red and the blue, they still defy us if we have never seen them. Hence, Dickinson's final point, perhaps evoked by an awareness of readers who responded to her verse, is that we live in the mind and its structures of reality, but that the structures are circumscribed by individual configurations based in our experience of it.[2] Our tracing of the poet's development of the dramatic monologues in relation to what we know of her life, or our knowledge of the configurations of reality in examples of literary works with which Dickinson was familiar, helps us to perceive ways in which she chalked the sun. She was, however, an experimental poet. Just as she did not limit herself to herself as subject—whatever the ambiguities of language or idiosyncrasies of style—she did not restrict the writing to a single poetic genre. And while we attend willingly to the poet's words, they are not "of ourselves and of our origins"[3] but, rather, of her origins. We continue, consequently, to try to recover those origins, their varied manifestations, and the conscious uses the poet made of them.

Attention to Emily Dickinson's letters is rewarding not only because of her autobiographical reflections but also because the poet reveals her "community," her search for words, and the pleasure they gave her when she found them. The fact that for her the epistolary form was often a private and intimate one, from which she could turn with ease to her poems or to which she could easily turn from the poems, strengthens the illusion that she was also writing about herself in the poems. Letters, on the other hand, are a social as well as a personal form: they can awaken in us the consciousnesses of the actualities or thoughts that the author wishes to evade or capture and share. The skill with which Dickinson makes us aware of the company she kept—intractable, vital, spectral words—is evident in the correspondence to which we are now privy.

As a schoolgirl, not yet seventeen years old, she expressed to a friend a writer's dissatisfaction with their "knowing each other only by symbols traced upon a paper" (L, 1:46). Yet the letters she wrote show that from the first they were exercises in finding words of her own. After having described domestic chores, family scene, and emotions of loneliness on a morning in April of 1852 to another friend, for example, she asks, "Do I paint it *natural?*" (L, 1:193). Writing, however, was more than that to her.

> Shall I take thee, the Poet said
> To the propounded word?
> Be stationed with the Candidates
> Till I have finer tried—
>
> The Poet searched Philology
> And . . .
> There came unsummoned in—
>
> That portion of the Vision
> The Word applied to fill . . .
> (#1126, c. 1868)

She never forgot that words were both contested and given. Dissembling as she did when she told Thomas Wentworth Higginson that "for several years" her "Lexicon" was her only companion (L, 2:404), she was not altogether fabricating if we make allowance for the energy she spent in tracing symbols on papers or the value she placed on the "consent of Language" (#1651, n.d.).

The Dickinsons, children and father at least, were alert to the importance of style and, as the letters repeatedly affirm, free in bantering about it. They criticized and educated one another. "I was highly edified with your *imaginative* note," Emily writes sarcastically to Austin on May 29, 1848, "and think your flights of fancy indeed wonderful at your age!" (L, 1:68). "Father says your letters," she again remarks, "are altogether before Shakespeare, and he will have them published to put in our library" (L, 1:122). Or, she commends the brother for a "good" letter the family has enjoyed: "*particularly* the notes on the agricultural convention. Miss Kelly's part of the performance was very fine indeed, and made much fun for us. Should think you would have some *discipline* in order to write so clearly amidst so much confusion." She adds that "Father seemed specially pleased with the story of the farmer" (L, 1:173).

The competition between the young ones to outdo the other in writing sometimes breaks out in a frenzy of words. "I have just finished reading your letter," the aspiring poet replies to Austin in June 1851. "I like it grandly—very—because it is so long, and also it's *so* funny—we have all been laughing till the old house rung again at your delineations of men, women, and things." She tells him: "I feel quite like retiring in the presence of one so grand, and casting my lot among small birds, and fishes—you say you dont comprehend me, you want a simpler style." So she gives him as good as he sends; she outdoes him; she ridicules him in language that is even fancier than his, and delights in taking his criticism of her to an extreme. "I strove to be exalted thinking I might reach *you* and while I pant and struggle and climb the nearest cloud, you walk out very leisurely in your slippers from Empyrean, and without the *slightest* notice request me to get down!" He must understand that she had aspired to great heights (elevated language) because he occupies such lofty regions. Very well, then, she promises, "I'll be the *simplest* sort of simple . . . a little ninny—a little pussy catty, a little Red Riding Hood, wear a Bee in my Bonnet, and a Rose bud in my hair, and what remains to do you shall be told hereafter." She has not yet finished with him.

She can also hurl barbs from down under: "Your letters are richest treats, and send them always such warm days—they are worth a score of fans, and many refrigerators—the only 'diffikilty' they are so very *queer*, and *laughing* such hot weather is *anything* but *amusing*. A little more of earnest and a little less of jest until we are out of August." She reminds him that he, too, needs advice of a practical sort when he descends from the stratosphere to the trials that ordinary mortals endure. She warns him to be "careful in working, eating and drinking when the heat is so great—there are temptations there which at home you are free from—beware the juicy fruits, and the cooling ades, and cordials, and do not eat *ice-cream*, it is so very *dangerous*." She learned long before Wallace Stevens that the only emperor is the emperor of ice-cream. For "our sakes Austin wont you try to be careful? I know *my* sake a'nt much, but Vinnie's is considerable—it weighs a good many pounds—when *skin and bones* may plead, I will become a *persuasion*." With such verbal facility, appropriating what she wants from Shakespeare's madcap Prince Hal, jesting Poins, and fat old Falstaff to point up her own skylarking,[4] she would try to best anyone she thought worthy of the wit.

Lavinia Dickinson's note, enclosed in the sister's letter, reads: "Emilie has fed you on air so long, that I think a little 'sound common sense' perhaps wouldn't come amiss[.] *Plain english* you *know* such as Father likes."[5] *Emilie's* long letter ends with a mix of plain American and biblical sanction for her roguery: "The railroad is a 'workin'—my love to all my friends. I am on my way down stairs to put the teakettle boiling—writing and taking tea cannot sympathize—if you forget me now your right hand *shall* [forget] its cunning" (L, 1:117–19).

While she often served as her brother's right hand, she never forgot her cunning. She may have cast her lot among small birds and big fishes, but she sounds like Brer Rabbit in the briar patch when she writes: "You know," she says to Austin, "it's quite a sacrifice for *me* to tell what's going on." If Lavinia told him all the news, however, the young poet had other resources and topics—for instance, a summer storm, "the very first of the season" in May 1852. "The air," she begins, "was really scorching, the sun red and hot, and you know just how the birds sing before a thunder storm, a sort of hurried, agitated song—pretty soon it began to thunder, and the great 'cream colored heads' peeped out of their windows." Although the prose is hardly notable, the observations of sun, birds, and clouds justify her continuing with assurance: "then came the wind and rain and I hurried around the house to shut all the doors and windows. I wish you had seen it come, so cool and so refreshing—and everything glistening from it as with a golden dew—" (L, 2:204). The final flourish of phrases is for anyone nurtured in the light.

The next spring she informs Austin: "I shall never write any more grand letters to you, but all the *little* things, and the things called *trifles*, and the crickets upon the hearth, you will be sure to hear" (L, 1:240). She reports to him once that she has "transplanted some crickets" and wonders whimsically if they will grow indoors. She joshes him by relating that their father said he "guessed you saw through things" in Cambridge: "Whether he meant to say you saw through *the Judges*, overcoats and all, I could not quite determine" (L, 1:231).

Or, with the strictest economy, she asks: "Has father written you that Edwin Pierce, our neighbor, was arrested last week, for beating a servant girl, tried, and fined two dollars and costs? Vinnie and I heard the whipping, and could have testified, if the Court had called upon us" (L, 1:259). She also remained willing to chide Austin when he failed to write well: "I have some things from you, to which I perceived no meaning. They were either very vast, or they didn't mean anything. I dont know certainly which." Then she invokes the authority of the mentor: "Father asked me what you wrote and I gave it to him to read—He looked very much confused and finally put on his spectacles, which did'nt help him much—I don't think a *telescope* would have assisted him" (L, 1:281). The Dickinsons, then, had their own writers' workshop at home. They were cognizant of two tenets essential to the education of the poet but sometimes in conflict: to give testimony as a sworn witness and to make a good tale of whatever one told. She was, of course, capable of being straightforward and matter-of-fact or of exaggerating or saying less than she felt, but she was, like all good stylists, a finicky student of right words.

II

Although the poet's devotion to language is unmistakable throughout her prolific correspondence, some of her best letters are those to Dr. and Mrs. Josiah G. Holland, with whom Dickinson shared literary interests and bon-mots. (During a friendship of over thirty years, she sent the Hollands a larger number of poems than anyone else beyond the family circle.) The first of almost one hundred extant letters to them is from the autumn of 1853 and begins: "It is cold tonight, but the thought of you so warm, that I sit by it as a fireside, and am never cold anymore. I love to write to you—it gives my heart a holiday and sets the bells ringing." She confesses, however, that she had written a "lofty" letter earlier but had not sent it because she thought they would laugh and call her sentimental. "If it wasn't for broad daylight and cooking-stoves, and roosters, I'm afraid you would have occasion to smile at my letters often, but so sure as 'this moral' essays immortality, a crow from a neighboring farm-yard dissipates the illusion, and I am here again." The self-consciousness of a twenty-three-year-old would-be poet ambiguously flirting with thoughts of "immortality" she knows the Hollands will think foolish is transparent, so she tells them she "solemnly resolved" to be "*sensible* . . . , wore thick shoes, and thought of . . . the Moral Law" (L, 1:263–64). Who was she to think of novelties of the sublime or aspire to supreme fictions? It was no doubt preferable to listen to the common crow and be a good girl—albeit the crow is a clever bird, as she would have known from observation, and sings sweetly when unattended, as she and they would have known from Shakespeare's Portia in *The Merchant of Venice*, if not from having heard the caw. Dickinson then writes a less "lofty" letter to the friends, belittles herself, and says she will clomp along like the country lass she pretends to be.

The confidence she developed as a writer is easily measured by a letter from early spring 1866 to Elizabeth Holland: "February passed like a Skate and I know March. Here is the 'light' the Stranger said 'was not on land or sea.' Myself could arrest it but we'll not chagrin Him.' One can only guess why she calls Wordsworth "the stranger"; perhaps she has not read him recently, but the allusion to the "Elegiac Stanzas," suggested to him by a painting of Peele Castle in a storm,[6] seems to be related to Dickinson's poem beginning

> A Light exists in Spring
> Not present on the Year
> At any other period—
> When March is scarcely here
>
> A Color stands abroad
> On Solitary Fields
> That Science cannot overtake
> But Human Nature feels.

The vision, concentrated on the intense clarity of the landscape just at the end of stark winter, is not fully articulated, but the mood is quietly expectant. The light

> . . . waits upon the Lawn,
> It shows the furthest Tree
> Upon the furthest Slope you know
> It almost speaks to you.
>
> Then as Horizons step
> Or Noons report away
> Without the Formula of sound
> It passes and we stay—
>
> A quality of loss
> Affecting our Content
> As Trade had suddenly encroached
> Upon a Sacrament.
>
> (#812, c. 1864–66)

Dickinson's sense of the ambient purity of the light that cannot be arrested is analogous to Wordsworth's regret that he is unable "to add the gleam," "the light that never was, on sea or land, / the consecration," denied those who trade in words, even when Nature is one of their pieties. Hence, Dickinson does not humiliate him.

There is no record that the poem went to Elizabeth Holland. Dickinson, tongue-in-cheek, counts on the correspondent to agree that there is no equaling the great romantic poet and chooses to let Noons report away. After pausing for breath in her letter, she mentions in the sentence following the ironic claim of superiority to Wordsworth that her nephew, Ned, has been ill, "maturing all our faces. He rides his Rocking-Horse today, though looking apparitional" and "tells that the Clock purrs and the Kitten ticks. He inherits His Uncle Emily's ardor for the lie."

The light-hearted letter concludes as if Dickinson were writing or on the way to writing another poem: "My flowers are near and foreign, and I have but to cross the floor to stand in the Spice Isles. The Wind blows gay today and the Jays bark like Blue Terriers. I tell you what I see. The landscape of the Spirit requires a lung, but no Tongue. I hold you few I love, till my heart is red as February and purple as March"(L, 2:449–50).

Dickinson has gone well beyond the youthful anxieties about high style and sentimentality. She never asks "do I paint it natural?" She has made both the phenomena and people that are the topics of the letter alive. We breathe the air; we share her affections and joys. We feel, as we read, that no one surpasses her in talking about the dullest of all topics—the weather, or the subtlest and least sensational of all human bonds—friendship. When she "paints," it is as an expressionist. Changes of season or differences of opinions are emotional events. "The lawn is full of south and the odors tangle, and I hear today for the first the river in the tree," she writes in early May 1866 to Elizabeth Holland. "You mention spring's delaying—I blamed her for the opposite. I would eat evanescence slowly"(L, 2:452).

No single rubric such as "expressionist," however, is an accurate designation for Dickinson's work. Another letter written to Elizabeth Holland in late November ("the Norway of the year") begins with a description primarily in the romantic mode that prepares for a poem in the neoclassical temper. The poet reports: "I saw the sunrise on the Alps since I saw you. Travel why to Nature, when she dwells with us? Those who lift their hats shall see her, as devout do God." She engages the reader in the experience without saying prosaically that the first snow had fallen on Pelham hills, or that she was up early, or that she finds in life as given the words by which to live it, but the imagery of sunrise on the Alps and the "worship of nature" are common to the romantics. She then inquires about the friends: "I trust you are merry and sound. The chances are all against the dear, when we are not with them, though paws of principalities cannot affront if we are by. . . . Today is very homely and awkward, as the homely are who have not mental beauty" (L, 2:455–56). The moralizing introduces a wittily didactic poem with which the letter ends:

> The sky is low, the clouds are mean,
> A travelling flake of snow
> Across the barn or through a rut
> Debates if it will go.
>
> A narrow wind complains all day
> How someone treated him;
> Nature, like us, is sometimes caught
> Without her diadem.
> (#1075, c. 1866)

The fine distinctions she makes between mean-spiritedness, neurotic indecision, and resentful talk are the poet's own, but the reductive pronouncement ("Nature, like us, is sometimes caught / Without her diadem") is worthy of that old aphorist, Alexander Pope himself.[7] If he could write "To err is human, to forgive divine," she could match him by asserting "To ache is human—not polite" (#479, c. 1862), or be as persuasive as he by observing in a poem on triumph that "left the Dead alone,"

> Could Prospect taste of Retrospect
> The tyrannies of Men
> Were Tenderer—diviner
>
> .   .   .   .
>
> A Bayonet's contrition
> Is nothing to the Dead.
> (#1227, c. 1870–73)

She was, in the spirit of the eighteenth century, a social poet interested in codes of civilized behavior, and she realized with the neoclassicists that effective criticism of human conduct depends on concentrated phrasing and verbal artistry. She knew well how to turn admonishment into trenchant symbol.

Dickinson's paradoxically intense and detached observations of life have their origins in her own temperament: "I would eat evanescence slowly." The quality of simultaneous excitement and aesthetic distance in much of her writing stems from her control over language; that in turn is the result of what Jean Garrique called "an insistent kind of self-schooling."[8] Although she had less formal education than the great men of the New England renaissance—Longfellow, Emerson, Thoreau, or Hawthorne—she learned much on her own from the writers she admired. She did not restrict her reading to literary genre or period. She studied not only the plays and sonnets of Shakespeare, not only the verse and prose fiction of the Victorian era, but also the masters of the age of reason and of romanticism. Growing beyond the help she had from her family, she did what every original writer does: she taught herself. Yet, as the correspondence implies, she was at ease with the Hollands because reading and writing were among their prepossessions. She took for granted that theirs were cultivated minds, and felt free to compare herself with "the Stranger" or to send along a small poem that she assumed they would appreciate for its censure of human foibles and its ridicule of pathetic fallacies.

The poet's letters to them are among her most high-spirited. The jokes are often private and the allusions occasionally inexplicable: "I hear," she comments, "you are feasting on Army Worms, Canker Worms, and Cut Worms, and envy you your salad—" (L, 3:782). Since she was writing in summer, the teasing may be in reference to birds or gardening. The humor is, however, often quite clear and felicitous. Thanking the Hollands for a gift of candy, she writes: "but better than Bonbons was the love—for that is the basis of Bonbons." Then, no less appreciative, she says: "The Doctor's Pun was happy—How lovely are the wiles of Words!" (L, 2:612).

Dickinson can also be obliquely critical of the authors with whose work she is comfortably at home. She may begin with a good-natured gibe at verbal pretensions that amuse her: "We," she writes, "are making a few simple repairs, what Dickens would call qualifications and aspects—and looking in Vinnie's Basket for the Lightning Rod, which she had mislaid, 'What *would* Mrs. Holland think!' said Vinnie? 'I would inquire,' I said." She then goes on to jeer at the "poetical": "I can always rely on your little Laugh, which is what the

Essayist calls the 'Immortal Peewee' " (L, 3:692–93). The compliment to the friend is at the expense of Higginson, whose "Life of the Birds" (1862) the poet knew well enough to deride. The "essayist" had written: "penetrating to some yet lonelier place, we find it consecrated to that lifelong sorrow which is made immortal in the plaintive cadence of the Peewee-Flycatcher" (L, 3:693). Since Higginson's mourning bird has become Dickinson's "mocking bird," it is likely that both she and Elizabeth Holland were familiar with the Pewee-Flycatcher's "confiding ways and gentle manner," which "have won the real affection of its human neighbors."[9] One wonders if the two women also knew that another of the poet's birds, the Phoebe (which "states its name" in an abrupt, buzzy bisyllable), is characterized by "imperfect adaptability" because of "occasional blindness." In any case, although the poet sometimes flattered Higginson by calling herself his "scholar," she had her wits about her. And mocking or magnanimous, she was rarely plaintive and seldom sentimental.

A significant factor in the friendship between Emily Dickinson and Elizabeth Holland was the common experience of "imperfect adaptability" because of problems they both suffered with their eyes. The letters from the poet to her friend are at least a partial record of the anxieties they shared and the reliance on language to sustain one another. Although Dickinson was a "recluse" in her later years, the observations of her world and an ear for words do not confirm a withdrawal of attentiveness to the life around her; instead, they reveal a zest for it. She liked to hear the news and to comment on it as much as she liked to tell it. "Dear Sister," a letter to Elizabeth Holland begins, "Father called to say that our steel-yard was fraudulent, exceeding by an ounce the rates of honest men. He had been selling oats. I cannot stop smiling, though it is hours since, that even our steelyard will not tell the truth." If weights and measures are not reliable, what can one count on in this familiar world?

The poet had just come home, probably in late October or early November 1865, from the second of the long periods she spent in Boston for medical treatment of her eyes. She gives the friend a progress report, including the resumption of housekeeping tasks: "Besides wiping the dishes for Margaret, I wash them now, while she becomes Mrs. Lawler, vicarious papa to four previous babes. Must she not be an adequate bride?" At the age of thirty-six, Margaret O'Brien, who was the first steady domestic help in the Dickinson household, had married a widower on October 18, 1865, and was leaving to take care of her new family: "I winced at her loss," the poet explains, "because I was in the habit of her, and even a new rolling-pin has an embarrassing element, but to all except anguish the mind soon adjusts." The experience of change upon the poet's return to what had once been customary might have been an episode in a history of pathos, but was instead an occasion for humor and subtle prose.

Although there was, for her, a sense of slight unreality about the familiar, even the winter atmosphere was delineated without resorting to pathetic fallacies: "It is also November. The noons are more laconic and the sundowns sterner, and Gibraltar lights make the village foreign." Strange as the commonplace seemed to her, she wrote of it without self-pity. And she had her own charming way of congratulating Josiah Holland on the fact that his *Life of Abraham Lincoln* (1865) was being translated into German: "tell the dear Doctor we mention him with a foreign accent, party already to transactions spacious and untold" (L, 2:444–45). The message to the successful writer, however, is not without its poignancy in relation to the estrangement she could have felt from her friends, but she could bear others' good fortune as generously as she bore others' troubles, even when she had her portion of anguish, too.

There is, furthermore, a noticeable lack of attention on Dickinson's part to her own visual problems in the letters of concern about Elizabeth Holland's handicaps, perhaps because the nuances in the expressions of sympathy would have made saying "I know from experience what you feel" tautological, or perhaps because their painful histories were different. During the Holland family's European residence in the years 1868–69, Mrs. Holland went to Paris for eye surgery, was confined to a dark room for an unspecified period, and was reported to see better than she did before the operation.[10] Upon their return to America, they visited the Dickinsons in October 1870. Writing on the morning after the visit, the poet begins: "I guess I wont send that note now, for the mind is such a new place, last night feels obsolete. Perhaps you thought dear Sister, I wanted to elope with you and feared a vicious Father." Cryptic as it is without a context, the humor seems to be in poor taste, if not outrageous. It sounds as though she is familiar with the view that Edward Dickinson was tyrannical and she was afraid of him. But secure in the fact that the Hollands had known the family a long time, the poet risks teasing the friends and

mocking herself. The remark suggests that she had said something
sotto voce to Elizabeth Holland because Dickinson goes on to say:
"It is not quite that!" Having read in the newspaper that Holland
"was mostly in New York" (where he was planning to start a new
magazine), she explains, she was worried about "who would read"
for Mrs. Holland. "The Doctor's sweet reply makes me infamous."

As the apology for whispering continues, the social comedy gives
way to Dickinsonian rhetoric, tongue-in-cheek:

Life is the finest secret.
So long as that remains, we must all whisper.
With that sublime exception I had no clandestineness.

The proprieties well out of the mouth, she dashes on:

It was lovely to see you and I hope it may happen again.
These beloved accidents must become more frequent.
We are by September and yet my flowers as bold as June.
Amherst has gone to Eden.
To shut our eyes is Travel.
The Seasons understand this.
How lonesome to be an Article! I mean—to have no Soul.
An Apple fell in the night and a Wagon stopped.
I suppose the Wagon ate the Apple and resumed it's way.
How fine it is to talk.
What Miracle the New is!
Not Bismark but ourselves.[11]

(L, 2:482–83)

Letting herself go, she may sound a little mad. But enjoying a rush
of words—an experiment in spontaneity—is an old trick as useful
to a writer as following one's stream of consciousness, which free-
association approximates. And the amenities were sustained without a sacrifice of freedom to *be* in Dickinsonian style. "The Soul," as
one of the finest poems proclaims, "selects her own Society" (#303,
c. 1862).

The indiscreet concern about who would read to Elizabeth Holland was not an idle one. The eye problem worsened. "Dont affront
the Eyes," Dickinson wrote in January 1871. Or "Beg the Oculist,"
she wrote in late November of the same year, "to commute your
Sentence that you may also commute mine. Doubtless he has no

friend and to curtail Communion is all that remains to him." Trying to encourage her, the poet continues: "This transitive malice will doubtless retire—offering you anew to us and ourselves to you. . . . Let me know your circumstance through some minor Creature, abler in Machinery if unknown to Love" (L, 2:486 and 492). Mrs. Holland was "obliged" in August 1872 "to have one of her eyes removed."[12] Dickinson comforts her: "To have lost an Enemy is an Event with all of us—almost more memorable than to find a friend. This severe success befalls our little Sister—and though the Tears insist at first, as in all good fortune, Gratitude grieves best. Fortified by Love, a few have prevailed." The language is characteristic of the way in which the poet found words to transpose—or contort—loss into gain. She nevertheless takes liberties with biblical scripture to protest Mrs. Holland's loss of an eye: " 'Even so, Father, for so it seemed faithful in thy Sight.' "[13] But Dickinson confesses suffering vicariously with her and praises the friend: "We are proud of her safety—Ashamed of our dismay for her who knew no consternation. It is the meek that Valor wear too mighty for the Bold" (L, 2:497).

After a visit from Mrs. Holland in the autumn of 1873, Dickinson writes: "Little Sister, I miss your childlike Voice—I miss your Heroism. I feel that I lose combinedly a Soldier and a Bird. I trust that you experience a trifling destitution. Thank you for having been" (L, 2:514). Although the manners occasionally flutter and falter, the *jeu d'esprit* in a simple "thank you for having been" enlivens the praise.

Appreciation of Elizabeth Holland's valor also reflects the poet's, but we must infer that. Writing four years later to her, Dickinson says: "Your letters have that peculiar worth that attaches to all prowess, as each is an achievement for your delicate Eyes. I fear you urge them too far, though to lag is stale to a rapid Spirit." Dickinson's affinity with her is so strong that she forgets the "little sister" had but one eye. The poet then scoffs at the idea that Elizabeth Holland would be considered dependent: "Doctor's 'Child Wife'— indeed, if not Mr. Copperfield's." It was permissible for Dickinson to describe the voice as "childlike" and to use "Little Sister" as a term of endearment, but for women of stamina "Child Wife" underestimated their inner reserves and self-sufficiency. The poet, it seems certain, would have resented the frequent view that she too was "childlike" or adolescent.[14] From a different view, she reports to Elizabeth Holland: "This is a stern winter, and in my Pearl Jail, I think of Sun and Summer as visages unknown" (L, 2:572).

In March of the same year, 1877, she again thanks the friend for words: "The vitality of your syllables compensates for their infrequency. There is not so much Life as *talk* of Life, as a general thing. Had we the first intimation of the Definition of Life, the calmest of us would be Lunatics!" But, once again, the relief from a stern winter is a matter of consequence to her: "There is a Dove in the Street and I own beautiful Mud—so I know Summer is coming. I was always attached to Mud, because of what it typifies—also, perhaps, a Child's tie to primeval Pies." And, without setting up as a metaphysician, she makes one of the wittiest of all her remarks to Elizabeth Holland: "God seems much more friendly through a hearty Lens" (L, 2:576).

As relaxed as the letter is, it bears the poet's mark—concision—bringing together gracious but direct words, sharp comments on human behavior, a light-hearted moment, and sage observation. The trifles are not, after all, trifles. And one almost never ceases to be surprised at the turn her mind will take or the turn of phrase. She had written, for example, years before:

> Much Madness is divinest Sense—
> To a discerning Eye—
> Much Sense—the starkest Madness—
> 'Tis the Majority
> In this, as All, prevail—
> Assent—and you are sane—
> Demur—you're straightway dangerous—
> And handled with a Chain—
>
> (#435, c. 1862)

The poem begins, as Denis Donoghue observes, "in very general terms as if reciting a familiar lesson," but turns "almost into a drama or a novel full of the individual event. There is no anticipating that chain or the savagery that made it, or that other kind of savagery in Emily Dickinson" who "placed it there without apology. Savagery is part of what she knew."[15] Fierce emotions and gentleness are inextricably linked in the poet's mimic "demur" with its connotations of mild protest. The link is feminine, and the nuances permit Dickinson to remain between both excesses and restraints. The "drama" in words is also part of what she knew.

There is no predicting what she will toss off in the letters or the poems unless one is prepared for them by keeping in mind that it was the wiles of words in which she invested almost everything. If one thinks of her as primarily a poet of "protestant self-excruciation,"[16] one has to disallow the poet's delight in reporting to Elizabeth Holland: "Even my Puritan Spirit 'gangs' sometimes 'aglay—' " (L, 3:798).

But it is almost as inaccurate to think that her "ancient glittering eyes were gay"; they were discerning. Although she was too disciplined to take it easy, too rigorous to be soft, she was not given to flagellating herself in order to be either a saint or martyr in what she called her quick career. She had no grand ambition to "master" life. She wanted rather to nurture it and the language that would express whatever she discerned for "Races—nurtured in the Dark."

She writes during the summer of 1878, for instance, to the Hollands in response to the news of the death of William Cullen Bryant, revered poet and advocate of liberal causes in their time:

> We thought you cherished Bryant, and spoke of you immediately when we heard his fate—if Immortality *be* Fate.
> Dear friends—we cannot believe for each other. I suppose there are depths in every Consciousness, from which we cannot rescue ourselves—to which none can go with us—which represent to us Mortally—the Adventure of Death—
> How unspeakably sweet and solemn—that whatever await us of Doom or Home, we are mentally permanent.
> "It is finished" can never be said of us. (L, 2:612–13)

The ambiguities of Dickinson's mature style are a far cry from the early symbols traced on paper. The inner consciousness,"from which we cannot rescue ourselves," was clearly present in the words of the nascent poet, but as it deepened she often seemed to believe, without knowing what her destiny would be in death, that the mind would not die. Yet she also repeatedly agonized over the fact that the adventure of the life of the mind was unequal to the adventure of death. So, did she mean that what she wrote would live after her? Remembering that "the Landscape of the Spirit requires a lung, but no Tongue," however, one can hardly rest in a reading of her words as an expression of her faith in the survival of the poems—a faith for which there is no more proof than there was for her when she said "if Immortality *be* Fate."

In spite of all the speculation about "the flood subject," as she denominated the overwhelming question of death and immortality, she remained close to the life about her. The gusto with which she describes "Father's Horace," in a letter to Mrs. Holland, suggests that under other circumstances she might have written short fiction comparable to that by the best of the local colorists. Horace Church died in April 1881, but that did not efface the realistic characterization:

> He had lived with us always, though was not congenial—so his loss is a pang to Tradition, rather than Affection—I am sure you remember him—He is the one who spoke patronizingly of the Years, of Trees he sowed in "26," or Frosts he met in "20," and was so legendary that it seems like the death of the College Tower, our first Antiquity.

She recalls that "he was at one time disinclined to gather the Winter Vegetables till they had frozen," and when her father (like daughter?) "demurred," Church replied: "Squire, ef the Frost is the Lord's Will, I dont popose to stan in the way of it." The poet's conclusion? "I hope a nearer inspection of that 'Will' has left him with as ardent a bias in its favor." In the same letter, she anticipates an issue of Dr. Holland's magazine, *Scribner's Monthly*, which was to include a picture of George Eliot. "Vinnie is eager to see the Face . . . , and I wince in prospective, lest it be no more sweet. God chooses repellent settings, dont he, for his best Gems?" (L, 3:693). Even an admirable woman might not escape the discerning eye of Dickinson. And sometime later, she described Horace Church as "the wise, but acrid Man." She also had a discerning ear.

One last gratitude, among many to the woman Richard Sewall calls Dickinson's "true spiritual sister" who "seems to have understood her best of all her friends,"[17] expresses also the intense devotion to language by which the poet sustained her fate and true uncertainties. She begins the letter, written to Elizabeth Holland probably in the summer of 1883, by expressing fear that a "poor friend has taken fright anew." The woman is unidentified, but the poet says that the "support of a Mother, an almost imbecile husband and two very sweet little Girls, hangs upon her Needle, so her sight is not luxury, but necessity." Dickinson then tells that "Father valued her much, often befriending her, and I love to fulfill the kindness that only Death suspends."[18] The poet does not say what she has done, and it seems that Mrs. Holland has assisted the woman too, because the letter continues:

> Forgive the personality. It seemed inevitable, and thank you again for your full sweetness, to which as to a Resevoir the smaller Waters go. What a beautiful Word 'Waters' is! When I slept in the Pond and ate Seraphs for Breakfast, I thought I should know all about it now, but 'Now' comes, and I dont—(L, 3:782).

Nevertheless, transforming the world she knew into words, whether she wrote letters or poems, she commemorated "Now," of which she thought forever was composed.

III

The poet's heightened consciousness of language is nowhere more evident than in her attention to the phenomenal world. The passion with which Dickinson observes nature—the scenes and the signs—was, as the letters substantiate, a matter of life and death for her sensibility. In no area of her work is she more versatile or more educated. She looks forward to the radical experiments of modern poetry and backward to tradition. There are poems in which the eyes are concentrated primarily on the object; but, since she is interested in the relations between what she called "the Outside" and the "in" (#1097, c. 1866), she also verifies the existence of the observer and often allows the observer to comment on the look of things. In sum, she likes images for their own sake, and she likes them for the poems she makes from them.

The purest vision is epiphanic:

> An Everywhere of Silver
> With Ropes of Sand
> To keep it from effacing
> The Track called Land.
> (#884, c. 1864–65)

There is no intrusion of personality upon the seascape stretching into the silence and the horizon. The ambience of moonlight over the still water and long line of beach is almost without tension, except for an awareness that the peace is momentary. The images themselves predominate. "In a poem of this sort," as Ezra Pound said of his own comparable imagist verse, "one is trying to record the precise instance when a thing outward and objective transforms itself or darts into a thing inward and subjective."[19]

Dickinson's poems, in fact, were among those most admired by the proponents of Imagism, which became a seminal influence on the development of modern poetry. Her response to the humming-bird (noted for traveling twice as fast as other birds) is frequently cited as a brilliant example of descriptive writing:

> A Route of Evanescence
> With a revolving Wheel—
> A Resonance of Emerald
> A Rush of Cochineal—
> And every Blossom on the Bush
> Adjusts it's tumbled Head—
> The mail from Tunis, probably
> An easy Morning's Ride—
> (#1463, c. 1879)[20]

The human presence, implied in all writing, is at first so withheld in the sensuous illumination of the ruby-throated hummingbird, its color, sound, and rapidity of movement, that the quip of the startled observer is surprising and as appropriate to an appreciation of the essence of the diminutive bird as the imagery itself. Both bird and bird-watcher quickly vanish into the quiet, leaving only the reverberations that darted inward.[21]

A poem in which the exposition can be excised without weakening the effect of the images tends, by contrast, to lose intensity. Twentieth-century poets like William Carlos Williams, who commended Dickinson's distaste for lingering,[22] forego overlong commentary. As a nineteenth-century poet, she could not resist a few remarks, but she usually kept them brief. In a poem describing the bat, for instance, the equilibrium is perfectly maintained. She says, without saying so, "Behold, the only mammal that can fly!"

> The Bat is dun, with wrinkled Wings—
> Like fallow Article—
> And not a song pervade his Lips—
> Or none perceptible.

His small Umbrella quaintly halved
Describing in the Air
An Arc alike inscrutable
Elate Philosopher.

Deputed from what Firmament—
Of what Astute Abode—
Empowered with what Malignity
Auspiciously withheld—

To his adroit Creator
Ascribe no less the praise—
Beneficent, believe me,
His Eccentricities—

(#1575, c. 1876)

She has not only looked at the bat, she has studied the creature; she knows that the bat's sound is so high in frequency the human ear cannot hear it, and that he can fly in the dark. A precision of language and an intelligent pleasure in the inscrutable world are necessary to write as an elated observer who neither gothicizes nor broods over the bat. If she turns it into an examplar, which no imagist would have done, all the better for the bat and the poem.

A poem which she once called a chill gift,[23] integrates the nuances of imagery with the emotions of a participant in the rites of nature:

Further in Summer than the Birds
Pathetic from the Grass
A minor Nation celebrates
It's unobtrusive Mass.

No Ordinance be seen
So gradual the Grace
A pensive Custom it becomes
Enlarging Loneliness.

*Antiquest felt at Noon
When August burning low
Arise this spectral Canticle
Repose to typify

Remit as yet no Grace
No Furrow on the Glow
Yet a Druidic Difference
Enhances Nature now
                    (#1068, c. 1866)
*Antiquer—Antiquest

The late summer, observed "religiously" according to custom by its celebrants, evokes a pensiveness and druidic difference that appear to be for the poet stronger than images of the season, but only if one assumes that imagery is restricted to the visual. The stridulations of snow crickets and unnamed insects, probably cicadas and grasshoppers—a minor nation—are spectral in that one hears without seeing them. The sensory activity of the poem is primarily aural: the repeated sibilants and the hard consonants pulse in the ears. They are the minor sounds—unobtrusive onomatopoeia—yet they are as close as the poet's voice can come to the inhuman "song" of a minor nation whose sounds "en masse" are simultaneously insistent, restful, and disquieting. One knows, in listening to them, that August is burning low. (Country people say, when they first hear them, that it will be six weeks until frost.) The warm light of high noon and the snow crickets in grass will give way to winter, its snow, and another kind of repose—by comparison with which the pathos of the canticle, haunting as it is, "enhances Nature now."

Experiencing an inner vision commensurate with observed objective natural phenomena, Dickinson goes beyond simple descriptive poems. A meditation on "afternoon" light is flawless in the language with which it sounds the inexplicable mutability of life:

There's a certain Slant of light
Winter Afternoons—
That oppresses, like the Heft
Of Cathedral Tunes—

Heavenly Hurt, it gives us—
We can find no scar,
But internal difference,
Where the Meanings, are—

None may teach it—Any—
'Tis the Seal Despair—

An imperial affliction
Sent us of the Air—

When it comes, the Landscape listens—
Shadows—hold their breath—
When it goes, 'tis like the Distance—
On the look of Death—

(#258, c. 1861)

The silent light falling obliquely across the winter sky weighs as heavily on our minds as bells ringing from a great cathedral; and although both light and sound are weightless, they are oppressive because they leave us with "a Slant" and "Tunes" signaling the experience of alienation and absolute quiet in the universe. If the whole "Landscape listens," there is only the sense of "Distance"; shadows, holding their breath in tense anticipation, only prefigure "the look of Death." The imagery of the poem—an annunciation of reality, the solitude of human existence, that all the tropes and icons of earth sustain—is sacramental, but it denies there is any ultimate meaning which earthly eyes and ears can perceive beyond the final word, Death.

If Dickinson can record the precise instance when a thing outward and objective transforms itself into a thing inward and subjective, she is equally adept at finding the words for the less-than-precise instance when the inward and subjective dart outward and articulate the objective. "As imperceptibly as Grief," she writes, "The Summer lapsed away— / Too imperceptible at last / To seem like Perfidy—" (#1540, c. 1864–65).

There are far too many experiments with form, angles of vision, and the possibilities of language to make the categorizing and labeling of them or her easy. When she wrote that "The Broad are too broad to define" (#1207, c. 1872), she may have been talking about herself after all. At least the assertion is hers. Having said that her business was circumference and truth, she said that her business was to sing, too. She sometimes talks, veering toward the colloquial: "Believe me," or "Further in Summer," or "There's a certain slant of Light." But she brings together the different and grammatically independent constructions of "circumference," "truth," and "to sing" in a "song"—another one of a kind in the more than seventeen hundred verses she wrote. The song returns to the theme of the relation between images of light, other natural phenomena, and the distance separating the living from the dead:

Under the Light, yet under,
Under the Grass and the Dirt,
Under the Beetle's Cellar
Under the Clover's *Root,

Further than Arm could stretch
Were it Giant long,
Further than Sunshine could
Were the Day Year long,

Over the Light, yet over,
Over the Arc of the Bird—
Over the Comet's chimney—
Over the Cubit's Head,

Further than Guess can gallop
Further than Riddle ride—
Oh for a Disc to the Distance
Between Ourselves and the Dead!
                    (#949, c. 1864–66)

*Foot

The rhythms of children's games, the jump-rope ritual or a coun-
ting-out formula, may seem inappropriate to the imagery of the
grave ("the Dark Sod—as Education," of which she writes in
#392, c. 1862), but they are subtly allusive in underscoring the
relationship between the ebullience of the young together in play
and the futile wish for the skill to hurl a discus to the dead light-
years away. The metrical evocation of the living, in all their vigor,
joy, and innocence, keenly aware that they are alienated from the
dead, is itself an ironic feat. Human prowess is of no avail in
altering the fatal distance between them. The poem may have
been influenced by examples in John Donne's verse, but I suspect
that Dickinson, however, watched children at play or remembered the games she enjoyed when she was a girl and did not have
to fetch image or tone from the old metaphysical. The music is
comparable to T. S. Eliot's "New Hampshire," which also em-
ploys the "counting out" for a "finger exercise" on the swift passage of time.[24]
  Placing a poem or two by Dickinson alongside minor pieces by
the great modern poets—Pound and Eliot—is not to claim more for
her than I have already claimed: that she is versatile. She did not
write The Pisan Cantos or The Waste Land of the nineteenth cen-

tury. She had no Poundian intentions of bringing distinctive work together in a "commedia agnostica" of epic scope and did not conceive of what Eliot called "the mythic method" by which to present "a continuous parallel between contemporaneity and antiquity." One of the early readers of Dickinson's poems, for instance, condemned them as "mere conceits, vague jottings," and said "they should have been allowed to perish as their author intended." She found no scheme, with or without relaxed connectives, by which to contain what have sometimes been considered the fragments she shored against her ruins. Yet, when she abandoned the practice of sewing the fair copies of the manuscripts together in fascicles during the later years, she continued to write her poems.

Even the singing palls as the poet returns again and again to themes that preoccupied her from youth:

> A Pang is more conspicuous in Spring
> In contrast with *the things that sing
> Not Birds entirely—but Minds—
> Minute Effulgencies and Winds—
> When what they sung for is undone
> Who cares about a Blue Bird's Tune—
> Why, Resurrection had to wait
> Till they moved the Stone—
>
>   (#1530, c. 1881)
>
> *those

The piercing sense of futility, or the self-indulgence, and the anguished voice that registered the "Pang" of spring despite the loveliness of "the things that sing"—anticipating Eliot's announcement that "April is the cruellest month," with which *The Waste Land* opens—are countered by the "rapid spirit" reminding one "Why, Resurrection had to wait / Till they moved the Stone." The juxtaposition of the idea of a transcendent reality and a literal imagination in another voice concludes the debate in one of the most telling moments in Dickinson's work. The contrarieties of mood in the poem are inextricable from her need to believe beyond belief in the miracles of Christianity and the promise of redemption. It is, however, consistent with her "sensible" habits of mind that human action and human wit are what save the day. The poem—as minor and exhausted as it is—locates the nineteenth-century woman between a "modern" and a traditional sensibility.

Never having written a position paper or a prologomenon, Dickinson did not alert readers to concepts of individual talent and literary tradition. She also did not flaunt by so much as a footnote origins that are overlooked in some of the most accomplished of the poems. She could not have written the variety of verse she wrote, however, had she not studied the literature of the past, within which she found there was a place for her own vision. That literature also gave her ideas for different "styles," as well as the sanction to write in whatever independent and outrageous ways she wanted. No pure imagist, for example, would have dared the inflated language of Dickinson's comic description in:

> These are the Nights that Beetles love—
> From Eminence remote
> Drives ponderous perpendicular
> *His figure intimate
> The †terror of the Children
> The ‡merriment of men
> Depositing his Thunder
> He hoists abroad again—
> A Bomb upon the Ceiling
> Is an improving thing—
> It keeps the nerves progressive
> Conjecture flourishing—
> Too dear the Summer evening
> Without discreet alarm—
> Supplied by Entomology
> With §it's remaining charm—
>   (#1128, c. 1868)

*This
†transport
‡jeopardy
§a

The mock heroics of the style, the humorous regard for the bombastic beetle, and the tongue-in-cheek homiletics are all of a piece. If one ignores the tone, the poem is another of Dickinson's renditions of the harrowing life, but as Robert Weisbuch points out, "charm and alarm are rhyming synonyms."[25] The terror belongs to "the Children," the merriment to the big brave "men." Or should a mock epic show us endangered men? The poet—with her big words, her entomology, her nerves progressive, her conjecture flourishing—stands among the children and the men.

In spite of the "terror," no one is either psychologically annihilated or metamorphosed into a Kafkaesque beetle crouching under a sofa. The Dickinsonian beetle is a bomb upon the ceiling, and from that remote eminence "drives" ponderous perpendicular, then hoists abroad again like Milton's Satan, hurled from heaven into hell, from which he ("Full fraught with mischievous revenge") flies toward the world. Dickinson's alarm is "discreet," and all the charm is in how she says "a thing." The high burlesque does not mock the great Puritan poet's epic, *Paradise Lost* itself, but a lowly pest and the idea of its educative power; the comic effect results from the disparity between the trivial theme, the thunderous beetle, and the lofty style.[26] When she said that she found ecstasy in living, it was sometimes true, because she also found ecstasy in writing; and she held to her early resolve to write about all the *little* things, the things she called *trifles*, but she did not promise to write about nothing else.

"The Devil—had he fidelity," she says, "Would be the best friend—/ Because he has ability—/ But Devils cannot mend." Faithlessness, she continues in a tone of obvious irony, is the virtue the Devil is unwilling to resign, and that is what prevents him from being "thoroughly divine" (#1479, c. 1879). Dickinson, it has been said, had no sense of "Sin"; it is, she writes as if she were outside the law, "a distinguished Precipice / Others must resist—" (#1545, c. 1882). She is not sure, given the nature of things, that it is possible for anyone to change radically. On that score, she is still a Puritan, and she knows treachery when she encounters it; but she abrogates the old Satan, the old rigidities, the old self-righteousness and hypocrisies, prefers profound seriousness based on doubt to shallow faith based on terror, and is not afraid to find joy in the "trifles" of this world, including the nights that beetles love.

IV

Describing "the Fly," Dickinson combines the perspective and language of Swift's Gulliver in the land of Brobdingnag with that of a woman who sometimes "hayed a little for the horse" (or the cows) in the barn and often "minded" the flies in a fastidious household:

> Those Cattle smaller than a Bee
> That herd upon the eye—

Whose tillage is the passing Crumb—
Those Cattle are the Fly—
Of Barns for Winter—blameless—
Extemporaneous stalls
They found to our objection—
On eligible walls—
Reserving the presumption
To suddenly descend
And gallop on the Furniture—
Or odiouser offend—

"Odiouser"? She prefers one of Gulliver's favorite words, faintly echoing Swift's excremental detail, to sound "wrong" so that nose and ear are equally repelled. At home with the bitter satirist who said he loved mankind too much to tell it pretty tales, she also would have liked the genial acerbities of a twentieth-century versifier such as Ogden Nash, who took liberties with proper grammar whenever they suited him. She is not too strict about the rhyme, starting with "Bee" and "eye," which are not quite in accord, but settling on "Fly," which brings the poem's two important words together. The perfect rhymes follow—usually but not always alternating as the house becomes a barn where the Furniture obtrudes—and are consonant with the final disclaimer:

Of their peculiar calling
Unqualified to judge
To Nature we remand them
To justify or scourge—
(#1388, c. 1876)[27]

This *jeu d'esprit* in which "pompous Latinisms cavort with pure Saxon to present the case . . . against the common fly," as Richard Sewall says of the poet's exuberant legalisms, is an instance among many of Dickinson's "stretching of the language at point after point."[28] She may, then, confidently leave to Nature the decision to send the matter back to a lower court. Read it, if you wish, as a criticism of the "herd."

Some of the poems about trifles and "little things" suggest that Dickinson, like Swift, or Hawthorne, Mark Twain, and a number of American women contemporary with her,[29] had an interest in writing for children as well as adults. Letters lend credence to the supposition. Writing for the young nephew and niece when they were on vacation in the summer of 1873, for instance, she reports: "Bun has run away—Disaffection—doubtless—as to the Supplies. Ned [who was twelve] is a better Quarter Master than his vagrant Papa." (Papa, she says, is very tired.) "The little Turkey is lonely and the Chickens bring him to call. His foreign Neck in familiar Grass is quaint as Dromedary." A turkey on the scale of a camel is as Swiftian as flies on the scale of cows.[30] Of the niece, not yet six, the aunt says: "I suppose the Wind has chastened the Rows on Mattie's impudent Hat and the Sea presumed as far as he dare on her stratified Stockings. If her Basket wont hold the Boulders she picks, I will send a Bin." Dickinsonian exaggeration and humor are in play, but the sense of proportions and the view of the world from the children's encounter with it are also at work.

Even when she exaggerates or is humorous, there is a subtle difference in remarks to the children's mother. The poet says to her, for instance, "Our parting was somewhat interspersed and I cannot conclude which went. . . . Vinnie drank your Coffee and has looked a little like you since, which is nearly a comfort" (L, 2:508). The tone is still playful but less direct. Sentiment becomes wit. In another letter to the vacationers two years earlier (1871), she begins almost as if she is writing to the children, although she is probably addressing the sister-in-law: "The Trees keep House for you all Day and the Grass looks chastened. A silent Hen frequents the place with superstitious Chickens—and still Forenoons a Rooster knocks at your outer Door." There is, so far, no reason to think the message is exclusively for the adult, but in the words that follow the distinction is clear: "To look that way is Romance. The Novel 'out,' pathetic worth attaches to the Shelf." She continues, less wittily, more "elegantly": "The Forests are at Home—the Mountains intimate at Night and arrogant at Noon, and lonesome Fluency abroad, like suspending Music." For the children, there are other words; the differences in vocabulary or even topics are not as salient as the imaginative gestures. She knows what the children want to hear and does not ask from them an awareness that is more complex than they can grasp. "Tell Neddie that we miss him and cherish 'Captain Jinks'" (the poet's nickname for the nephew alludes to a popular song about the horse marines). And "Tell Mattie that 'Tim's' Dog calls Vinnie's Pussy names and I don't discourage him. She must come Home and chase them both and that will make it square" (L, 2:489–90).

During another holiday period, the aunt writes for the children:

" 'Pussum' cries and I hear, but it is too select a grief to accept solace. Tell Mattie Tabby caught a Rat and it ran away. Grandpa caught it and it stayed. He is the best Mouser. The Rabbit winks at me all Day, but if I wink back, he shuffles a Clover. What Rowen he leaves, Horace will pick for the Cow" (L, 2:512). Receiving a reply from the nephew, she writes: "Ned—Bird—It was good to hear you. Not a voice in the Woods is so dear as your's." She tells him, "Papa is living with me. He is a gentle Passenger. It will be an excellent day when you and Mattie come. The Robins have all gone but a few infirm ones and the Cricket and I keep House for the Frost. He is very tidy." She says she has borrowed honey from "a religious Bee, who can be relied on" and is "saving a Miller for Mattie. It laid six eggs on the Window Sill and I thought it was getting tired, so I killed it for her" (L, 2:513). She missed what she called Ned's "Circus Airs in the Rowen" (L, 2:509).

There are more letters to him than to the niece, but he was five years older and there were more years in which to write to him. The first note to Ned was written on the occasion of his third birthday, in June 1864, when the poet was in Boston for the treatment of her eyes. She calls him "My little Uncle," asks him to remember her "till" she comes "Home a hundred miles to see his Braided Gown," and describes "a Man who drives a Coach like a Thimble, and turns the Wheel all day with his Heel—His name is Bumblebee" (L, 2:432). On one of Mattie's birthdays, probably her twelfth, the poet sent a "little Bouquet": "It's Father is a very old Man by the name of Nature, whom you never saw." There was also some advice to proud young Mattie: "Be sure to live in vain and never mingle with the mouse—like Papa's Tongs—" (L, 2:517). To Gilbert, born in 1875 and the third of the Dickinson children, the first note is dated about 1881, when he was six and had started to school. It is about his having asked for "a little Plant" to carry to his teacher. Aunt Emily sends one "from her Crib." She counted on all of them to appreciate that she shared their perspectives; the children knew she was "grown up."

The affinity the poet felt with children reached beyond those of the immediate family to friends of the young Dickinsons and to the children of neighbors. There are also notes to them or frequent messages for them in letters to their parents. The attention she paid to children seems, rather than an evidence of the poet's immaturity, a measure of the range of her imagination and a refusal to condescend to them. They were, she knew, open to experience, were curious about the natural world, saw it anew, and loved the sound of words. She wrote of "Austin's Baby" Gilbert, at the age of three, that he "says when surprised by statements—'There's *sumthn*—else—there's *Bumbul*—Beese" (L, 2:633).

Children not only delighted her, as they delight many adults; children also gave her ideas for verse, some of it fanciful and not always among the best poetry she wrote. It is occasionally superior light verse. An example is "I know some lonely Houses," a poem which has had a mixed reception among readers who have thought it melodramatic, based "on Emily's irrational fear of robbery and violence by night," yet "nevertheless largely comic, in the purely entertaining manner of a ghost or murder story"; "essentially feminine and occasionally coy," but "full of small surprises in impressionist imagery"; "a statement about the poetic mind and about insight and awareness"; and "intricately wrought" in the verbal as well as the metrical effects.[31] It happens to be particularly suitable for young listeners, is original, and has (I think) no intention of expressing much of anything except the joy of letting the fancy go:

> I know some lonely Houses off the Road
> A Robber'd like the look of—
> Wooden barred,
> And Windows hanging low,
> Inviting to—
> A Portico,
> Where two could creep—
> One—hand the Tools—
> The other peep—
> To *make sure All's Asleep—
> Old fashioned eyes—
> Not easy to surprise!
>
> How orderly the Kitchen'd look, by night,
> With just a Clock—
> But they could gag the Tick—
> And Mice wont bark—
> And so the Walls—dont tell
> None—will—
>
> A pair of Spectacles ajar just stir—
> An Almanac's aware—
> Was it the Mat—winked,
> Or a Nervous Star?

The Moon—slides down the stair,
To see who's there!

There's plunder—where—
Tankard, or Spoon
Earring—or Stone—
A Watch—Some †Ancient Brooch
To match the Grandmama—
Staid sleeping—there—

Day—rattles—too
Stealth's—slow—
The Sun has got as far
As the third Sycamore—
Screams Chanticleer
"Who's there?"

And Echoes—Trains away,
Sneer—"Where"!
While the old Couple, just astir,
Fancy the Sunrise—left the door ajar!
                              ·(#289, c. 1861)

*Gauge the sleep
†Antique

The cadence of a voice telling a story to children, the freedom in the rhymes, and the whimsical tone match the lively images. There is nothing comparable to it in all of Dickinson's work, and it suggests that the poet would try anything at least once.

The verse narrative, if it is written for children, as I think it is, would indicate that the poet had an interest in "juvenile" literature, even before the birth of the young Dickinsons next door. It is, however, likely that the noticeable increase, from the mid-sixties to the end of her life, in descriptions of "Several of Nature's People"—to use a familiar phrase from the famous poem on the snake, "A narrow Fellow in the Grass"—was motivated by conversations with the children she often entertained. "A narrow Fellow" is described from the point of view of an adult talking to a boy[32] about the fascination and fear of snakes. The persona notes that the snake "likes a Boggy Acre / A Floor too cool for Corn." Yet, "when a Boy, and Barefoot— / I more than once at Noon / Have passed, I thought, a Whip lash/ Unbraiding in the Sun / When stooping to secure it / It wrinkled, and was gone." The images are both immediate and remembered. "But never met this Fellow / Attended, or alone / Without a tighter breathing / And Zero at the Bone—" (#986, c. 1864–66). The eyes are on the snake; the empathy is with the boy. (Or anyone at the mercy of "a snake in the grass"?)

In keeping with the topics she chose for messages to the children when they were on holiday, she wrote more than one verse about their small "people." She preferred the less well-behaved ones. There is a rather ordinary poem about a dog that reminds her of a boy who "gambols all the living Day / Without an earthly cause"; and a cat dwelling in a corner—"Her martial Day forgot / The Mouse but a Tradition now / Of her desireless Lot"—reminds the poet of "another class" who "neither please nor play" (#1185, c. 1871). With dispatch and amused authority, she declares: "The Rat is consisest Tenant. / He pays no Rent. / Repudiates the Obligation—" (#1356, c. 1876).[33] Is she or isn't she the rat's advocate? And of a rat caught in a trap, she writes gleefully although sermonically: "A Rat surrendered here / A brief career of Cheer / And Fraud and Fear. / Of Ignominy's due / Let all addicted to / Beware. / The most obliging Trap / It's tendency to snap / Cannot resist." The New England primer is pre-text for every word,[34] and the lesson is not yet over: "Temptation is the Friend / Repugnantly resigned / At last" (#1340, c. 1873–77). If the vocabulary seems larger than the readers, children like big words, which Dickinson happily taught her pupils.

To Gilbert, age six, she sent a dead bee with some high-flown lines of verse for his other "school" teacher. It was titled "The Bumble Bee's Religion":

> His little Hearse like Figure
> Unto itself a Dirge
> To a delusive Lilac
> The vanity divulge
> Of Industry and Morals
> And every righteous thing
> For the divine Perdition
> Of Idleness and Spring—
> (#1522, c. 1881)

She adds, for Gilbert to read, " 'All Liars shall have their part'— Jonathan Edwards— / 'And let him that is athirst come'—Jesus—" (L, 3:701).

The bee is one of the poet's favorite "symbols."[35] There is, for example, a verse letter to: "Bee!" signed "Yours, Fly." Perhaps it is a parody on the banalities one writes to friends; perhaps it was for the children. It sounds "dashed off," implying that the correspondent is as busy as the proverbial bee: "I'm expecting you! / Was saying Yesterday /To Somebody you know / That you were due." Then there is brief news of the frogs, and birds, and clover as inducement to Bee. "You'll get my letter by / The seventeenth; Reply / Or better, be with me—" (#1035, c. 1864–66). She could hardly miss a chance for a pun. If there is a common "doctrine" in the poet's variations on the image of the bee, it is that he vagariously *is*. "Auto da Fe—and Judgment—/ Are nothing to the bee—/ His separation from His Rose—/ To Him—sums Misery—" (#620, c. 1862); he is "Traitor" with "Silken Speech and Specious Shoe" (#896, c. 1864–66); or buccaneer in "Black, with Gilt Surcingles," he rides "abroad in ostenation" and subsists "on Fuzz" (#1405, c. 1877),[36] is exhilarated by "His [own] oriental heresies" and fills "all the Earth and Air / With gay apostasy" (#1526, c. 1881). He is male, erotic, adventurous, daring. "A Bee his burnished Carriage" (no Hearse for this one) "Drove boldly to a Rose." The rose, in Dickinson's metaphor, "received his visit / With frank tranquility / Withholding not a Crescent / To his Cupidity." The poet again does not resist a chance for the pun on "Cupidity," and the light rhyme scheme ironically counters the opprobrium of the final quatrain. "Their Moment consummated—/ Remained for him—to flee—/ Remained for her—of Rapture / But the Humility" (#1339, c. 1873–74). This poem, more than any of the others on the bee, is one that readers find embarrassing. But is she Victorian school marm, repressed virgin, or feminist poet? Or is she following one image through a series of variations? When she took up the topic of bees and flowers, which were especially popular among the sentimentalists of the period, she was more daring, more observant, and less serious than they. She enjoys the bee's freedom and zest; she commends, welcomes, admires, envies, parodies, and criticizes him. She deliberately or playfully varies the significance of the image. She is also probably writing for the children as well as the adults. You see, she is saying, this is the way things are—sometimes.

Among the best of the kindergarten lessons on the bee is another entertainment:

> A single Clover *Plank
> Was all that saved a Bee

A Bee I personally knew
From sinking in the sky—

Twixt Firmament above
And Firmament below
The Billows of Circumference
Were sweeping him away—

The idly swaying Plank
Responsible to nought
A sudden Freight of Wind †assumed
And Bumble Bee was not—

This harrowing event
Transpiring in the Grass
Did not so much as wring from him
A wandering "Alas"—

                         (#1343, c. 1875)

*spar
†took on

Such was the fate of at least one Dickinson bee with the boldness to
wander, alas. And the flower, idly swaying, was the irresponsible
one this time around.

The poet has, characteristically, still other words of "worldly
wisdom" derived from the observations of "little" and "big" people
she "knew" personally. The clover, Dickinson's "Purple Democrat"
(#380, c. 1862), and the spirited bee also figure in a little social
criticism that sums up her attitudes toward the "emblems": "The
Pedigree of Honey / Does not concern the Bee—/ A Clover, any time,
to him, / Is Aristocracy" (#1627, c. 1884). She is hardly indifferent
toward the common clover and draws from it another lesson: "The
Clover's simple Fame / Remembered of the Cow—/ Is better than
enameled Realms of notability. / Renown perceives itself / And that
degrades the Flower—" (#1232, c. 1872). The images have been
subordinated in the pronouncement, but the subjective values contain them.

If some of these poems were for children as well as adults, Dickinson was also teaching both of them the religion of the eyes,[37] nature's catechism, and what she called the "vision of the word." It is
not certain which of the verses, except "The Bumble Bee's Religion," went exclusively to the pupils next door, but their visits to

the Homestead were frequent, and who knows what she read to them or told them? Notes were for special occasions, and the children saved the notes. They confirm that she teased as she taught them. She wrote once: "Dear Ned, You know that Pie you stole— well, this is that Pie's Brother—Mother told me when I was a Boy, that I must 'turn over a new Leaf'—I call that Foliage Admonition—Shall I commend it to you?" She sent another note shortly thereafter to Ned's mother on "the solaces of theft." And when the boy was stung by a hornet, she wrote: "Dear Ned—You know I never liked you in those Yellow Jackets" (L, 2:622, 630, and 587). She sent him, after he had suffered epileptic seizures and was ill in February 1877, "A Field of Stubble, lying sere / Beneath the second Sun—" (#1407) as "a Portrait of the Parish" with a note rejoicing that he was better. She also sent him, when he was probably again ill, "The Bible is an antique Volume—/ Written by faded Men / At the suggestion of Holy Spectres." But Eden is the "ancient Homestead—/ Satan—the Brigadier—/ Judas—the Great Defaulter—/ David—the Troubadour . . . " (#1545, c. 1882). She prefaced the poem with a note: " 'Sanctuary Privileges' for Ned, as he is unable to attend" (L, 2:577 and 3:732). It was the purpose of poetry, she thought, to provide sanctuary privileges as well as a means of bringing up the children in the ways she thought they should go.[38] Mattie, the poet said, was "the North wind of the family" and tended to be a snob. Perhaps those are reasons, to make a wild guess, that the aunt sent her and her friend Sally Jenkins a poem on "The Butterfly upon the Sky / That does'nt know it's Name / And has'nt any tax to pay / And has'nt any Home" but "Is just as high as you and I, / And higher, I believe, / So soar away and never sigh / And that's the way to grieve—" (L, 3:704). Perhaps, on second guess, Mattie liked things that fly.

Writing for children is one of the many interests Dickinson had in common with other nineteenth-century authors, as well as yet another confirmation of the resilience with which she responded to the world. Stimulated by "trifles," she also shared with family and friends the play of language for registering quickened moments of perception and the values she found in them to enlarge the vision of that world.

7

"Experiment to me / Is every one I meet": Points of View

I

Although Emily Dickinson wrote few dramatic monologues but many "trifles" after 1865 when she returned home from Boston, there is throughout the work keen attention to human behavior. Assuming a point of view that has the authority of "I know" or the perspective of an "invisible" but observant poet, she tries out different means of depicting the actions of other people, their mental and emotional states. How successful was she?

"Experiment to me / Is every one I meet,"[1] the poet says, and she does not sound disinterested in the findings. The word *experiment* indicates a preoccupation "with issues of evidence, inference, and knowledge."[2] The "I" of the poem therefore asks of every *one*, "If it contain a Kernel?" And "The Figure of a Nut" (in a nutshell? to be cracked?) tempts the poet to pun: "But Meat within, is requisite / To Squirrels and to Me" (#1073, c. 1864–66). Understandably skeptical about whether one can know another's soul, or inner being, Dickinson also knows one is customarily alert to signs that will confirm the claims of humankind. "I like a look of Agony / Because I know it's true." Evidence? "Impossible to feign / The beads upon the Forehead / By homely Anguish strung" (#241, c. 1862). We may take "Experiment to me" and "I like a look of Agony" as the poet's position papers; but whatever strategy Dickinson uses, readers' eyes are often on the inward thrust, and a concentrated focus on the "self"-centered percipient obscures an assessment of the poet's outward thrust.

Breaking free of the "I," which gives us the illusion that she is the persona in the dramatic monologues, the poet observes, "The lonesome for they know not What— / The Eastern Exiles—be—" (#262, c. 1861), "What Soft—Cherubic Creatures— / These Gentlewomen are—" (#401, c. 1862) and "Color—Caste—Denomination— / These are—Time's Affair" (#970, c. 1864); or she describes natural phenomena such as "An Everywhere of Silver" (#884, c. 1864), the season "Further in Summer than the Birds" (#1068, c. 1866), and "the Nights that Beetles love—" (#1128, c. 1868). Choosing among them, a critic decides that the satire of "These Gentlewomen" expresses the poet's "gigantic self-hatred";[3] or another comments that "the cricket" in "Further in Summer than the Birds" is "singer, persona for the poet," and that there is "some identification" between "her own plight and the cricket's," as well as that "the birds represent the conscious, civilized ego, while the crickets represent . . . regression to the Druidic Self."[4] Texts yield to psychobiography, although the basis for deciding that a poem's images and insights are self-centered varies according to the reader's predisposition.

Describing herself as observer, for instance, the poet sees the moon as less and more than human. She begins as if she were writing a novel of manners:

> I watched the Moon around the House
> . . . .
> I gazed—as at a stranger—
> The Lady in the Town
> Doth think no incivility
> To lift her Glass—upon—
>
> But never Stranger justified
> The Curiosity
> Like Mine—

And the suggestion of a novel of manners turns macabre. There is, a critic writes, "a wistful note in the speaker's voice as she describes . . . the moon . . . as a bodiless woman":

for not a Foot—nor Hand—
Nor Formula—had she—

But like a Head—a Guillotine
Slid carelessly away—
Did independent, Amber—
Sustain her in the sky—

Or like a Stemless Flower—
Upheld in rolling Air
By finer Gravitations—
Than bind Philosopher—

No Hunger—had she—nor an Inn
Her Toilette—to suffice—
Nor Avocation—nor Concern
For little Mysteries

As harass us—like Life—and Death—
And Afterwards—or Nay—

"As we see Dickinson marvel at the moon's independence, her autonomy, her unconcern for an 'Avocation' or life's 'little Mysteries,' and her lack of *hunger*," according to the critical view, "it becomes clear that the self-absorbed poet is defining the moon in terms of herself, projecting upon that orb all that she, by sharp contrast, is not—or so she claims." In the "psychological, metaphoric portrait of herself as the poet daughter," the critic concludes, "the sense of hunger is directly related to the woman's lack of power . . . in her own house and the father's house beyond: this deprivation makes 'Possibility.' "[5] The ambivalent images of the moon do contrast with more human and gross earthly concerns that bind philosopher and poet, but their concerns are larger than those of the poet as daughter, head on shoulders and "glass" in hand for an unobstructed although brief look at the moon that "seemed engrossed to Absolute— / With shining—and the Sky." There are limits to the poet's vision:

The privilege to scrutinize
Was scarce upon my Eyes
When with a Silver practice
She vaulted out of Gaze—
And next—I met her on a Cloud—

                    Myself too far below
                    To follow her superior Road—
                    Or it's advantage—Blue—
                                (#629, c. 1862)

The privileged moment over, the mortal poet has lost the muse and
the vision: an ironic vision of a thoughtless, severed head.

     With no hint of the novel of manners and no headnotes, or foot-
notes, for the reader, she writes a poem for the legendary Joan of
Arc: "A Mien to move a Queen— / Half Child—Half Heroine. . . . " A
critic comments, once again, that the poem is a "self-conscious self-
portrait" in which Dickinson appraises "the effect her physical,
psychic, and intellectual self has upon other people."[6]

     Although there is no record that she read Robert Southey's *Joan
of Arc* (1796), Dickinson seems to have adapted his dramatic narration of the history of the eighteen-year-old heroine for a twenty-
five-line poem. Both Southey and Dickinson write as omniscient
authors. The narrative by the English poet has many characters for
whom there are often long and tiresome speeches in ten books of
verse with pages of notes, followed by *The Vision of the Maid of
Orleans* in three books with additional notes.

     Southey calls her "Child" and compares her to "a youth who
from his [sic] mother's arms, / For his first field impatient, breaks
away." She is received, Southey says, "With cordial affability" by
the queen: "With her Joan lov'd to pass / Her intervals of rest," and
to her Joan told of being roused to "uneasy wonder." Or, "Sad and
sick at heart, / Fain to her lonely chamber's solitude / the Maiden"
retired. She is more than once tearful.[7] Dickinson writes, with typical concision, of "An Orleans in the Eye / That puts it's manner by /
For humbler company / When none are near / Even a Tear—/ It's
frequent Visitor."

     Southey, describing the battle dress of the "martial Maid," says
"The white plumes nodded o'er her helmed head"; Dickinson amusingly gives her "A Bonnet like a Duke—/ And yet a Wren's Peruke /
Were not so shy / Of Goer by." Southey dwells lovingly on the
spiritual significance of the folk tradition that Joan, with other
young girls, would go to dance and sing under "the fairy's tree"
which stood near their village. Southey's Joan recounts the influence of the strange and fearful pleasures, the "holy quietness," the
"solitude and freedom" of the "blessed spot" ("a green grass plot"
on which "an ancient oak" grows beside "The Fountain of the

Fairies") and "Tales of the Elfin tribe," of whose "midnight revelry" she had first heard with "a delightful wonder."[8] Dickinson is less reverential and less "poetic" than Southey. She barely touches the lore by saying of Joan's "Hands—so slight— / They would elate a Sprite / With Merriment."

Southey also attends to Joan's persuasive powers, her "mild tone," her rebukes, or her forceful commands and passionate convictions. He says the heroine inspired amazement, awe, and wonderment; "with eager hush the crowd" listened. Or, when she placed "the crown of France" on the brow of Charles VII, the "assembled multitude / In awful stillness witness'd: then at once, / As with a tempest-rushing noise of winds, / Lifted their mingled clamours. Now the Maid / . . . waved her hand, / And instant silence followed." Southey's poem ends with Joan's charge to the king, at whose knees she pleads solemnly for a righteous reign.[9]

Dickinson writes that Joan has "A Voice that Alters—Low / And on the Ear can go / Like Let of Snow— / Or shift supreme— / As tone of Realm / On Subjects Diadem." Attention to the king is scant (subjects' diadem). The focus is on Joan at the height of victory. She is:

> Too small—to fear—
> Too distant—to endear—
> And so men Compromise—
> And just—revere—
> (#283, c. 1861)

The poem is from a woman's perspective, giving to the Maid of Orleans "tone of Realm" and reverence but aptly including the note that men neither feared nor loved her. Both Dickinson's brief transposition and Southey's thunderous scenes, however, belong to their era. Although Joan of Arc had been declared innocent in 1456, canonization was discussed in 1875; she was pronounced venerable in 1902, beatified in 1909, and canonized in 1920. Dickinson's sketch of "Saint Joan" is, then, in accord with the historical moment, and reference to it is as germane as the poet's personal history to our reading of the modest poem.

The verses on "individual" people who caught her imagination *are* steeped in the poet's predilections and personality. That is particularly true of the "protest" poems. One of the most resonant of them begins:

> It always felt to me—a wrong
> To that Old Moses—done—
> To let him see—the Canaan—
> Without the entering—

She wonders if Moses really were a historical person, but "the
Romance / In point of injury" surpasses the story of either Stephen
or Paul:

> For these—were only put to death—
> While God's adroiter will
>
> On Moses—seemed to fasten
> *With tantalizing Play
> As Boy—should deal with lesser Boy—
> To †prove ability.
>
> The fault—was doubtless Israel's—
> Myself—had banned the Tribes—
> And ushered Grand Old Moses
> In Pentateuchal Robes
>
> Upon the ‡Broad Possession
> 'Twas little—§He should see—
> Old Man on Nebo! Late as this
> ‖My justice bleeds—for Thee!
>   (#597, c. 1862)

*In
†show supremacy
‡Lawful Manor
§But titled Him—to see
‖One

The variation on the phrase "that old Moses," as it opens to the full
sound of "Grand Old Moses" and lengthens to "Old Man on Nebo,"
is terminated with the words "justice bleeds—for Thee!" It is a
simple matter for the poet to say "bleeds" instead of "pleads,"
which a person of lesser ability would have chosen, but for Dickinson the strength of the feeling is in the right word, even if she is
only "one justice." The poem, however, is really another quarrel
with God: a big Boy.
    She again uses a familiar story like that of "It always felt to me—
a wrong" in a poem also based on legendary figures about whom

she again makes no effort to use words that are "value free." They express the poet's opinion:

> Tell as a Marksman—were forgotten
> Tell—*this Day endures
> Ruddy as that coeval Apple
> †The tradition bears—
> *till now
> †Heroism

The story, she says, is humble and stately. "Tell had a son—The ones that knew it / Need not linger here," but she assumes the part of storyteller as teacher:

> Tell *would not bare His Head
> In Presence
> Of the Ducal Hat—
> Threatened for that with Death—by Gessler—
> Tyranny bethought
>
> Make of his only Boy a Target
> That surpasses Death—
> *could

There is, in contrast to the poem on Moses, no criticism of God. Tell is described as

> Stolid to Love's *supreme entreaty
> Not †forsook of Faith—
>
> ‡Mercy of the Almighty *begging—
> Tell his Arrow sent—
> God it is said replies in Person
> When the cry is meant
>   (#1152, c. 1869)
> *sublime
> †forgot
> ‡power
> §asking

The emotional distance between the statements "God it is said replies in Person" and "When the cry is meant" is in turn reflected in the distance between an interpreter and participants in the trial.

The restraint with which the poet voices consternation about what a gesture of freedom might have cost had Tell not been a man of self-control, skill, and Christian faith is less eloquent than the rhetoric of protest against God's treatment of Moses, who also, as she says in another poem, "was'nt fairly used" (#1201, c. 1871). For one critic, Dickinson was like Moses, "given a glimpse of the promised land and forbidden to enter it"; another writes that Moses' vindication became the poet's.[10] There is no commentary on her poem for Tell.

Whether based on the life of someone Dickinson knew or had only heard or read about, another verse describes a fatal moment for an unnamed man. Although she provides no antecedent for "it," in the first line of the narrative, he apparently had received bad news:

> He scanned it—staggered—
> Dropped the Loop
> To Past or Period—
> Caught helpless at a sense as if
> His Mind were going blind—
>
> Groped up, to see if God were there—
> Groped backward at Himself—
> Caressed a trigger absently
> And wandered out of Life.
>   (#1062, c. 1864–66)

The poem is read by one critic as "a suicide wish."[11] It is also read as a depiction of the "actual process of suicide." Adrienne Rich says, however, "the precision of knowledge . . . is such that we must assume that Dickinson had, at least in fantasy, drifted close to that state in which the 'Loop' that binds us to 'Past or Period' is 'dropped' and we grope randomly at what remains of abstract notions of sense, God, or self, before—almost absentmindedly— reaching for a solution." This, Rich writes appreciatively, "is a poem in which the suicidal experience has been distanced, refined, transformed through a devastating accuracy of language. It is not suicide that is studied here, but the dissociation of self and mind and world which precedes."[12] Dickinson, then, "seems" capable of anything. She is a protean poet.

Like any other writer, she is *in* every poem she wrote; and in the poems, she "was the single artificer of the world / In which she sang, / . . . she was the maker." She was not, however, a poet of whom we can say that "there never was a world for her / Except the one she sang . . . ," even though it "was her voice that made / The sky acutest at its vanishing." She, too, raged for order.[13] And it was often a blessed rage, but not always; nor was rage her only reaction, because she well knew that the bodiless moon's road was "Superior— / Its advantage—Blue—"; "Men Compromise—," or are "caught helpless"; "God's will" is "adroiter,' and men must beg "Mercy of the Almighty." If we judge by the response of innumerable readers (of whom I have selected only a few), however, Dickinson failed to convey the great interest she had in "every one" she met.

II

Why, as adroit as she was with words, that failure? Putting aside for the moment the matter of different readings based on a common assumption that the author and her characters are one, I would like to consider other reasons for prevailing attitudes toward the poems about people whom the poet described with minimal reference to herself. While there is a profusion of "experiments," there is also an unstated principle that I think Dickinson tended to follow when she wrote poems about people.

She knew all kinds of them and had opportunities to observe them as closely as she observed nature or other writers' ways of depicting character. In the letters, from which I have in earlier chapters quoted passages describing people, it is clear that she liked characterizing them. She spoke of Amherst commencement ceremonies as "the Gravities," most professors as "Manikins" [sic], and the governor of the state as "Pope," whom she wished to Rome (L, 2:410, 3:824, and 2:367). A rotund woman "rolls down the lane to church like a reverend marble" (L, 2:470).[14]

Or "Mother had a new tooth Saturday, you know Dr S had promised her one for a long time. 'Teething' didn't agree with her, and she kept her bed, Sunday, with a face that would take a premium at any cattle show in the land." As if the mother had not suffered enough, the daughter continued: "Came to town next morning, with slightly reduced features, but no eye on the left side. Doubtless we are 'fearfully and wonderfully made' and occasionally grotesquely." (Dickinson was writing to relatives.) In the same letter, written in October 1863 (?), the poet reported:

> L goes to Sunderland, Wednesday, for a minute or two; leaves here at 6 ½—what a fitting hour—and will breakfast the night before; such a smart atmosphere! The trees stand right straight when they hear her boots, and will bear crockery wares instead of fruit, I fear. She hasn't starched the geraniums yet, but will have ample time, unless she leaves before April. (L, 2:428)

Or, when the child next door was away on a visit, she wrote, "Grandma moans for Neddie, and Austin's face is soft as Mist when he hears his name" (L, 2:464).

For Ned, ten years later, she wrote about Dennis Scannell, gardener and handyman, whose wife had died three years before the escapade the poet probably watched from an upstairs window:

> Dennis was happy yesterday, and it made him graceful—I saw him waltzing with the Cow—and suspected his status, but he afterward started for your House in a frame that was unmistakable—
> You told me he had'nt tasted Liquor since his Wife's decease—then she must have been living at six o'clock last Evening—
> I fear for the rectitude of the Barn—
> Love for the Police—
>
> (L, 2:641)

There is a paucity of this kind of "human interest" in the poems. Commenting on the behavior of people, Dickinson may make aphoristic assertions such as "Much Madness is divinest Sense— / To a discerning Eye— / Much Sense—the Starkest Madness" (#435, c. 1862), or " 'Speech' is a prank of *Parliament*— / '*Tears*' a trick of the *nerve*—" (#688, c. 1862). She will observe, as a "mob" psychologist, that "The Popular Heart is a Cannon first— / Subsequent a Drum— / Bells for an Auxiliary / And an Afterward of Rum—" (#1226, c. 1870–73). The reclusive poet even writes "society verse": The Show is not the Show / But they that go— / Menagerie to me / My Neighbor be— / Fair Play— / Both went to see" (#1206, c. 1872). Perhaps she had to stay home to write of "show-offs." But there is not a pinpointing of an individual.

Or seeming to enjoy a sense of "negative superiority," a Dickinson persona declares: "I'm Nobody! Who are you? / Are you— Nobody—too?" Once again, the daughter of the great Dickinson goes her joyful way. "Then there's a pair of us! / Don't tell! they'd advertise—you know!" The poet leaves herself open for approval by those who have a disdain for self-important people (like the "Pope" she wished to Rome?) and criticism by those who think the poem a "pose" or a rationalization of obsessive behavior. For Alice James, who said Dickinson's "being sicklied o'er with T. W. Higginson makes one quake," the verse revealed "the cheap farce and the highest point of view of the aspiring soul."[15] Yet it is more usual to think that "young Emily Dickinson's morbid aversion to fame makes Thoreau look almost gregarious."[16] Still, with tongue not quite in cheek, she renders the sentence: "How dreary—to be— Somebody! / How public—like a Frog— / To tell one's name the livelong June— / To an admiring Bog!" (#288, c. 1861). So, the poet as social critic rhymed her way to glory. Everyone is free to fill in the images of "Nobody"; and while the images of "Somebody" characterize another kind of person, as does the word "Manikins," they do not compare with the realism of the hyperbolic Dickinson describing mother's swollen face: "No eye on the left side."

The poet also likes realistic detail in the descriptions of scenes from nature, although (as Robert Frost said about some of the verse he wrote) it is realism with the dirt washed off. She writes of "An Antiquated Tree" cherished by the crow in "Corporation Coat" (#1514, c. 1881), compares "The reeling Oriole" to "The splendor of a Burmah" (#1466, c. 1879), or says "Glass was the Street—in tinsel Peril / Tree and Traveller stood—" but "Hearty with Boys the Road— / /Shot the lithe Sleds like shod vibrations" (#1498, c. 1880). She writes with equal gusto:

> A Bird came down the Walk—
> He did not know I saw—
> He bit an Angleworm in halves
> And ate the fellow, raw,
>
> And then he drank a Dew
> From a convenient Grass—

And then hopped sidewise to the Wall
To let a Beetle pass . . .
                    (#328, c. 1862)

In the poems about an individual from the point of view of the observer, however, Dickinson customarily concentrates on a type of person and a single characteristic to which she responds.

Passing judgment on a theologically liberal minister, she is epigrammatic: "He preached upon 'Breadth' till it argued him narrow." The observation is probably common folk wisdom, but the poet's long phrasing of it is uncommonly expressive. Both the cadences and choice of words are right. The equal strength, measured by the word count in the clauses for the "broad-minded" and the "narrow-minded" yoked together by "till," is imbalanced wittily in the force of the verb *argued*, by which the man loses the case or the cause that he *preached upon*. An eight-line depreciation of him follows (he is compared to fool's gold), and ends by citing his own authority as reproof: "What confusion would cover the innocent Jesus / To meet so enabled a Man!" (#1207, c. 1872). Dickinson, who could be daring, sent a copy of the poem to Higginson.[17] The skillful verse has no visual imagery, and although we know the man, we do not "see" him, unless we associate him with Higginson, who had been to see her in 1870. But the poem gives the reader no help. There is, moreover, no reason that it should, just as there is no reason for a description of features or look. The man is a type.

Dickinson, who had heard many preachers, wrote another sketch of a type that contrasts with the one characterizing the man of "liberal persuasion." The sketch is wired with sound. And the man has tremendous power over "you":

He fumbles at your Soul
As Players at the Keys
Before they drop full Music on—
He stuns you by degrees—
Prepares your brittle *Nature
For the Etherial Blow
By fainter Hammers—further heard—
Then nearer—Then so slow
Your Breath has †time to straighten—
Your Brain—to bubble Cool

Deals—One—imperial—Thunderbolt—
That ‡scalps your naked Soul—

When Winds §take Forests in their Paws—
The ‖Universe—is still—

(#315, c. 1862)

*substance
†chance
‡peels
§hold
‖Firmament

Since she identifies the man only as "He," opinions differ about
whether he is "lover," "a great preacher," "a hell-fire preacher," the
Calvinist Nobodaddy, "God," "the poet," "one soul mastering another," "masculinity" which the poet fears, or her own power "exte-
riorized in masculine form." (There has also been speculation that
he is the Reverend Charles Wadsworth.)[18] He is a "performer" who
knows exactly what he's doing. So does Emily Dickinson. And she
not only knows what he's doing; she knows what she is doing.

Readers "hear" the man and witness the impact of the preacher
on the congregation. While there is no visual image like "the reverend marble" rolling down the lane to church, the poet's characterization is comparable to the sketch of L, who "hasn't starched the
geraniums yet," but the trees "stand right straight when they hear
her boots."

As an observer Dickinson may include herself among the "you,"
stunned, then scalped, but she may be listening, watching, and
analyzing the performance without having been a victim at all.
She is fascinated, repelled, and funny. From the man's first clumsy
efforts at feeling his way to the final taking hold with "Paws," there
is a brute force without mercy, although the music is both "full"
and "faint" as he "Hammers" away at the soul. The "Etherial
Blows" may be spiritual or they may lack *substance* (a word the
poet originally used for the listener); they may be delicate and
refined, but they are blows. The poet mixes her metaphors, but
there is temporary respite for the listener. Brought to the boiling
point, the victim barely has time to cool off before being struck
by a thunderbolt. Dickinson's ubiquitous dashes are especially effective in the line "Deals—One—imperial—Thunderbolt" (from
heaven? the voice of God?): the action is slow, deliberately paced,
and sure, as the man comes in for the lightning-quick kill. The final

couplet is summary and judgment: the poet's. The change from the singular "He" to plural "Winds" suggests there are others like him, while "Forests" and "The Universe" suggest audiences. Violent, destructive windstorms may also be big bags of wind. The witty poet may have learned something from preachers. She learned early that she could stand against their power, and when she wrote "He fumbles at your soul," she knew she had comparable command of the "word," if not of audiences. We not only disagree about whether she is describing a man who has delivered a sermon. We don't know whether he was large or small, in Indian war paint or television tan. What we know is that he is a person of "brute force" and uses it without compunction. It is possible that she envied him, but I doubt it.

The third of the sketches of "famous" men in Dickinson's copybooks is carefully understated and sparse. The persona frankly expresses a feeling of awe toward a kind of man whose verbal habits also fascinate the poet:

> I fear a Man of *frugal Speech—
> I fear a Silent Man—
> Haranguer—I can overtake—
> Or Babbler—entertain—
>
> But He who weigheth—While the Rest—
> Expend their †furthest pound—
> Of this Man—I am wary—
> I fear that He is Grand—
>
> (#543, c. 1862)

*scanty
†inmost

The poet's comment on those who "Expend their furthest pound," in contrast to the frugal man, underwrites her refusal to use the expected word, *expound*, but the expectation itself is fulfilled with "furthest pound." As prodigious as she was with "speech," she was not prodigal in its use. The repetition of "I fear," as if she protests too much, indicates an ambivalence—similar to the uncertainty about the adjectives "frugal" (or "scanty") and "furthest" (or "inmost")—in the characterizations of the grand man and those who "expend" all the weighty words they have. As a poet, knowing the lure of words, she was also wary of them; and, knowing that words serve a profound need, she respected the dignity of silence but dreaded absolute silence.

There are, in fact, two poems that do not belong to the character sketches but are variations on the theme of "I fear a Man of frugal Speech." The first contrasts the need for human speech and fear of eternal quiet: "Silence is all we dread. / There's Ransom in a Voice— / But Silence is Infinity. / Himself have not a face" (#1251, c. 1873). The second has religious implications: "Speech is one symptom of Affection / And Silence one— / The perfectest communication / Is heard of none— / / Exists and it's indorsement / Is had within," which is followed by a paradoxical comment affirming faith: "Behold, said the Apostle, / Yet had not seen!" (#1681, n.d.). A third poem completes Dickinson's meditations on silence and encompasses the other two, as well as the complexities of the attitudes in the character sketch. "There is," the poet declares, "no Silence in the Earth—so silent / As that endured / Which uttered, would discourage Nature / And haunt the World" (#1004, c. 1864–66). Metaphysical questions may seem rather tenuously connected to the lines "I fear a Man of frugal Speech— / I fear a Silent Man," but she herself wrote, unforgettably, that "The Jehovahs—are no Babblers—" (#626, c. 1862)

She pays tribute to an admirable man, of whom she writes:

> Fate slew Him, but He did not drop—
> She felled—He did not fall—
> Impaled Him on Her fiercest stakes—
> He neutralized them all—
>
> She stung Him—sapped His firm Advance—
> But when Her Worst was done—
> And He—unmoved regarded Her—
> Acknowledged Him a Man.
>
> (#1031, c. 1864–66)

This old-fashioned, straightforward poem engages the imagination less than the man himself. Yet the strong, sure verbs and the relentless rhythms expressing the repeated attacks upon him are matched by rhythms that snap back in the account of the man's continued opposition to Fate. The space between the pronoun *She* at the beginning of the last stanza and the final line—"Acknowledged Him a Man," the predicate for which "She" is the subject—establishes the distance between the antagonists. And since the opening word of the poem is "Fate," it is fitting that the last word is "Man."

There is a small group of verses that seem hardly worth mentioning except for the record of Dickinson's interest in writing about other people. As usual, they have no names: "His Cheek is his Biographer— / As long as he can blush / Perdition is Opprobrium— / Past that, he sins in peace—" (#1460, c. 1879), or "His Heart was darker than the starless night / For that there is a morn / But in this black Receptacle / Can be no Bode of Dawn" (#1378, c. 1876), or "Her Grace is all she has— / And that, so least displays— / One Art to recognize, must be, / Another Art, to praise" (#810, c. 1864–66). But these quatrains are glimpses of essential qualities of the people about whom the poet writes. They have been almost lost among the major poems.

Other verse, in the same category, may describe a woman the poet has observed:

> Her smile was shaped like other smiles—
> The Dimples ran along—
> And still it hurt you, as some Bird
> Did hoist herself, to sing,
> Then recollect a Ball, she got—
> And hold upon the Twig,
> Convulsive while the Music *crashed—
> Like Beads—among the Bog—
>   (#514, c. 1861)
>
> *broke

The strained simile of the bird that has been gun-shot and the spasms of sound breaking like a strand of beads suggest that the poet is trying too hard. Perhaps the verse is well forgotten, but it belongs to the record of an effort to describe another human being whose pain the poet perceives. A second poem, describing a man who has suffered, is better:

> The Hollows round His eager Eyes
> Were Pages where to read
> Pathetic Histories—although
> Himself had not complained.
> Biography to All who passed
> Of Unobtrusive Pain

> Except for the italic Face
> Endured, unhelped—unknown.
> (#955, c. 1864–66)

The poet "reads" the life. Even though she begins with a visual image, as she did in "His Cheek is his Biographer— / As long as he can blush" and "Her smile," the description becomes "poetry," relying on figures of speech, similes and metaphors, to reveal the person "within." It is the person "within" that is of primary interest in "His Heart" and "Her Grace." All of these verses, then, recall the poet's description of grandma, who "moans" for an absent grandson, and a father whose face is "soft as Mist" when he hears the son's name. The innovative poet wants to suit words to the temperament and the life of the emotions for which the outward and visible or other sensible signs are often significant but not absolutely requisite for portrayals of character in verse. In "The Hollows round His eager Eyes," the ironic point is that the man suffers in silence, which other people recognize but are helpless and unable to understand because he endures the pain in silence.[19] And once she exclaims: "To Whom the Mornings stand for *Nights*, / What must the Midnights—be!" (#1095, c. 1866).

If these poems, "Her smile was shaped like other smiles—" and "The Hollows round His eager Eyes," confirm that Dickinson is an authority on pain, they also express a sympathy for the other. She observes with compassion that

> The Ditch is dear to the Drunken man
> For is it not his Bed—
> His Advocate—his Edifice—
> How safe his fallen Head
> In her disheveled Sanctity—
> Above him is the sky—
> Oblivion *bending over him
> And †Honor leagues away.
> (#1645, c. 1885)
>
> *enfolding him with tender infamy
> †Doom a fallacy—

The man is oblivious, but he is also forgotten or unknown. There is not much to say about him; but the images of the ditch as bed, disheveled sanctity for the fallen head, and the sky above him are details that neither sentimentalize nor criticize the troubled man for whom the ditch is ironically "dear." The realism in the description, however, has none of the sense of the individual that Dickinson's notes on Dennis Scannell, gardener and handyman, had. And while one's ignorance of the history of the fallen man is the sum of all the points of the poem, just as the "ignorance" of the people who passed the man with "the italic Face" is pertinent to that characterization, the poet might easily have imagined histories for both of them. She chose, however, not to do so, except as an observer whose knowledge is restricted.

Men were more frequently observed in the biographical verse than are women, whereas they are more frequently given voice in the dramatic monologues. There are, however, a few efforts to sketch women: "What Soft—Cherubic Creatures—," "A Mien to Move a Queen," "her Grace is all she has," and "Her Smile was shaped like other smiles." There is also an important biography of a woman who keeps her own counsel:

> She rose to His Requirement—dropt
> The Playthings of Her Life
> To take the honorable Work
> Of Woman, and of Wife—
>
> If ought, She missed in Her new Day,
> Of Amplitude, or Awe—
> Or first Prospective—Or the Gold
> In using, wear away.
>
> It lay unmentioned—as the Sea
> Develop Pearl, and Weed,
> But only to Himself—be known
> The Fathoms they abide
>   (#732, c. 1863)

"She rose to his Requirement—dropt—," a poem going in two directions simultaneously, as it does in the first line, has yet another single movement downward (to darkness?), which the word "dropt" emphasizes. The effect is similar to the first line of "He preached upon 'Breadth' till it argued him narrow—" or of "Fate slew Him, but He did not drop—," although the dash before "dropt" in "She rose to His Requirement—dropt" gives the word even stronger stress. The private life—the life too deep for fathoming, known only to the old man of the sea, where the woman who "rose" is submerged and "abides" with him—is perhaps deprived of amplitude or awe; that is uncertain. If the woman has her reserves, the poet has her reservations, too. Is the choice of the image of "weed" an afterthought of the poet's word "pearl," or are they of equal value (pearl and weed?), or are they polarities? There is no answer, just as there is no agreement on whether the phrase "honorable Work" is ironic or approving; the ambivalent poet leaves the questions for those living in the sea, or the scuba diver. It is, however, one of the finest biographies.

The perceptions of character in these poems are not those of a self-aggrandizing voice or a self-indulgent writer. Nor are the poems mimetic representations of the "other." They are rather extrapolations of the inner dynamics of representative kinds of men and women, not every man or every woman, nor everyone or anyone. The poet recognizes that what one can perceive may be restricted. She hears and reacts as she does to the man who "fumbles at" the soul because he is a performer who "reveals" himself. She recognizes the superficial and the profound persons, those with sensitive consciences and histories of pain, the "dark" heart, and the woman of grace. She knows there are men of spiritual strength and persistence who defy fate. She sees and responds to the man in the ditch as she does because he has escaped into oblivion. She refuses to draw inference about a woman whose life is too deep for sounding. Dickinson, as an observer, understands the obligations of the poet to render fine discriminations and, when there is sufficient evidence, to make judgments. The poems, on the whole, are well-made.

The austerity of texture, or the lack of realistic detail in most of these biographies, in comparison with the passages from Dickinson's letters, which have many stylistic qualities in common with the verse but are richer in their particularities, must be by design. It was not because she had little interest in people or lacked the skills to write about them.

Dickinson even invests objects with human qualities and delights in the language that designates the differences between them. Classifying two items on the basis of their "familial names," she also caricatures a daughter in contrast to a forbearing father:

> The parasol is the umbrella's daughter,
> And associates with a fan

While her father abuts the tempest
And abridges the rain.

The former assists a siren
In her serene display
But her father is borne and honored,
And borrowed to this day.
                                                (#1747, n.d.)

Critics have paid no attention to this lighthearted poem. Although it gives pleasure, it is probably not one meriting serious attention. I cite it because I like it and because it would be amusing to take it as one about which we could write parodies of our own seriousness in reading Dickinson. I also cite it as an example of people observed and to say that among the variables in Dickinson's verse there are more descriptions of people than we have taken into account, that the poems are not all of the same kind, and that some of them are slight, even minor. Had there been only the verse in this category, Dickinson would not have achieved the stature she is now accorded. We cannot say the same about the dramatic monologues or the nature poems.

III

Dickinson, furthermore, is valued as a writer who delves into common states of "being" and brings up words that are more expressive than the abstract language by which human emotions are designated. Readers have always recognized that she is superior in the depiction of feeling itself; she is, as Vivian Pollak said of her, "a psychological realist."[20] It is generally assumed that she investigates states she herself experienced and also often assumed that she intends—or presumes—the verses of this kind to speak of universal experiences.

Since she has received enormous and thoughtful attention for the poems that probe the realities of subjective experience, I will comment on fewer of them than the achievement warrants. The practice of reading from the poet's life to the poetry and from the poems to the life should, I would argue, be extended beyond that closed circle to include the evidence that Dickinson also took notice of other people and what she could learn from them. Like any authority on human emotions, she does not limit herself to observations of herself. When she said to Susan Dickinson, "With the exception of Shakespeare, you have told me more of knowledge than anyone living," the poet could hardly have been more generous in recognizing an indebtedness to a friend. She had other teachers, too, and she must often have adapted, collated, or conflated not only what she learned from reading but what she learned from the people she knew. There is at least one example of the use she made of a letter from Samuel Bowles, who wrote to the Dickinsons while he was in Switzerland: "There has been plenty of sight seeing, but that is not life; Nature is very beautiful, very wonderful, . . . but it is not *life*. . . . Of all nature, *human* nature is the most interesting and quickening to me." Bowles continues:

> One can *exist* on snow peaks, and apple orchards—can dream of pansies and buttercups, . . . but to *live*, one needs contact with the higher life of humanity, but of that life, I have had nought this summer. The Alps are marvellous. . . . They will oppress you, however, with their cold, hard forms,—they stand out awful, in their majesty and severity. No wonder John Calvin lived and cradled in Switzerland. . . . It is a regular Old Testament scenery, this of the higher Alps.[21]

Dickinson's persona begins: "I thought that nature was enough / Till Human nature came / But that the other did absorb / As Parallax a Flame." The poem then moves quickly to the religious allusions:

> Of Human nature just aware
> There added the Divine
> Brief struggle for capacity
> The power to contain
>
> Is always as the contents
> But give a Giant a room
> And you will lodge a Giant
> And not a smaller man
> (#1286, c. 1873)

The poem, read in the context of the letter (which Susan Dickinson saved and reprinted in a reminiscence of Bowles after his death), may be the poet's tribute to him. As he struggled with the wish for human company to share the solitude and grandeur of the Alpine peaks, he began to think about a great old "divine" and to contain the loneliness. Bowles, in other words, lodged a "Giant" (Calvin) in the landscape that was home to him, as the "Giant" in turn had struggled with a conception of God that would contain the cold, hard mountains. The poem absorbs the moment.

Since the poet drew on many sources for the poems, it is not always possible to know when she is primarily exploring her own feelings and when she is making use of what she learned from others. And because she exploits qualities inherent in different perspectives, the meanings of the poem itself may be dependent on the point of view, whether or not the experience is personal.

She writes, for example, a narrative hardly distinguishable from the dramatic monologues. An interior monologue, usually considered as autobiographical—and it may well be—the poem recounts from the perspective of an "I" a remembered romantic meeting:[22]

> Again—his voice is at the door—
> I feel the old *Degree*—
> I hear him ask the servant
> For such an one—as me—
>
> I take a *flower*—as I go—
> My face to *justify*—
> He never *saw* me—*in this life*—
> I might *surprise his eye!
>
> I cross the Hall with *mingled* steps—
> I—silent—pass the door—
> I look on all this world *contains*—
> *Just his face*—nothing more!
>
> We talk in †*careless*—and in *toss*—
> A kind of *plummet* strain—
> Each—sounding—shyly—
> Just—how—deep—
> The *other's* ‡one—had been—
>
> We *walk*—I leave my Dog—§at home
> A *tender—thoughtful* Moon

> Goes with us—just a little way—
> And—then—we are *alone.* . . .
> *not please
> †venture
> ‡foot
> §behind

The narrative is, as it has to be, in the present tense. The specific details of the servant, the flower, the dog left behind, and the Moon (none of which is visualized, although the moon is charged with "tender thoughtfulness" that leaves the lovers alone) give discrimination to the memory, in which it is not important to recall, if one could, anything more about matters secondary to the memorable event. The narrative is rather a testament to memory's need to relive the emotional impact of a passionate experience. The last stanza verifies the theme:

> I'd give—to live that hour—*again*—
> The *purple*—in my *Vein*—
> But *He* *must *count the drops—himself*—
> My *price* for *every stain!*
>
> (#663, c. 1862)
>
> *should

The movement of the narration, from the first "Again" and "the *mingled* steps" to the last "*again*," includes both the talk "in *careless*" and "in *toss*" (not the words themselves but the quality of the words) that anticipate the cost of the meeting: the pain of unspecified dire consequences. The memory itself lives on the feeling of the "old degree" and a "plummet strain," yet the woman would like to relive the brief happiness more than once again. Dickinson never wrote a more personal-impersonal poem. It is both subtle and obvious: subtle in the language that carries two states of being concurrently, and obvious in its knowledge of the mind in the act of recollecting a significant hour in one's life. And one usually relives the encounter many times. To have written the poem from any point of view but that of first-person singular would have been a mistake, if possible at all.

Another poem begins with the persona's stating: "I measure every Grief I meet / With narrow, probing, Eyes— / I wonder if It weighs like Mine— / Or has an Easier size." The persona speculates about the others, how long "They" have suffered and how "They" cope with the hurt. "I note that Some—gone patient long— / At length renew their smile— / An imitation of a Light / That has so little Oil—," and continues to wonder whether Years ("Some Thousands . . . such a lapse") of time will give them balm, or will "they go on aching still / Through Centuries of Nerve— / Enlightened to a larger Pain." The persona is told there are many who grieve and from "various Cause":

> Death—is but one—and comes but once—
> And only nails the eyes—
>
> There's Grief of Want—and Grief of Cold—
> A sort they call "Despair"—
> There's Banishment from native Eyes—
> In sight of Native Air—
>
> And though I may not guess the kind—
> Correctly—yet to me
> A piercing Comfort it affords
> In passing Calvary—
>
> To note the fashions—of the Cross—
> And how they're mostly worn—
> Still fascinated to presume
> That Some—are like My Own—
> (#561, c. 1862)

The need of the grief-stricken to look for others in a similar emotional state is not uncommon, and a grieving person is often reminded—"told"—that others also suffer. There is "a piercing comfort" in mutual recognition and understanding; yet no two experiences are exactly alike, and everyone has a different "style" in which he or she clothes the sorrow. Each therefore grieves alone, feeling the ineffectiveness of any attempt to influence the way others wear their grief or to resist one's own sense of isolation from them. The poet's analysis is painfully honest. The persona is fascinated by the question of why, when we are not alone, we are forever alone. The perspective of the "I," the solitaire, is essential to the poem.

Dickinson, however, returns to the analysis of grief in a poem written from the point of view of an author who attempts to characterize the emotion itself:

> Grief is a Mouse—
> And chooses Wainscot in the Breast
> For His Shy House—
> And baffles quest—
>
> [And/or] Grief is a Thief—quick startled—
> Pricks His Ear—report to hear
> Of that Vast Dark—
> That swept His Being—back—
>
> [And/or] Grief is a Juggler—boldest at the Play—
> Lest if He flinch—the eye that way
> Pounce on His Bruises—One—say—or Three—
> [And/or] Grief is a Gourmand—spare his luxury—
>
> [But] Best Grief is Tongueless—before He'll tell—
> Burn Him in the Public Square—
> His *Ashes—will
> Possibly—if they refuse—How then know—
> Since a Rack could'nt coax †a syllable—now.
>   (#793, c. 1863)

*embers
†an answer

The structure of the poem also expresses the attempt to characterize the emotion, which has not only "various Cause" but different qualities. The progression, from the image of grief as a mouse hiding away in a dark place that cannot be "got at" to the image of one burned as a martyr on the public square because he is unwilling to tell his grief, is countered by the fact that grief cannot be told. The poem itself is a trying out of alternative images, none of which is adequate for "Best Grief" (the reader might say "worst grief," the most profound, the most painful), which is inexpressible. How, then, can one say what the suffering is "like"; and how, then, know what another suffers? Then or now. To have written the poem in a "personal" voice would have undercut the meanings.

The poet may write a poem in which an "I" indicates that the

persona is speaking either from experience or observation. The
verse begins with an observation, a generalization in emblematic
language:

> Not with a Club, the Heart is broken
> Nor with a Stone—
> A Whip so small you could not see it
> I've known
>
> To lash the Magic Creature
> Till it fell,
> Yet that Whip's Name
> Too noble then to tell.

The heart, the Magic Creature, whiplashed, tongue-lashed, devastated, is then described as responding magnanimously, like a bird
that sings "unto the Stone" with which a boy has killed it. Leaving
the dead alone, the observer comments,

> Shame need not crouch
> In such an Earth as Our's—

and then speaks directly to Shame:

> Shame—stand erect—
> The Universe is your's.
> (#1304, c. 1873–74)

When the whip is not arrested and feels no shame, there is nothing to
hinder that whip, shame objectified, from taking possession of the
world once shared. Because Dickinson sang of a broken heart, however, this poem has baffled many readers who think it a confession of
her own shame at being hurt and not telling it. Perhaps. But there is
no cause for victims who behave nobly or generously to feel
ashamed; they may feel bitter—and the tone of the final words addressed to "Shame" is bitter—because it is well understood that "the
other" need not crouch if there is no fear of being hit or exposed. The
poem is an examination of both a psychological phenomenon and a
moral dilemma, hardly peculiar to an acutely sensitive poet. No one
likes to squeal. The assertion, "I've known," however, prepares for

the imperative: "Shame—stand erect." The monologue might have been written by an invisible poet, but the "I" as witness strengthens the rebuke and the command.

Even in poems like "Grief is a Mouse," written from the point of view of an author observant rather than the "personal I" or "representative I," the language persuades us that the author observant is observing herself. Among the most well known is "After great pain, a formal feeling comes—" (#134, c. 1862), a generalization one recognizes as accurate only if one has experienced the feeling, whatever the cause of the pain that induced the emotional state. A less well-known poem about pain and anguish is "A Weight with Needles on the pounds—" (a torture instrument worthy of Poe):

> To push, and pierce, besides—
> That if the Flesh could resist the Heft—
> The puncture—cooly tries—
>
> That not a pore be overlooked
> Of all this Compound Frame
> As manifold for Anguish
> As Species—be—for name—
>
> (#264, c. 1861)

The excruciating figures of this fragment seem to derive from the poet's reading: "On every step of the stairs there was placed a roller, sparked with barbed points all round, so as to impede the ascent of the rioters"—unemployed workers—"if they succeeded in forcing the doors" of a barricaded factory in England.[23] The fact that Dickinson apparently rewrote the passage may reveal that she was masochist, sadist, or critic, but the figures are painful to anyone who is conscious of suffering or is appalled by an imagination that concocts devices for relentless torture.

When the poet speaks about human need, the attitude is not really different from that of most people; she merely states it pointedly for us: " 'Faith' is a fine invention / When Gentlemen can *see* / But *Microscopes* are prudent / In an Emergency" (#185, c. 1860). Or she steps back and considers a familiar moment: "How News must feel when travelling / If News has any Heart / Alighting at the Dwelling / 'Twill enter like a Dart. . . ." She amusingly wonders "What News will do when every Man / Shall comprehend as one / And not in all the Universe / A thing to tell remain?" (#1319, c.

1873–74). She listens to the mentally lifeless and describes them: "They talk as slow as Legends grow / No mushrooms in their minds / But foliage of sterility / Too stolid for the wind—" (#1697, n.d.). The poet's perceptiveness, however, is not detached from their infirmity. But, in other situations, the feelings are different: "A transport one cannot contain / May yet, a transport be— / Though God forbid it lift the lid— / Unto it's Extasy!" (#184, c. 1860), and "The Thrill came slowly like a Boon for / Centuries delayed / Its fitness growing like the Flood / In sumptuous solitude—" (#1495, c.1880).

Nevertheless, the personal pronoun "I" does not occur in any of these verses, picked out from dozens of Dickinson's examinations of "the human experience" which is not exclusively her own and does not claim to be always her own. People may rely on "faith," but they "feel" they want modern medicine. They are quick to tell the news but forget that it may pierce those to whom it is told. If all people understood as "one," an unlikely event, misapprehension and idle curiosity, as well as the pleasure of telling the news, would cease. The slow speech of the old expresses little or no emotion; although they are still alive, one cannot penetrate their minds or being—they are unmoved and unmoving. One desires to contain ecstasy. And the thrill for which we secretly waited a very long time overwhelms our solitude with sumptuousness when it finally comes. The author's perspectives are appropriate to the observations. They tell us much about Dickinson, who probed at will the world around her but withdrew from it to transmit both the close connections and distinct differences between that world and the innermost self.

Poems delineating psychological states from the perspective of the pronominal "we" are not as numerous as those written from other points of view, but Dickinson is impressive when she depicts a communal experience. She writes, for example, of attendance upon the dying:

> The last Night that She lived
> It was a Common Night
> Except the Dying—this to Us
> Made Nature different
>
> We noticed smallest things—
> Things overlooked before
> By this great light upon our Minds
> Italicized—as 'twere.

The poem, in seven stanzas, focuses both on the woman and those waiting while she died. The final lines are:

> She mentioned, and forgot—
> Then *lightly as a Reed
> Bent to the Water, †struggled scarce—
> Consented, and was dead—
>
> And We—We placed the Hair—
> And drew the Head erect—
> And then an awful leisure was
> ‡Belief to regulate—
>   (#1100, c. 1864–66)

*softly
†shivered
‡with nought/our faith

The spare imagery of the narrative both relieves the emotions and makes them more acute. United in grief, "We" are left with both private anguish and doubt.[24]

An occasional poem uses the editorial "we"and is discursive: "Immortal is an ample word / When what we need is by / But when it leaves us for a time / 'Tis a necessity . . ." (#1205, c. 1870–73); or "We do not know the time we lose—/ The awful moment is / And takes it's fundamental place / Among the certainties—" (#1106, c. 1867). Dickinson is particularly good when she develops an image for an abstraction: "Exultation is the going / Of an inland soul to sea / . . . Bred as we, among the mountains, / Can the sailor understand / The divine intoxication / Of the first league out from land?" (#76, c. 1859); or "They leave us with the Infinite. / But He—is not a man— / His fingers are the size of fists— / His fists, the size of men— / And whom he foundeth, with his Arm / As Himmaleh, shall stand—" (#350, c. 1862). She likes to give words a sense of immediacy: "Eden is that old-fashioned House / We dwell in every day / Without suspecting our abode / Until we drive away . . ." (#1657, n.d.).

Filling a single term, "one dignity," with images and action, she writes:

> One dignity delays for all—
> One mitred Afternoon—
> None can avoid this purple—
> None evade this Crown!

Coach, it insures, and footman—
Chamber, and state, and throng—
Bells, also, in the village
As we ride grand along!

What dignified Attendants!
What service when we pause!
How loyally at parting
Their hundred hats they raise! . . .
                          (#98, c. 1859)

The scene, the occasion, the people, are described as a novelist would describe them: the poet's attitude toward the "dignity" is both exclamatory and critical, but we see the scene. It has panache, and Dickinson did not have to hear from Bowles that "nature was enough / Till Human nature came."[25]

While she tried her hand at different kinds of verse, she was too much the poet to have thought it suitable that she describe village "characters" in verse as she did when she wrote a letter or watched birds. Writing in a period that saw the rise of realism in American fiction,[26] she was also a poet in an era that conceived of poetry as the delineation of the "ideal." She adhered to an unstated principle for verse; she aimed for the intrinsic qualities, the essence of character and situation. The dramatic monologues which reveal the inner being of a character, as well as the poems that depict emotional and mental states for which the terms are abstract, freed Dickinson from the necessity of a realistic manner. She went for "insights" that are psychologically valid. Following the principle of idealization of character for the "biographies," the poet was limited in what she could legitimately say from the outside looking in. She relied on varying degrees of selective realism that indicate the essence of the character, but she excluded attention to details that would have enriched the texture of the biographies. Even the imagist poems, which are alive with evidence that Dickinson was a keen observer of the phenomenal world, "dart inward and become subjective."

The principle, which yielded the powerful dramatic monologues and permitted the fine nature poems but, by comparison with them, made for a relative dearth of biographical sketches, encourages us to subscribe to a belief in Dickinson's self-absorption. The priority given to her personal experience, as well as the life of the mind or her imagination, tempts us to neglect the engagement between the "me" and "not me" in the poems. While a regard for Emily Dickinson as a "solitaire," which the biography does not fully substantiate, particularly in view of the family relationships, reinforces the emphasis on the poet's subjectivity, both the romantic readings of the poems as a record of "thwarted experience" and the psychobiographical readings of them as a record of dispossession sacrifice much that was vital to the imaginative intelligence of the writer.

Critical evaluation of Dickinson's poetry, furthermore, coincided with the age of realism in fiction, which influenced the work of poets who (whether or not they accepted the tenets of the realists) were publishing at the time. Among them, the best was E. A. Robinson, whose first book of verse appeared in 1896—the date of the publication of the last of the three initial volumes of selections from Dickinson's poems. Robinson, whose characters have names like Richard Cory, Luke Havergal, Cliff Klingenhagen, and Flammonde, tends also to idealize them, but there are stronger strains of realism in the depiction of the types than we find in Dickinson's sketches of people.

If Robinson is one of her successors, to say nothing of Robert Frost, who thought her a little crazy but admired her poems on death, Dickinson is in a long tradition of the poet as the biographer of souls. To recognize that she accepted the tradition can dispel some of the disparities and contradictions in our readings of the poetry.

8

Words Engender Poems

Since the life around Emily Dickinson is blatantly present in the words by which she enacted what she had to say, she did not like them to be banal. She wanted to renew the common language and make it uncommon. Others talk about being *chilled to the bone;* she writes "Zero at the Bone." A snake in the grass is a "narrow Fellow in the grass." A hostile eye may be "jaundiced," but to her it is "yellow." The pejorative "fair weather friend" becomes "A Shady friend—for Torrid days." A formal portrait, by comparison with "daily faces," is "a fine, pedantic sunshine— / In a satin Vest!" and the pictures of the dead are "fair—fictitious People."

She puts language to the test. She may question what Richard Sewall terms "the vulnerable adage":[1] "They say that 'Time assuages'— / Time never did assuage / . . . Time is a Test of Trouble— / But not a Remedy— / If such it prove, it prove too / There was no Malady—" (#686, c. 1863); and "Till Death—is narrow Loving—" (#907, c. 1864), or "Peace is a fiction of our Faith—" (#912, c. 1864–66).[2]

She debates with herself the belief accepted among orthodox Christians that "This World is not Conclusion." The proposition to be considered is the topic sentence of the poem that follows:

199

A *Species stands beyond—
Invisible, as Music—
But positive, as Sound—
It beckons, and it baffles—
Philosophy—dont know—
And through a Riddle, at last—
Sagacity, must go—
To †guess it, puzzles scholars—
To gain it, Men have borne
Contempt of Generations
And Crucifixion, shown—
Faith slips—and laughs, and rallies—
Blushes, if any see—
Plucks at a twig of Evidence
And asks a Vane, the way—
Much Gesture, from the Pulpit—
‡Strong Hallelujahs roll—
Narcotics cannot still the §Tooth
That nibbles at the Soul—

                                     (#501, c. 1862)

*sequel
†prove
‡Sure
§Mouse

She understood the history of humankind, even if she had not heard of religion as the opium of the people. The dialectic on traditional faith is integral with the questioning of the language she heard in a community dedicated to words: "The Channel of the Dust—who once achieves—," she wrote, "Invalidates the Balm of that Religion / That doubts as fervently as it believes" (L, 2:574).³ "Good Night! Which put the Candle out?" (#259, c. 1861). The world may be conclusion.

Or God is love? "God is a distant—stately lover—" (#357, c. 1862). Omnipresent? "If God could make a visit— / Or ever took a Nap— / So not to see us—but they say / Himself—a Telescope / Perennial beholds us—" (#413, c. 1862). In an equally and deceptively simple "little" poem, she entertains a concept and an image of the philosophers of the Enlightenment. If, as they said in the Age of Reason, God is a great clockmaker and the universe a master clock, Dickinson asks why not a hatmaker, too? Consider, she says, the hardy dandelion:

It's little Ether Hood
Doth sit upon it's Head—
The millinery supple—
Of the sagacious God—

*Till when it slip away
A nothing at a time—
And Dandelion's Drama
Expires in a stem.
                    (#1501, c. 1880)
*And then doth

The eighteenth-century argument for the existence of a rational, beneficent and wise Deity from the evidence of "design" in nature goes pouff. And the poet takes the poems wherever she finds them.

She brings together several points common to religious thinking: the advice to pray (ask and it shall be given) and the belief that God cares or at least knows about the fall of every sparrow. "Of Course—I prayed— / And did God Care? / He cared as much as on the Air / A Bird—had stamped her foot— / And cried 'Give me'—" (#376, c. 1862). Such resistance convinced Dickinson she was alive. To express the conviction in taut and vigorous images is proof that she was alive, especially to what she heard around her.

Not all of these poems are deeply felt, but they are not trite. One which is far more moving in its relation to religious concepts and the vocabulary of faith central to the work of Dickinson is the poem beginning "Behind Me—dips Eternity— / Before Me—Immortality." The final stanza reads:

'Tis Miracle before Me—then—
'Tis Miracle behind—between—
A Crescent in the Sea—
With Midnight to the North of Her—
And Midnight to the South of Her—
And Maelstrom—in the Sky—
                    (#721, c. 1863)

This cosmic vision, praised for being entirely original as an experiment in verse, incites a terror that even the unresolved doubt of "This World is Not Conclusion" does not lead one to expect. The reversal of the poles—foreshadowed by the facile shifts in wording from eternity *behind*, immortality *before* to miracle *before* and miracle *behind*—is hardly beatific: midnight to the north and midnight to the south of the crescent in the sea and maelstrom in the sky. The imagery of the natural world in awesome disorder is the imagery of a dark night of the soul. That, too, is essential to a full appreciation of what Dickinson was and what she wrote. Had she accepted the shibboleths of conventional Christianity, she would not only have been a different poet but a less disquieting one.

There are other visions that entertained her. Some of them are indebted to the pleasure she took in writing what Wallace Stevens called "poems of earth," but they also express the exuberance with which she restored life to moribund language. Describing a sunset, one may be able to say no more than that it was dazzling or "a show." She writes of a great American sunset as if it were a traveling circus that had just left town:

> I've known a Heaven, like a Tent—
> To wrap it's shining Yards—
> Pick up it's stakes, and disappear—
> Without the sound of Boards—
> Or Rip of Nail—Or Carpenter—
> But just the miles of Stare—
> That signalize a Show's Retreat—
> In North America—
>
> No Trace—no Figment of the Thing
> That dazzled, Yesterday,
> No Ring—no Marvel—
> Men, and Feats—
> Dissolved as utterly. . . .
> (#243, c. 1861)

"Celestial phenomena"? Fanciful? Witty? Even a more descriptive phrase may be turned into a conceit that seems bad early verse unless it is read as the poet's play with a common image—"a golden sunset": "I never told the buried gold / Upon the hill—that lies— / I saw the sun—his plunder done / Crouch low to guard his prize. / . . . That was a wondrous booty— / I hope twas honest gained. / Those were the fairest ingots / That ever kissed the spade!" She pirates the words and asks, "Whether as I ponder / Kidd will sudden sail—" (#11, c. 1858–59).

Others may speak of the floor of the forest and, finding it covered with pine needles, say it is "like a carpet." Dickinson's reply: "Of Brussels—it was not— / Of Kidderminster? Nay— / The Winds did buy it of the Woods— / They—sold it unto me / / It was a gentle price— / The poorest—could afford— / It was within the frugal purse / Of Beggar—or of Bird." She describes the "small and spicy Yards—" and "the hue—a mellow Dun"; the "carpet" is composed of "Sunshine—and of Sere—" but "principally—of Sun— / / The Wind—unrolled it fast— / And spread it on the Ground—" (#602, c. 1862).

The descriptive techniques are comparable to those in a favorite verse among children who know Dickinson. "I like," she says, "to see it lap the Miles— / And lick the Valleys up— / And stop to feed itself at Tanks— / And then—prodigious step / / Around a Pile of Mountains— / And supercilious peer / In Shanties—by the sides of Roads." This elaboration of the nineteenth-century term for the train, "the iron horse," is a tour de force. Of the mountain route "made" by the train, she says: "And then a Quarry pare / / To fit it's Ribs / And crawl between / Complaining all the while / In horrid— hooting stanza—" (a loud, clamorous mechanical sound—hooting). The stanzas run on as she sees the horse "Then chase itself down Hill— / / And neigh like Boanerges— / Then—punctual as a Star / Stop—docile and omnipotent / At it's own stable door—" (#585, c. 1862). The buildings that house trains are still called "car barns," although so far as the records show, no one has ever named either horse or train for Boanerges, the sons of thunder, who offered to call down fire from heaven upon the inhospitable. Recognizing a "poetic" turn of phrase or a riproaring sound when she heard it, the poet must have had a good time writing these "unsophisticated" poems. What about the poet as "iron horse"? Or a "son of thunder"? And why not? (The manuscript shows "I like to hear it" as an alternative for the familiar opening line.)

Dickinson even writes a six-stanza poem on the fond old figure "Mother Nature": "the Gentlest Mother," who is "Impatient of no Child—," whether the child is feeble or dull or wayward, but mildly restrains the rampant and the impetuous. The mother's conversation and household are fair; her affection infinite, and her care "infiniter" (#790, c. 1863). Is the conceit a description of Nature at "her" best, the "nature" of an ideal mother, or the poet's "real" mother? The poem is hardly "objective"; the poet also saw and depicted storm, blight, and bouleversement in the natural world, just as she made disparaging remarks about her mother. The characterization, then, is perhaps sentimental, especially if one remembers only the poet's saying that she never had a mother—with one kind of truth in the overstatment; but there are qualities of Emily Norcross Dickinson in Emily Elizabeth Dickinson's affectionate characterization of "nature," and however one reads the imagery, it is both true and not true of Nature and the poet's mother. The vehement child, however, has something of young Emily one sees fleetingly in the letters. And as a poet, she may be like the subject of another "observation" of "waywardness":

> A Drunkard cannot meet a Cork
> Without a Revery—
> And so encountering a Fly
> This January Day
> Jamaicas of *Remembrance stir
> That send me reeling †in. . . .
>   (#1628, c. 1884)
>
> *Prospective
> †on

Knowing all kinds of people and hearing *usual* words for describing them, Dickinson can integrate the responses as if stereotypes themselves had their validity. There is hardly a comparison more worn by use than that in which a person is said to be *hard as stone*. (Dictionaries no longer cite the phrase to illustrate "simile.") The poet picks up the cliché and breathes new life into it:

> A face devoid of love or grace,
> A hateful, hard, successful face,
> A face with which a stone
> Would feel as thoroughly at ease
> As were they old acquaintances—
> First time together thrown.
>   (#1711, n.d.).

Of course, two of a kind, ironically at ease with each other—and we identify them by the company they keep. Another common phrase by which Dickinson sketches a character is that for describing words that "cut to the quick": "She dealt her pretty words like Blades— / How glittering they shone— / And every One unbared a Nerve / Or wantoned with a Bone." The poet quickly turns to "excuse" the woman: "She never deemed—she hurt— / That—is not Steel's Affair— / A vulgar grimace in the Flesh— / How ill the Creatures bear." But words can kill; hence the poet must report on the victim, too: "The Film upon the eye / Mortality's old Custom— / Just locking up—to Die" (#479, c. 1862). In poems like these two, Dickinson seems to be writing almost for the sake of seeing what she can do with the cliché.

She also uses "tried and true" metaphors for depicting psychological responses to danger. The expression "saved by a hair's breadth," for instance, is incongruous among the other images with which it first occurs in "That after Horror—that 'twas *us*— That passed the mouldering Pier— / Just as the Granite Crumb let go— / Our Savior, by a Hair—" (#286, c. 1861), and the poet does not take the hackneyed phrase further in the narrative. She has not, however, finished with it, and returns to work out the tensions latent in the image when she found what she wanted to do with it:

> Crisis is a Hair
> Toward which the forces creep
> Past which forces retrograde
> If it come in sleep
>
> To suspend the Breath
> Is the most we can
> Ignorant is it of Life or Death
> Nicely balancing.
>
> Let an instant push
> Or an Atom press
> Or a Circle hesitate
> In Circumference
>
> It [Crisis]—may jolt the Hand
> That adjusts the Hair
> That secures Eternity
> From presenting—Here—
> (#889, c. 1864–66)

Perhaps the poet is holding horror in check, but she is also echoing the sounds of *h* and *r* in "Hair" and "Here," which are superior to the conventional rhymes of "Breath" and "Death." And there is not an anemic sound in the penultimate stanza: "Let an instant push," "an Atom press," "a Circle hesitate / In Circumference." The poem is written with a steady hand and keen ear. A third poem uses the "adjusted Hair" again and in a different mood:

> *We like a Hairbreadth 'scape
> It tingles in the Mind
> Far after Act or Accident
> Like paragraphs of Wind
>
> If †we had ventured less
> The ‡Gale were not so fine
> That reaches to our utmost Hair
> It's §Tentacles divine.
>   (#1175, c. 1870)
>
> *I
> †I
> ‡*Breeze*
> §Resonance

"Act or Accident" may be less hilarious than "paragraphs of Wind"—or "horrid hooting stanza"—but a poet who risks the monstrous image "tentacles divine" in order to complete a "breezy" rhyme scheme cannot be too threatened this time. Crisis, like the bumblebee, evoked more than one kind of response. "Was it not crisis, all the time, in our hurrying Home?" she wrote late in life, but she obviously enjoyed some of the harrowing occasions to her "utmost Hair."

There are other platitudes she transforms into new poems that become psychological events. Nervous? Weak in the knees? Fearful? Need support? It's not a matter of life and death; put it in perspective, coward; take a deep breath:

> If your Nerve, deny you—
> Go above your Nerve—
> He can lean against the Grave,
> If he fear to swerve—
>
> That's a steady posture—
> Never *any bend
> Held of those Brass arms—
> Best Giant made—

If your Soul †seesaw—
Lift the Flesh door—
The Poltroon wants Oxygen—
Nothing more—
                (#292, c. 1861)

*one
†stagger

If one wishes to read these poems as autobiographical—and they may be, since all human beings need occasionally to take a deep breath and cope with crises—Dickinson at least knew how to cope, whether or not she coped. But the poems seem engendered by words.

Knowing, too, that *joy* and *glee* are synonyms, she has no difficulty in sustaining the old metaphor "I could dance with joy" in one of the happiest poems she ever wrote:

I cannot dance upon my Toes—
No Man instructed me—
But oftentimes, among my mind,
A Glee possesseth me,

That had I Ballet knowledge—
Would put itself abroad
In Pirouette to blanch a Troupe—
Or lay a Prima, mad,

And though I had no Gown of Gauze—
No Ringlet, to my Hair,
Nor hopped for Audiences—like Birds,
One Claw upon the Air,

Nor tossed my shape in Eider Balls,
Nor rolled on wheels of snow
Till I was out of sight, in sound,
The House encore me so—

Nor any know I know the Art
I mention—easy—Here—
Nor any Placard boast me—
It's full as Opera—
                (#326, c. 1862)

This wit is usually read as a poem about art. Joy *is* an art. But is the poet "gleeman" or "minstrel"? No, the poet is dancer out of sight in sound, still full as comic opera.

It is not chance that "But often times, among my mind, / A Glee possesseth me" and "I felt a Funeral, in my Brain" are tenuously connected by the similar phrasing *among my mind* and *in my brain*, as well by the date now assigned to each of the poems (c. 1862, although the latter was previously dated c. 1861). If Emily Dickinson was mentally disturbed in the early sixties, the latest analysis of the condition is that she was a manic-depressive. Or was she, to use an old-fashioned notion, a poet "possessed"? Had she been a detective assigned to recover stolen goods, she would have succeeded because she would not have scrupled to identify with the thieves. That is among the values of the imagination.

Had she ever seen a ballet? There is no mention of it in the correspondence. She went, before she shunned society, to funerals, but death—despite the prolific configuration of words associated with it—was never for Dickinson a metaphor for madness or possession. Although she, so far as we know, did not send "I felt a Funeral" to any of the people who constituted the small private audience for the poems, she enclosed "I cannot dance upon my Toes," along with "Before I got my Eye put out," in a letter written in August 1862 to Higginson.[4] The poet's choosing to pair the two poems was deliberate. They represent her confidence in herself and her art, whether or not "any" recognized it.

The dramatic imagination, the evidence of a poet expert beyond "experience" (creation but the gambol of her authority), the verisimilitude in the descriptive points (the hilarious detail in "hopped" like "Birds, / One Claw upon the Air"), and the development of the metaphor for an emotion (joy)—all come surely together in "I cannot dance upon my Toes." It is, however, only one of hundreds of great poems "among" the poet's mind.

Coda

When Dickinson said in one poem and of that poem alone, "This is my letter to the World / That never wrote to Me— / The simple News that Nature told— / With tender Majesty" (#441, c. 1862), is she to be believed? Many readers have accepted the poem in good faith, but she is cagey. She needs to be watched. In fact, the "World," a public audience such as she now has, never wrote to her. Perhaps she was a better poet because she was not "ruined by success." That is a "romantic" notion. There was, after all, a strong romantic strain in Dickinson. The poem itself, turning back on the assertion that the world never wrote to "Me," says nature told the news.

She was often at ease with nature. There is the moment of equanimity in the valediction: "Image of Light, Adieu— / Thanks for the interview— / So long—so short— / Preceptor of the whole— / Coeval Cardinal— / Impart—Depart—" (#1556, c. 1882). The manuscript shows that she considered "Fellow of the Light" as a possible first phrase for the farewell. Or "Winter instantly becomes / An infinite Alas—" when the poet hears "a shouting Flower— / The Proclamation of the Suns" (#1519, c. 1881). She observes, in an autumnal mood, that "The Cricket drops a sable line / No more from yours at present" (#1635, c. 1884). And "Mountains straight reply" to words themselves. The "world"—nature, people, words themselves—spoke to her, and she listened.

One "confessional" poem states: "I heard, as if I had no Ear / Until a Vital Word / Came all the way from Life to me / And then I knew I heard" (#1039, c. 1865). At another time, she wrote, "A Word is dead / When it is said, / Some say. / I say it just / Begins to live / That day" (#1212, c. 1872).

Illustrating again Dickinson's capacity to develop the meanings inherent in common language, one poem is the most uncommon of all of them because in it the *Word* itself is personified and speaks:

> My Life had stood—a Loaded Gun—
> In Corners—till a Day—
> The Owner passed—identified
> And carried Me away—
>
> And now We roam *in Sovreign Woods—
> And now We hunt the Doe—
> And every time I speak for Him—
> The Mountains straight reply—
>
> And do I smile, such cordial light
> Upon the Valley glow—
> It is as a Vesuvian face
> Had let it's pleasure through—
>
> And when at Night—our good Day done—
> I guard My Master's Head—

'Tis better than the Eider-Duck's
†Deep Pillow—to have shared—

To foe of His—I'm deadly foe—
None ‡harm the second time—
On whom I lay a Yellow Eye—
Or an emphatic Thumb—

Though I than He—may longer live
He longer must—than I—
For I have but the §power to kill
Without—the power to die—
                              (#754, c. 1862–63)

*the
†low
‡stir
§art

To conceive of the word itself as persona is elementary; to anal-
ogize *word* and *loaded gun* may seem more "fantastic" than imaginative. But the incongruous figure of speech, evoking the history of
life on the American frontier, is powerful in its suggestiveness.
Words are weapons. Both words and weapons "speak," "report,"
"explode," and "illuminate" (at the time of a gun's report there is a
moment of light). Both have the capacity to guard, to defend, to
protect, to ward off evil, to harm; they are prized by owners, hunt-
ers, sportsmen and women—or poets—who know them to be harmless if "unloaded," but know, too, that loaded guns or words "go
off" indiscriminately unless one learns (is "Master" of) the use of
deadly weaponry.

In the alternate version of the poem, the lines "For I have but the
power to kill, / Without—the power to die," read "For I have but the
power to kill, / Without—the art to die." The exchange of the words
power and *art* confirms the play with resemblance between *gun* and
word. Emily Dickinson's belief in both the power and the art of
language is her most consistent belief. "We used to think," she
wrote to Joseph Bardwell Lyman, "when I was an unsifted girl and
you so scholarly that words were cheap and weak. Now I don't
know anything so mighty."[5]

Writing as much as she did, she did not always find it an act of
grace. "Your thoughts dont have words every day / They come a

single time / Like signal esoteric sips / Of communion Wine / Which while you taste so native seems / So easy to be / You cannot comprehend the price / Nor its infrequency" (#1452, c. 1878). In a characteristic transubstantiation, she begins another poem with sacramental imagery: "A Word made Flesh is seldom / And tremblingly partook / Nor then perhaps reported . . ." (#1651, n.d.). The poem continues: "A Word that breathes distinctly / Has not the power to die . . . ," which recalls not only "I don't know anything so mighty [as words]" but also the word as gun, loaded gun, "without the power to die."[6]

The figure of the poet as hunter is an attractive one among many others. Dickinson, for instance, liked "sovereign woods," where she listened in silence for sound and movement to which she matched both daring and skill. Hunting down thoughts and emotions wherever she found them, she brought them to bay because she was empowered by language.

Since she wrote for her own satisfaction or, when it suited her, for people she knew, she seems somewhat quixotic. The fact that she had primarily a private audience when she was living, however, cannot be separated from the history of women's public powerlessness. Nor can it be separated from the failure of past judgments with regard to writers as different as Melville and Dickinson who roamed freely outside the range of their contemporaries. But Dickinson, the lone woman of genius in nineteenth-century American poetry, assumes heroic proportions which have been countered by conventional views of a woman limited because she was a woman. (She probably never carried a gun, although she had "hayed a little for the horse.")

It was Dickinson's friend Samuel Bowles who said, after reading her poem on the snake in which she observed that "He likes a Boggy Acre / A Floor too cool for Corn—": "How did that girl ever know that a boggy field wasn't good for corn?"[7] We continue to ask how that "girl" knew what she knew in relation to the world in which she became a poet. It was a woman's world, seen from the perspective of a woman of stamina in a nineteenth-century household, where life was lived always and necessarily in detail that suggests a realistic novel or, on occasion, a novel of manners. It was a life of family, friends, neighbors, acquaintances, "the help," the quick and the dead; involvement with current events and crises at home or in the country; sermons, visits, and teas, housekeeping and caring for the sick, talk and gossip, writing notes and letters, reading everything in sight, gardening, a closeness to nature and nature's creatures, and the observance of local color and customs. Taking part in all that life, she also took it in and emerged as a poet. There is not a scintilla of evidence that she was ever bored with or unmindful of the abundance, enigmas, or denials she encountered. When there were no "guests"—and sometimes when there were—she made guests for herself.

Persisting under circumstances that were both favorable and unfavorable for realizing an extraordinary gift, she made use of what she learned from either personal experience or the experience of others in life and literature. The result is a poetry characterized by shared enthusiasms and intensities, as well as insights that she called skirmishes in her own mind—the stress and conflicts that came with the quotidian responsibilities of a woman who wanted to surpass herself and succeeded in doing so. Dickinson's truths and fictions are not, however, always in her own image. They express, rather, her sense of the world.

Since the world left much to be desired, study of the ways in which the poet worked to give an account of it does not support a reading of all the poems as the creation of an "autobiographical" life. The poems are self-conscious—but not self-enclosed—literary performances. Dickinson, histrionic but hardly hysterical, was a writer whose perceptions extended far beyond the "I" (sight and subjective intelligence) in the search for the meanings she made or was unable to make of the particulars of a world in flux. The images and situations, the impulses and attitudes expressed in the poems, consequently, contradict one another from poem to poem. They are disparate parts of a world.

Although there is little rhetorical development once she discovered that she was a virtuoso, she continued over the years to experiment with a diversity of genres and the exploitation of points of view. While we yearn for a script that will connect the poems to a matrix experience, we find that she had more than one muse and was willing to risk writing about more than she was fated to be: an ingenious poet whose modulations of theme, sound, and rhythms are appropriate to the play of voices that have survived our stories and hers.

In the critical efforts to distinguish between fact and speculation, between knowledge about the work of a resilient woman and "myths" about *that girl*, we free ourselves for an appreciation of a gratifying and haunting record of human experience. It is a record encompassing triumph and failure, grief and goodness, pain and anguish and anger, chaos and order, belief and doubt, solitude and society, joy and ecstasy, trifles and tragedy, love and comedy and epiphany, wisdom and art. As the poet's life developed and deepened, grew strong and weakened in an intrepid devotion to that art, Emily Dickinson always had her words about her.

Notes

Introduction

1. *The Letters of Emily Dickinson*, ed. Thomas H. Johnson and Theodora Ward (Cambridge, Mass., and London, 1958), 2:545.

2. Jay Leyda, *The Years and Hours of Emily Dickinson* (New Haven, 1960), 2:302–3.

3. See Emily Stipes Watts, *The Poetry of American Women* (Austin and London, 1977), 82–147.

4. Leyda, 2:474.

5. Ibid., 472–73.

6. Virginia Woolf, *A Room of One's Own* (New York, 1929), 4. Toril Moi, discussing the troublesome aspects of an "insistence on the identity of author and character" in relation to patriarchial ideology, also argues that it is "necessary to reject critical practice . . . that relies on the author as the transcendental signified of his or her text." See *Sexual/Textual Politics* (London and New York, 1985), 61–63.

Chapter 1: Occupation: At Home

1. Quoted in obituary, *New York Times* (3 April 1955).

2. *The Poems of Emily Dickinson*, ed. Thomas H. Johnson (Cambridge, Mass., 1955). All poems quoted subsequently in this chapter are from Johnson's text.

3. "Art," in *Collected Poems of Herman Melville*, ed. Harold P. Vincent (Chicago, 1947), 231.

4. E. C. Gaskell, *The Life of Charlotte Brontë* (New York, 1857), 1:40–41.

5. Jay Leyda, *The Years and Hours of Emily Dickinson* (New Haven, 1960), 1:20.

6. Ibid., 40–44.

7. On the other hand, Eugene Field (1850–95), a poet and journalist who had

been a young neighbor of the Dickinsons, wrote, from St. Louis in 1879, that he failed "to recognize any bliss in vegetating in that humdrum, old fogy hamlet of Amherst" (ibid., 2:313). As a young woman, Susan Gilbert also wanted to escape "the plain humdrum of old Amherst."

8. Ibid., 1:146, 194, 196, 203, passim.

9. Ibid., 207.

10. Ibid., 2:478. Emily Fowler Ford, with whom the Dickinson sisters read Shakespeare, remembered the poet as mingling "freely in all the companies and excursions of the moment and the evening frolics." Ford also described her friend's "demure manner which brightened easily into fun, where she felt at home, but among strangers she was rather shy, silent, and even deprecating."

11. Richard B. Sewall, *The Lyman Letters* (Amherst, 1965), 54.

12. Leyda, 1:213. Even before the trip to Ware, Lavinia had crossed her mother. See diary for May: "Walked with Howland. Displeased Mother *thereby*" and "Howland . . . called. Mother displeased again. . . . Not happy" (ibid., 1:198–99).

13. Ibid., 206–28, passim. "Twombly" is unidentified, but Lavinia also saw him in Boston.

14. Sewall, *The Lyman Letters*, 71.

15. Leyda, 1:229.

16. Ibid., 251. Ford said the poet "was not beautiful yet she had great beauties. Her eyes were lovely auburn, soft and warm, and her hair lay in rings of the same color all over her head, and her skin and teeth were good. . . . When 'we girls' named each other flowers, and called her sister, the *Pond Lily*," Ford recalled that the poet quipped, "And I am the *Cow Lily*," a reference to "the orange lights in her hair and eyes" (ibid., 2:478). The detail about the skin casts strong doubt on a photograph labeled "Emily Dickenson 1860" that Sewall reprints as a frontispiece for volume 2 of *The Life*. Sewall observes: "Opinions vary as to whether it is an authentic picture of Emily Dickinson, the poet." The woman in the photograph has obviously flawed, warty skin. The only verified picture of the poet is one taken when she was at Mount Holyoke in 1847–48 and commonly reproduced as if she never outgrew late adolescence. It can be classified as a cliché.

17. The valentine to Howland was published on February 20, 1851, in the *Springfield Republican* (Leyda, 1:234).

18. Nearly two years later, she chided Austin: "if it is'nt probable that you are coming [home] *some time*, I think I shall take the stage, or run away myself" (L, 1:239).

19. *A Room of One's Own* (New York, 1929), 48–51. Sandra M. Gilbert and Susan Gubar, in *The Madwoman in the Attic* (New Haven and London, 1979), consider Dickinson as one of Judith Shakespeare's "avatars": a "betrayed Eurydice" whose self-burial was self-willed, and whose "*corpus* lay bloody and unnoticed, not at a crossroads but in a corner" (59, 87, 463–64). Gilbert and Gubar then ask, "How did this apparently 'gentle spinster,' as [John Crowe] Ransom calls her, come so close to being 'Judith Shakespeare'?" Their answer, in part, is that she became "an angel of destruction" (582–83).

20. Ellen Moers, *Literary Women* (Garden City, New York, 1976), 60. See also Joanna Russ, *How to Suppress Women's Writing* (Austin, Texas, 1983), for the view that Dickinson "had no money," but "As for the leisure that, one would suppose, attended this odd sort of poverty," she "seems to have had it (although she participated in the family housekeeping and nursed her mother during the latter's last

illness) . . ." (7). The "although" is larger than Russ supposes. See also Wendy Martin's comments, in *An American Triptych* (Chapel Hill and London, 1984), on Dickinson's having enjoyed "freedom from pragmatic and utilitarian concerns," as well as "leisure and privacy to pursue her interests" (90).

21. Sewall, *The Life of Emily Dickinson* (New York, 1974), 2:465, 607. Sewall mentions "the busy home," "the comings and goings of her family, whose every action and mood were vital to her," and stresses the "stable family situation that at least left her free to develop as she would."

22. Leyda, 1:170. The poet's phrasing, in December 1853, was "this beleagured family as yet in want of time" (L, 1:275).

23. Sewall, *The Life*, 2:420.

24. See "Economy," in *The Variorum Walden*, ed. Walter Harding (New York, 1962), 66.

25. Leyda, 1:195, 197–98, 205, 210.

26. Ellen E. Dickinson, married to a cousin of the poet, wrote in 1892 that "Emily Dickinson was a past mistress in the art of cookery and housekeeping." Ellen Dickinson recalled that when the poet was engaged in making desserts or breads for the household dinners, "she had her table and pastry board under a window that faced the lawn, whereon she had a pencil and paper to jot down any pretty thought that came to her, and from which she evolved verses, later" (Leyda, 2:482).

27. Sewall, *The Life*, 1:60. "I cannot," Sewall says, after reviewing all the available evidence, "look upon the Dickinson household as fear-ridden" (1:61).

28. Leyda, 1:118 (recorded in George Gould's notebook).

29. Ibid., 2:200.

30. In the course of lengthy discussions with a pious friend, Abiah Root, when they were sixteen, Emily said: "I feel that the world holds a predominant place in my affections. I do not feel that I could give all for Christ, were I called to die" (L, 1:38).

31. Martha Dickinson Bianchi, *Emily Dickinson Face to Face* (Boston and New York, 1932; reprinted, 1970), 43.

Higginson, however, said that Dickinson's father "was not severe I should think but remote" (L, 2:475). The poet herself, writing to Joseph Lyman, who had lived with the family when he was a student at Amherst College, said her father seemed to her often the oddest sort of foreigner: "Sometimes I say something and he stares in a curious sort of bewilderment though I speak a thought quite as old as his daughter." She further observed: "in the morning I hear his voice and methinks it comes from afar & has a sea tone & there is a hum of hoarseness about (it) & a suggestion of remoteness as far as the isle of Juan Fernandez." See Sewall, *The Lyman Letters*, 70–71.

32. Bianchi, 46.

33. Millicent Todd Bingham, *Emily Dickinson's Home* (New York and Toronto, 1955), 414.

Chapter 2: Duplicities and Desires

1. Jay Leyda, *The Years and Hours of Emily Dickinson* (New Haven, 1960), 1:58.

2. Richard B. Sewall, *The Life of Emily Dickinson* (New York, 1974), 1:76.

3. Leyda, 1:209–10.

4. Sewall, *The Lyman Letters* (Amherst, 1965), 70. When Edward Dickinson went as a delegate to the National Nominating Convention of the Whig Party in Baltimore

during June 1852, the daughter reported to Austin that their father "writes he should think the whole world was there, and some from other worlds," that "it will do him the very most good of anything in the world," and that she feels happy to have him "at last, among men who sympathize with him, and know what he really is" (L, 1:213).

5. Sewall, *The Life*, 1:117.

6. Ibid., 116.

7. Leyda, 1:351.

8. When Austin's family was out of town during January 1875, the poet wrote to Elizabeth Holland that he "lived with us four weeks. It seemed peculiar—pathetic—and Antediluvian. We missed him while he was with us and missed him when he was gone. All is so very curious" (L, 2:537). In March 1883, she wrote: "my Brother is with us so often each day, we almost forget that he ever passed to a wedded Home" (L, 3:765).

In the same year (1833), Mabel Loomis Todd published *Footprints*, a short novel in which a young woman falls in love with a quiet, lonely man—a forty-year-old physician—for whom life's mysteries are cold and bleak. See Phillips, "Mabel Loomis Todd," in *American Women Writers* (New York, 1982), 4:243–47.

The similarities between the poet's comments about Austin and Todd's characterization of her hero are too close to be coincidental. By that time, a liaison had developed between Austin and Todd, who had come to Amherst in 1881 with a one-year-old daughter and husband David, an astronomer appointed to the faculty of the college.

Knowing as early as mid-September 1882 that Mrs. Todd and Austin were in love, the poet sent a note to Susan Dickinson: "Had 'Arabi' only read Longfellow, he'd have never been caught—," signed it "Khedive," and added a postscript: "Shall fold their Tents like Arabs, and as silently steal away—" (L, 2:739). (The rebel Egyptian Ahmed Arabi Pasha was defeated at Tel-el-Kebir on September 13, 1882.) Emily Dickinson drew clear lines around the people to whom she was closest. She never received Mabel Todd but exchanged notes and small favors with her, sent her poems, and corresponded with her parents. The poet's expression of gratitude, in the fall of 1882, for the knowledge her sister-in-law had "told me" was a reminder to Susan Dickinson of their old ties when she needed them strengthened.

9. Sewall, *The Life*, 1:126.

10. Ibid., 247.

11. *Charlotte Brontë* (New York, 1857), 1:133–34, 140–41. Having given Susan Dickinson a copy of the book in 1858 (Leyda, 1:361), Emily Dickinson also wrote a quatrain in tribute to the novelist: "I would distill a cup, / And bear to all my friends, / Drinking to her no more astir. / By beck, or burn, or moor!" (#16, c. 1858). She wrote a second verse (#148) for Brontë in 1859.

12. See Karen Dandurand, "New Dickinson Civil War Publications," *American Literature* 56 (March 1984): 17–27.

13. Persuaded by Lavinia Dickinson to undertake the formidable task of editing a selected group of work by the poet for publication, Mabel Todd sought the help of Higginson. Charming as she could be, she had to argue with him and to read nearly a dozen poems for him before she convinced him of their "rugged music." She was the only person who was not surprised by the attention the work received. See Sewall, *The Life*, 1:220–21, and Todd's preface to *Poem's: Second Series* (1891), reprinted in *The Recognition of Emily Dickinson*, ed. Caesar R. Blake and Carlton F. Wells (Ann Arbor, 1964), 42–44.

14. Reading the letters as autobiography is not as hazardous as reading the poems for the facts of the writer's life, but it requires caution, too. When it is possible to check what she says in the correspondence against other records, I find that she is more often truthful than not and that she did not represent herself falsely to people she loved and knew well. She sometimes alludes to situations about which we have to guess, and she also leaves much unsaid or said obliquely. The letters are, nevertheless, rich in observations and insights pertinent to an assessment of the writer at work.

15. Ten years later, Dickinson wrote to him: "Must I lose the Friend who saved my life, without inquiring why?" (L, 2:649).

16. Leyda, 2:49.

17. Ibid., 1:352.

18. See 525 (December 1877), 547 (c. March 1878), and 619 (October 1879) to Mrs. Holland (L, 2:596, 608, 647).

19. Wadsworth was one of the most popular preachers of his day. He served the Arch Street Presbyterian Church in Philadelphia from 1850 to April 1862, the Calvary Church in San Francisco from May 1862 to October 1869, and the Alexander Church in Philadelphia from late 1869 until his death April 1, 1882. Both Mark Twain and Samuel Bowles wrote about hearing Wadsworth preach when they were in San Francisco (See Leyda, 2:102, 112), but the fullest account of him as a preacher is in Josephine Pollitt's *Emily Dickinson: The Human Background* (New York, 1930; reprinted, 1970). Pollitt describes the large congregations at Arch Street Church: every pew was filled, the aisles and stairs were "choked," the galleries and vestibules crowded, so there was a question of how the preacher could possibly reach the pulpit. "Suddenly a trap door opened in the floor of the pulpit, and the tall, slim figure of Dr. Charles Wadsworth emerged from the basement" (110). Pollitt, among many others, assumes that Dickinson heard him preach. Dickinson's comment about "legerdemain"—if it refers to him—would tend to confirm the supposition.

20. Marianne Moore, "Emily Dickinson," *Poetry* 41 (January 1933): 219–26.

21. *The Master Letters of Emily Dickinson*, ed. R. W. Franklin (Amherst, 1986), 12–19, 22–29, 32–45.

22. *The Life*, 2:520. See Sewall's thoughtful and sensitive analysis of the style of the letters (2:512–20).

23. Millicent Todd Bingham, in *Emily Dickinson's Home* (New York and Toronto, 1955), 374, notes that Austin was "quite definite. He said that at different times Emily had been devoted to several men. He even went so far as to maintain that she had been several times in love, in her own way."

24. Bingham, *Emily Dickinson: A Revelation* (New York, 1954), 1–3, 77. Austin also saved the letters to Lord.

25. In the rough draft of the "Master" letter for which there is no salutation, Dickinson wrote: "Low at the knee that bore her once unto (royal) wordless rest, (now—she) Daisy (stoops a) kneels, a culprit—tell her her (offence) fault—Master— if it is (not so) small eno' to cancel with *her life*, (Daisy) she is satisfied—but punish—do(not)nt banish her—Shut her in prison—" (*The Master Letters*, 25). The variation of the phrase "kneels, a culprit," when she writes "I never knelt to other" in the letter to Lord twenty-one years later, may indicate that the pain of the earlier experience had been repressed or had receded so far in Dickinson's memory that it

was less significant than is often posited. At least, one does not at fifty-two remember everything one has said years earlier.

26. Leyda, 2:268.

27. Bingham says that after Lord's resignation from the court in December 1882, he lived for more than a year "with the ever-present consciousness that sudden death was impending," but the fact that he recovered sufficiently to make his five-day visit to Amherst, September 8–12, somewhat reassured Emily Dickinson, and she "was beginning to conquer her fear lest Judge Lord might die" (*A Revelation*, 61–63).

28. Gossip and hearsay which followed fast upon Emily Dickinson's fame also contributed to the conception of her as a weird and eccentric, fearful "virgin recluse." Her withdrawal from the community in later years and something of the prima donna in her character, as well rumors not always from kindly motives, added credibility to the literary head-game she played with Higginson.

Mabel Todd, giving herself a family background more distinguished than it was, also knew how to make it "difficult to recognize which elements of her story were more tenuous than others, or that the whole was a gentle distortion." And she, too, contributed to the popular conceptions of the poet as "a character," "rare and mysterious." Todd wrote on September 15, 1882: "Emily is called in Amherst 'the myth.' " "She has not been out of the house for fifteen years." See Polly Longsworth, *Austin and Mabel* (New York, 1984), 13, 3–4.

Chapter 3: The Prickly Art of Reading Emily Dickinson

1. For a recent example of this view, see Sandra M. Gilbert and Susan Gubar, *The Madwoman in the Attic: The Woman Writer and the Nineteenth-Century Literary Imagination* (New Haven and London, 1970).

2. *The Master Letters of Emily Dickinson*, ed. R. W. Franklin (Amherst, 1986), 26, 32, 40, 43.

3. In addition to Thomas H. Johnson, a major proponent of the Wadsworth thesis, others who have accepted it are: George F. Whicher, in *This Was a Poet: A Critical Biography of Emily Dickinson* (New York, 1938), 99–112, 322–24; Albert J. Gelpi, *Emily Dickinson: The Mind of the Poet* (Cambridge, Mass., 1965), 21–25, 110–11, 182; William Robert Sherwood, *Circumference and Circumstance: Stages in the Mind and Art of Emily Dickinson* (New York and London, 1968), 66–103, passim; and William H. Shurr, *The Marriage of Emily Dickinson* (Lexington, Ky., 1983).

4. Jay Leyda, *The Years and Hours of Emily Dickinson* (New Haven, 1960), 2:34.

5. Genevieve Taggard, *The Life and Mind of Emily Dickinson* (New York, 1930; reprinted, 1967).

6. Millicent Todd Bingham, *Ancestors' Brocades* (New York, 1945), 254.

7. Josephine Pollitt, *Emily Dickinson: The Human Background* (New York, 1930; reprinted, 1970), 164–65.

8. Winfield Townley Scott first suggested Bowles in the article "Emily Dickinson and Samuel Bowles," in *Fresco: The University of Detroit Quarterly* (Fall 1959): 7–17. More extended analyses of the relationship appear in David Higgins, *Portrait of Emily Dickinson* (New Brunswick, N.J., 1967), 16–84, passim, 116–18; Ruth Miller, *The Poetry of Emily Dickinson* (Middletown, Conn., 1968), 111–43, 144–88, passim; and Richard B. Sewall, *The Life of Emily Dickinson* (New York, 1974), 2:469–531. See Shurr's persuasive arguments against the Bowles thesis (136–42).

9. John Evangelist Walsh, *The Hidden Life of Emily Dickinson* (New York, 1971). The poet described Lord as her father's "closest friend" (Leyda, 2:258).

10. Rebecca Patterson, *The Riddle of Emily Dickinson* (Boston, 1951) and *Emily Dickinson's Imagery* (Amherst, 1979).

11. John Cody, *After Great Pain: The Inner Life of Emily Dickinson* (Cambridge, Mass., 1971), 163, 178, 182–84, 346.

Polly Longsworth also believes that "Emily was quite literally in love with" Susan Gilbert. "Withdrawal, the only defense Emily ever took against Sue (though it always dissolved at the merest approach to contriteness on Sue's part), was the attitude of the wounded lover." Emily's letters "to 'dear Susie,' whose kisses and comforts she sorely missed, were unmistakably love letters, more persistently and lyrically romantic than what she was writing to other friends, although they did not far exceed the nineteenth-century tolerance for intimacy between females." Longsworth also comments that "Emily wrote love letters of another kind to Austin." See *Austin and Mabel* (New York, 1983, 92–93).

12. Sewall, *The Lyman Letters* (Amherst, 1965), 69.

13. Leyda, 2:475.

14. Ibid., 213.

15. Cody, 29, 403, passim. There are several variations of this reading; but, among more than fifty critics who have commented on the poem, Robert Weisbuch most clearly disagrees with the interpretation of the poem as a fall into madness. See *Emily Dickinson's Poetry* (Chicago, 1975), 105–6.

16. *The Manuscript Books of Emily Dickinson*, ed. R. W. Franklin (Cambridge, Mass., and London, 1981), 2:334, 341–42. Poems quoted in this chapter will be from Franklin.

The phrase "Finished knowing," for which the poet considered the alternative, "Got through knowing" in the last line, is related to a later poem: "There is a finished feeling / Experienced at Graves— / A leisure of the Future— / A Wilderness of Size" (#856, c. 1864–66).

17. Theodora Ward, *The Capsule of the Mind: Chapters in the Life of Emily Dickinson* (Cambridge, Mass., 1961), 54–55.

In *Lyric Time* (Baltimore and London, 1979), Sharon Cameron states that "people do not feel funerals and certainly not in the brain." Arguing that "the poem is not about actual death" but asking why the funeral is "rendered in such literal terms, terms that might well lead a careless reader to mistake its very subject," she concludes that the poem is an allegory "of repression in terms of death . . . the death of consciousness." The "odd order of the poem's events," in which "the funeral precedes death, necessitates a figural reading" and "makes perfect sense within it" (96–98).

18. Clark Griffith, *The Long Shadow: Emily Dickinson's Tragic Poetry* (Princeton, 1964), 206–7, 247.

19. See David Porter, *Dickinson: The Modern Idiom* (Cambridge, Mass., and London, 1981), 114, 120–21, 124, 182–85, 227–28, 293–94.

20. Thomas W. Ford, *Heaven Beguiles the Tired: Death in the Poetry of Emily Dickinson* (University, Miss., 1966), 131–35. Shira Wolosky's *Emily Dickinson: A Voice of War* (New Haven and London, 1985) brilliantly traces the ramifications of the national conflict in relation to the problems of theodicy and finds that the "war broadened the problem . . . beyond the question of personal sorrow to embrace the whole order of existence" (68).

21. Wolosky, 37.

22. Barton Levi St. Armand, in *Emily Dickinson and Her Culture* (Cambridge, New York, and Melbourne, 1984), says the war "provided an epic background" for the poet's acting out her "intense" and "private war of romance"—the "conflict between the deacon and the Madonna." He thinks the letter is "unusually detailed," summarizing "the gossip and newspaper accounts" of the death and burial of "this young Amherst hero," as well as a "curious document" showing her "vicarious participation in the great conflict," but the "calculated hero worship demonstrates that Stearns had somehow become a symbol of her own assassinated self-hood." He, like the poet, "was a manic-depressive of the spirit, a victim of New England theology" (104–15). Reading the poem as a response to the funeral also, St. Armand believes that "a full dress rehearsal of Stearns's obsequies entailed" the poet's "own descent into the Valley of the Shadow, which now included psychological as well as physical death." For St. Armand, "The drums of a wartime funeral service merge with the tolling bells of simple village rites to produce a surreal cacophany, a Dead March that grates upon the very soul. External and internal death are merged, and though Dickinson 'finishes knowing,' we are left with . . . ambiguity" (107–8).

23. Dickinson sent Bowles a copy of the poem "Victory comes late" (#690) probably in "late March, 1862" (L, 2:399). The battle at New Bern was a Union victory.

24. Leyda, 2:50; Ford, 132–34; and St. Armand, 102.

25. James Reeves, "Introduction," *Selected Poems of Emily Dickinson* (London, 1959), xxxix. For John Emerson Todd, also, "I felt a Funeral" is "perhaps the poet's subtlest treatment of madness" (*Emily Dickinson's Use of the Persona* [The Hague, 1973], 85). Suzanne Juhasz, in *The Undiscovered Continent: Emily Dickinson and the Space of the Mind* (Bloomington, 1983), says the poem uses "death as a metaphor for madness" (78).

26. See John Crowe Ransom's view that "the setting could have only existed" in the poet's "exotic imagination" and his comparison of the poet with Thomas Hardy, in *A Collection of Critical Essays*, ed. Sewall (Englewood Cliffs, 1963), 91–92.

27. We can judge the impact of the circumstances of Frazar Stearns's death on her by a comment she made in a letter of condolence to Maria Whitney sometime after the death of Samuel Bowles in January 1878: " 'tis not what well conferred it, the dying soldier asks, it is only the water" (L, 2:634). The poet also wrote to Louise Norcross in mid-July 1871 about an Amherst memorial for Stearns and remarked: " 'We conquered but Bozzaris fell' " (L, 2:488).

28. Henry W. Wells, *Introduction to Emily Dickinson* (Chicago, 1947), 182.

29. Ward, 65–66. She believes, however, that the poet could never have been psychotic because "the insane cannot explain themselves" (55).

30. Sewall, *The Life*, 2:646. "The speech," Sewall notes, "reminded all Amherst of Frazar Stearns's death only four months before" (647).

31. See Sherwood, who finds the poet's aloofness to be "thoroughly aristocratic" and speaks of her "decision to announce (ironically in the midst of the Civil War) her private secession from society" (111, 152). In *Emily Dickinson: When a Writer Is a Daughter* (Bloomington, 1982), Barbara Mossberg comments on the poet's taking "the civil war and the events of those years . . . the politics of secession, division, and conflict *inside* her father's house—and inside the mind of an individual in captivity there"; Mossberg also thinks that "I felt a Funeral" describes "the burial of the consciousness and senses" and is the persona's "chronicle of her own demise" (17, 30–31).

32. Another of the Commencement speakers at Amherst College on the day that Otis Lord spoke was Henry Ward Beecher, who told the audience, "it might be expected, perhaps," that he would choose a literary subject, but since they were "so near the edge of revolution," he must treat of "questions of the hour . . . the storm in the North, and the earthquake in the South" (Sewall, *The Life*, 2:646).

33. References to places of battle in #596 leave no doubt that the poem is related to the war. Whicher, Ford, Sewall, and Wolosky have discussed it. Wolosky also observes that in #639, Dickinson identifies "with soldiers, no longer as types only, but in the flesh," that the poem "does not entirely exclude the metaphoric level," and that whether it "finally addresses an internal or an external state, it is certainly situated in the external world" (56).

34. Dickinson placed "They Dropped like Flakes" in Fascicle 28, which also includes "A Dying Tiger—moaned for Drink" and "He gave away his life" (*Manuscript Books*, 639, 645–46, 664). Perhaps three others poems in group 28 were stimulated by the poet's response to the war "brought home." They are: "How Many Flowers fail in Wood— / Or perish from the Hill" (#404). "The Test of Love—is Death— / Our Lord—'so loved'—it saith—" (#573), and "For largest Woman's Heart I Knew— / 'Tis little I can do—" (#309).

35. The wife of General McClellan attended Amherst Academy in her girlhood and thereafter spent two summers in Amherst. When the McClellans visited the town during June 1869, the local paper mentioned that the Honorable Edward Dickinson received a call from them (Leyda, 2:139–40).

36. Ford comments on the clash of fact and religious faith (132), and Wolosky discusses the nature imagery as a figure for the violence of war (37–38) in "They Dropped like Flakes."

37. Douglas Robillard, "Introduction," *Poems of Herman Melville* (New Haven, 1976), 17.

38. Ruth Miller notes that Dickinson "was not a social poet" but that "Color—Caste—Denomination" approaches "a comment on the Civil War." Miller adds: "There are poems that genuinely lament the sacrifice of young men to the violence of battle . . ." (232–33).

39. Leyda dates the fragment in relation to an item in the December 20, 1862, issue of the *Springfield Republican:* "A new edition of Robert Browning's poetical works is announced by London; also a new long poem by him, entitled 'Christmas Eve and Easter Day' " (2:72).

40. "It should be noted also that, if Emily in fact came near a breakdown during this period, no mention of it in the annals of her family or friends has so far come to light" (Sewall, *The Life*, 2:491–92).

41. Sewall, *The Lyman Letters*, 76.

42. Leyda, 2:101; 1:xliii; 2:192.

43. Sewall, *The Lyman Letters*, 73–75, and *The Life*, 2:606–7, n. 9.

44. Cody, 267, 355, 415, 423, 437.

45. Martin Wand and Richard B. Sewall, " 'Eyes Be Blind. Heart Be Still': A New Perspective on Emily Dickinson's Eye Problem," *The New England Quarterly* 52 (September 1979): 402–6. Jerry Ferris Reynolds, in " 'Banished From Native Eyes': The Reason for Emily Dickinson's Seclusion Reconsidered," argues that her symptoms "would suggest a diagnosis of systemic lupus erythematosus." See *The Markham Review* 8 (Spring 1979): 41–48.

46. Wand and Sewall, 405–6.

47. Millicent Todd Bingham, *Emily Dickinson's Home* (New York, 1955), 203, and Leyda, 1:263.

48. Gerald W. Jackson, "The 'Covered Vision' of Emily Dickinson" (master's thesis, Wake Forest University, May 1974), 7–20.

49. Henry W. Williams, *A Practical Guide to the Study of the Diseases of the Eye: Their Medical and Surgical Treatment*, 3d ed. (Boston, 1873), 34, 133–34, 144. The book went through six editions from 1862 to 1881.

50. Jackson, 20. Cody reads the detail, "For caution of my Hat, He says, the Doctor wipes my cheeks," as follows: "This suggests that the patient is weeping and that the physician has the role of consoler. It *could* mean that eye medication is overflowing from her eyes or inducing lacrimation during a treatment, but for a physician to apply medication without removing the patient's hat would be an extraordinarily odd procedure" (417–18).

51. Williams, 135.

52. Martha Dickinson Bianchi, *Emily Dickinson Face to Face* (New York, 1930; reprinted, 1970), 25.

53. Leyda, 2:133.

54. Todd recalled coming to play and sing "in the long, lonely drawing room"; the poet "sat outside in the darksome hall, on the stairs" to listen; she never came in to speak to the guest but would send her a note of thanks. See Sewall, *The Life*, 1:218.

55. Leyda, 2:258.

56. Ibid., 272–73.

57. Bianchi, 66–67.

58. Leyda, 2:406.

59. Ibid., 441. Mrs. Brown spoke of Emily Dickinson "as a most unusual woman—a real old maid."

60. Walsh notes that Adams Drug Store in Amherst still preserves the book containing prescriptions for all the Dickinsons, from 1882 to 1885. At least a dozen, perhaps as many as twenty, were for Emily Dickinson; "the most powerful specifics seem to have been digitalis and belladonna" (*The Hidden Life*, 274).

61. Bianchi, 170–71.

62. *Emily Dickinson: A Revelation* (New York, 1954), 107.

63. *The Manuscript Books* 1:xii–xiii; 2:1336.

64. Eileen Joyce Schaurek, Joyce's sister, recalled his efforts to protect the threatened sight: "He wrote at night mostly, mostly at night and he lay across the bed on his stomach when he wrote, with a huge blue pencil, a huge blue pencil like a carpenter's pencil and a white coat on him to reflect on the paper, to give reflection because his sight was so bad. He always wrote with a white coat on him to give him a kind of white light." From the "Archive Recording," quoted in *The World of James Joyce* (Columbia, S.C.: South Carolina Educational Television Network, 1983), 13. Joyce's daughter, Lucia, said also that the physical strain of writing was damaging to his eyes and that she saw him in tears when he could not read his own words.

65. Bianchi, 17.

66. See Leyda, 1:196.

67. Although the meanings of "terror" and "woe" differ, "terror" and "tremble" are etymologically close, as Dickinson was apt to have known.

68. Sewall observes that the poet uses the metaphor to indicate "what seems to have been a temporary pause in her writing, perhaps through illness or fatigue. Surely she is talking about more than her domestic handiwork" (*The Life*, 2:397–98).

69. Not only has the relation of the poem to the distaff work of the poet been largely ignored, but the poem has been linked with "I felt a Funeral, in my Brain" because images in both are said to demonstrate "the performance of language and not a representation of the world." Asserting that "when language breeds, removed from exterior referents, it becomes almost pure locution, and meaning cannot be established," David Porter cites as an example "Dickinson's invention of 'a dotted Dot.' " Apparently unfamiliar with fine needlework, smocking, or embroidery, he says that "no seamstress could envision what has existence only in Dickinson's words" and that lines 7–12 of the poem consist of "words . . . coupling . . . with no restraint from things" (121).

70. See Robert Lair, *A Simplified Approach* (Woodberry, N.Y., 1971), 65–66, but especially Cody, 423.

71. Higginson wrote to his sister Anna: "Last night [December 27, 1876] the Warings had their novel wedding festival of a dozen people. . . . The Woolseys were bright as usual & wrote some funny things for different guests—one imaginary letter to me from my partially cracked poetess of Amherst, who writes to me & signs 'Your scholar' " (Quoted in L, 2:570). See also L, 2:518.

72. Three of Dickinson's poems use images that may have been suggested by her visual history: "Renunciation—is a piercing Virtue" with the phrases, "The putting out of Eyes—" and "that Covered Vision—Here—" (#745, c. 1863); "The Poets light but Lamps—," in which the poet speculates that, even though they go out, "If vital Light / Inhere . . . / Each age [is] a Lens / Disseminating their / Circumference—" (#883, c. 1864); and "The Admirations—and Contempts—of time— / Show justest— through an Open Tomb—," of which she says " 'Tis Compound Vision— / Light— enabling Light— / The finite—furnished— / With the Infinite— / Convex—Concave Witness—" (#906, c. 1864).

Chapter 4: The Histrionic Imagination

1. Poems quoted in this chapter are, unless indicated otherwise, from *The Manuscript Books of Emily Dickinson*, ed. R. W. Franklin (Cambridge, Mass., and London, 1981).

2. *The Contemporary Writer*, ed. L. S. Dembo and Cyrena N. Pondrom (Madison and London, 1972), 138–40.

3. Sandra M. Gilbert and Susan Gubar praise "the magnitude of the poetic self-creation Emily Dickinson achieved through working in a genre that has been traditionally the most Satanically assertive, daring, and therefore precarious of literary modes for women: lyric poetry." Dickinson's life, they argue, "became a kind of novel or narrative poem in which, through an extraordinarily complex series of maneuvers, aided by costumes that came inevitably to hand, this inventive poet enacted and eventually resolved both her anxieties about her art and her anger at female subordination." Gilbert and Gubar touch all the bases. Understood "as an elaborate set of dramatic monologues, her poems constitute the 'dialogue' in an extended fiction whose subject is the life of that supposed person who was originally called Emily Dickinson." See *The Madwoman in the Attic* (New Haven and London, 1979), 582–84.

4. William Shurr finds that the poems tell a story of a love "consummated" between Emily Dickinson and "a well-known clergyman" (the Reverend Charles Wadsworth) in the spring of 1860. "Though the affair was relatively brief and based

on only a few personal intimacies," pregnancy or the fear of pregnancy resulted; "the crisis disturbed Dickinson physically and mentally during a whole summer, probably the summer of 1861, [and] led her to confide in Higginson vaguely about 'the terror—since September—I could tell to none.' " See *The Marriage of Emily Dickinson* (Lexington, Ky., 1983), 7, 195–96, and passim.

5. See the comments of Christopher E. G. Benfey in the introduction to *Emily Dickinson and the Problem of Others* (Amherst, 1984), 1–2. Although he considers Dickinson a lyric poet, he is interested in what she says about the question "Am I alone in the world?" Dickinson suggests, he argues persuasively, "that while our relation to other [minds] may not be one of certainty"—"knowledge taken as certainty"—the relation "may be one of nearness" (6), and "that we can relinquish *certainty* in our relations to others, . . . yet acknowledge our relatedness to them" as well as "some larger communion" (64).

Saying that Dickinson's "only subject was herself," Susan Juhasz believes that the poet "persistently categorizes" personal, private experience "as everyone's," and "populates her inner world with a society of selves." But the "many poems about the mind with their social as well as geographic metaphors let us see how necessary it was for her to be in relationship; for that was how . . . as a woman she could not help but define her humanity." See *The Undiscovered Continent* (Bloomington, 1983), 30, 172.

6. The theatrical antecedent is the soliloquy: the speech in a play at the moment a character reveals both a dramatic situation and a response to it. The speech usually suggests basic elements in the character's nature and often the deepest roots of that nature. The auditor or auditors may be clearly implied, but not necessarily.

Another antecedent of the dramatic monologue is the ballad. See, for instance, Michael S. Harper's comment on his use of the ballad form "because it is economical and dramatic and does not require too much right-sounding rhyme." *Fifty Contemporary Poets: The Creative Process*, ed. Alberta T. Turner (New York, 1977), 141. Dickinson's preference for the traditional ballad or common hymn meters is well known; irregular and dissonant rhymes are also characteristic of many of her poems.

7. *The Poems of Emily Dickinson*, ed. Thomas H. Johnson (Cambridge, Mass., 1955).

8. Jack Capps, *Emily Dickinson's Reading* (Cambridge, Mass., 1966), 88–89, 134–36, 138; Richard B. Sewall, *The Life of Emily Dickinson* (New York, 1974), 2:717.

9. Ellen Moers, *Literary Women* (Garden City, N.Y., 1976), 61.

10. The young poet wrote c. 1858 to Mary and Samuel Bowles: "I rode with Austin this morning. He showed me mountains that touched the sky, and brooks that sang like Bobolinks. Was he not very kind?" (L, 2:334). She probably refers here to an unidentified man for whom she used the name of her brother Austin as a cover (see L, 2:398, 402).

11. Millicent Todd Bingham, *Emily Dickinson's Home* (New York, 1955), 367. Also see Sewall, 2:418, 571–72.

12. "In so far as it concentrates on the life that is left behind, it is wholly successful; in so far as it attempts to experience the death to come, it is fraudulent, however exquisitely, and in this it falls below her finest achievement." Yvor Winters, *Maule's Curse* (Norfolk, Conn., 1938), 154. But see Jane Crosthwaite's coherent reading of the poem as the poet's "encounter with death"—"the force which drives the carriage of life," in "Emily Dickinson's Ride With Death," *Massachusetts Studies in English* 7 (4) and 8 (1) (1981): 18–27.

13. Vivian R. Pollak, *Dickinson: The Anxiety of Gender* (Ithaca and London, 1984),

55. While Pollak does not believe that "Dickinson's poems necessarily reenact actual events" and seeks "to dispel the misconception that her language is necessarily or even exclusively self-referential" (10), the critic also thinks that the poet's "subject is herself" (132).

14. William Howard, studying the words Dickinson used from "special sources," found that the second largest group was from "housewifery." The first group was scientific and academic. See "Emily Dickinson's Poetic Vocabulary," PMLA 72 (March 1957): 230. Jean McClure Mudge, in *Emily Dickinson & the Image of Home* (Amherst, 1975), records the frequency with which the poet uses words relating to space. She reports that "house" and "world" are used seventy-four times each; the word "home" is used eighty-six times; and cognates of *house* and *home*, "such as *houses, household, housewife* and *homes, homesick, homeless, homestead*, increase the number of poems from 160, the total use of *house* and *home*, to 210, or about 12% of her known poems" (229–30).

15. See Charles R. Anderson, *Emily Dickinson's Poetry* (New York, 1960), 100–102, and Matthew 6:28–30.

16. Jay Leyda, *The Years and Hours of Emily Dickinson* (New Haven, 1960), 1:344.

17. Ibid., 352.

18. Ibid. During January of 1858, Dickinson received from a maternal cousin a copy of Wadsworth's sermon ("Religious Glorifying"?)—the first real evidence of the poet's having any knowledge of the minister. Leyda speculates that her correspondence with him may have begun at that time when she sought advice on "the nervous illness" of her mother (1:352; lxxxvii).

19. Mary Shepard, writing February 9, 1860, from Amherst to her nephew, L. M. Boltwood, reports: "Among the callers, we have had—*Mrs.* Edward Dickinson, last Thursday P.M., appearing as well as *4 years ago*, when last she was here" (ibid., 2:7). Boltwood's mother and the poet's mother were schoolmates (L, 2:488). Mary Shepard again writes on July 12, 1863: "Mrs. Edward Dickinson . . . is . . . now quite herself" (Leyda, 2:81).

20. Sewall, *The Life of Emily Dickinson* (New York, 1974): "Fortunately, for her balance, she had her chores, her cooking, her sewing, whatever cleaning she could not pass off on Vinnie, and always, of course, Nature and her writing" (2:533).

21. Sewall, *The Lyman Letters* (Amherst, 1965), 14.

22. Leyda, 2:268. Lavinia Dickinson confirms that the elder sister took the major responsibility for the care of their mother. Writing in 1895, "to extinguish all untruth relating to" the poet, Lavinia explains: "Emily's so called 'withdrawal from general society,' for which she never cared, was only a happen. Our mother had a period of invalidism, and one of her daughters must be constantly at home; Emily chose this part and, finding the life with her books and nature so congenial, continued to live it, always seeing her chosen friends and doing her part for the happiness of the home" (Sewall, *The Life*, 1:153). The statement that the withdrawal was "only a happen" has been cited by those who disagree without paying attention to the account of the family situation. Chronic difficulties with the eyes would also have made it preferable for the poet to chose the duties that required staying at home.

23. According to Franklin's dating of the manuscripts, there were fair copies of 148 poems in fascicles 1–7, c. 1858–59, the time at which Dickinson began to assemble the sequences or "books"; there were 145 poems in fascicles 8–14, c. 1860 and 1861 (1:1–304). Franklin assigns more than 374 poems to 1862. An assigned date confirms that a poem had been written but does not necessarily mean "date of

composition." It is almost dizzying to contemplate the number of poems attributed to 1862. The record suggests, however, that the poet had more leisure time to write but also to take stock, perhaps to revise, and to make fair copies of previous work.

24. Sewall designates "the puzzling years . . . roughly, the years 1858–62," which would include "the terror since September" 1861 (*Life*, 2:465). Mrs. Dickinson's illness beginning in 1856 and her recovery in 1860 must have been one factor in "the puzzle." Dickinson clearly bore much of the strain of those years.

25. In *The Modern Poetic Sequence* (New York and Oxford, 1983), 45–73, M. L. Rosenthal and Sally M. Gall examine the psychological and poetic coherence of fascicles 15 and 16. But, they conclude, "a thorough study of all forty fascicles lies ahead. It promises to be one of the great voyages of discovery in modern criticism" (73). Ruth Miller, in *The Poetry of Emily Dickinson* (Middletown, Conn., 1968), first explored the possibility that each of the individual packets can be read as a coherent narrative.

Chapter 5: Listening to Literary Voices

1. "Whispers of Immortality," in *Collected Poems 1909–1962* (New York, 1963), 45.

2. Martha Dickinson Bianchi, *Emily Dickinson Face to Face* (New York, 1930; reprinted, 1970), 28. Bianchi identifies the story as "Circumstance," which seems to be confirmed by the poet's comments to T. W. Higginson: "I read Miss Prescott's 'Circumstance,' but it followed me, in the Dark—so I avoided her—" (L, 2:404). It is the tale of a frontier woman seized by a panther during a solitary walk through the Maine woods at nightfall. "The fiend" bears the woman up into the branches of a wind-rocked fir tree, gnashes, paws, and brutally bloodies her as they twist about and swing over the "horid tomb yawning" below. In the "agony" of the long cold night, she tries to ward off the repeated attacks of the beast by singing: first a cradle-song, then a wild sea chant, a gay reel, a lively Irish jig, and finally "the old Covenanting hymns" that renew her faith in God. The cock crows; the woman's husband appears with a gun; she loses her voice; there is a rifle crack; she is saved. But, returning home with her husband, she finds it in smoking ruins. The poet takes the tale as source for a series of complex images she put to use.

If one compares "Circumstance" and Dickinson's "psycho-drama," addressed to an unidentified "you," in " 'Twas like a Maelstrom, with a notch" (#414, c. 1862), her comments that the story followed her in the dark and so she avoided Prescott become yet another instance of the poet's dissembling to Higginson. He apparently admired Prescott's work, which was widely published in current periodicals. See the comparison worked out by Maryanne M. Garbowsky in "A Maternal Muse for Emily Dickinson," *Dickinson Studies* 41 (December 1981): 12–17.

3. Poems quoted in this chapter are from *The Manuscript Books of Emily Dickinson*, ed. R. W. Franklin (Cambridge, Mass., and London, 1981).

4. See *Jane Eyre*, ed. Jane Jack and Margaret Smith (Oxford, 1969), 549, 558, 568, 577. The poet, according to M. L. Rosenthal and Sally Gall, "flaunts her imagination" in "a developed imagery of fear and withdrawal, an internal stocktaking that confesses failure to cope adequately with blazing life." Citing the poem as an example that epitomizes a process the critics think common to Dickinson's work, they analyze the "riddling qualities" of the verse: "we have an emotional state whose basis is a mystery. . . . All the *poem* gives us is its affect of passionate recollec-

tion of wounded withdrawal. The stanzas present so many centers of evocation that we need no 'story.' And still they have the *form* of narrative and refer to unspecified crucial events." See *The Modern Poetic Sequence: The Genius of Modern Poetry* (New York and Oxford, 1983), 50–53. On the other hand, Jane Donahue Eberwein notes that Dickinson "seems to have tried out some of the literary miseries life had denied her, as when she fantasizes blindness in 'Before I got my eye put out' in apparent attempts to experience vicariously the sufferings of . . . Rochester" (*Dickinson: Strategies of Limitation* [Amherst, 1985], 113).

    5. *Jane Eyre*, 57–60, 68, 89–90, 151, 304, 415–16.

    6. Ibid., 13, 24, 31–32, 39, 87.

    7. Ibid., 552, 555, 557.

    8. Ibid., 562, 556, 558, 567–68, 559.

    9. Ibid., 568–70.

    10. Albert Gelpi, *The Tenth Muse* (Cambridge, Mass., and London, 1975), 253–54. John Emerson Todd writes that the "persona performs duties of both clergyman and nurse as she sings hymns and dispenses 'Balm' to her lover," but he also assumes that Dickinson "portrays the death" of the man. See *Emily Dickinson's Use of the Persona* (The Hague, 1973), 39–40.

    11. *Jane Eyre*, 573, 576–77. Jane's poem precedes by at least fourteen years an allusion to Rochester and to her in one of Dickinson's letters to a friend. Thanking Elizabeth Holland for a favor in the autumn of 1876, the poet writes: "You remember from whom I quoted, when you brought me the Clover? 'I find your Benefits no Burden, Jane' " (L, 2:562). The novel was clearly one Dickinson knew well.

    12. See Jay Leyda, *The Years and Hours of Emily Dickinson* (New Haven, 1960), 1:xxi, but also William Shurr, *The Marriage of Emily Dickinson* (Lexington, Ky., 1983), 708.

    13. *Jane Eyre*, 570 and 576. I suspect that there are other poems for which scenes in the book are seminal influences. "A Door just opened on the street— / I—lost— was passing by—" (#953, c. 1864–65) probably derives from the wandering Jane's experience after her departure from Thornfield; and "My period had come for Prayer" (#564, c. 1862) may be inspired by her account of praying at night on a north-midland heath.

    "There came a Day at Summer's Full / Entirely for me—" (#332, c. 1861), which Shurr argues is Dickinson's "central marriage poem" (12, 17, 23, 38, 60, 98, 132), seems to be her monologue for Lucy Snow, "the little English Protestant" who, after many obstacles, was united in love with the Belgian Catholic Paul Emmanuel in Brontë's novel *Villette*. Paul, having given Lucy a pledge of marriage before he sailed for Guadaloupe, was drowned in a storm at sea when he was returning to her three years later. The intertextual evidence, particularly the religious imagery in the novel and the poem, as well as the narrative of what Shurr terms the poet's "anomalous marriage" within the verse, can bear scrutiny. For instance, "The day" in the novel is the Feast of the Assumption (August 15), of which Dickinson's heroine says, "I thought that such were for the Saints, / Where Ressurections—be—"; or Dickinson's apparent version of the final episodes in the novel reads that the two lovers were "Bound to opposing lands—" but also "Each—bound the other's Crucifix— / We gave no other Bond— // Sufficient troth that we shall rise— / Deposed—at length, the Grave— / To that new Marriage, / Justified—through Calvaries of Love." (The poet's manuscript shows "Revelations" as an alternate word for "Resurrections.")

    At least one of Dickinson's poems, the difficult "Like Eyes that Looked on

Wastes—" (#458, c. 1862), with its mirror imagery (read as a reflection of Dickinson's narcissism or lesbianism), may have its source in the description of the wasted face and mirror scene of the dying Catherine Earnshaw Linton, the heroine of Emily Brontë's *Wuthering Heights*. See, however, Vivian Pollack's analysis of the poem, in which she says Dickinson "implicates" herself and Susan Dickinson equally in "homosexual terror" (*Dickinson: The Anxiety of Gender* [Ithaca and London, 1984], 145.

Nothing that Dickinson's "interest in the gender" of the Brontës, George Eliot, and Elizabeth Barrett Browning "seems to have overshowed [sic] her interest in what they wrote," Karl Keller suggests that "several" of Dickinson's "love poems may actually derive from *Jane Eyre* and *Wuthering Heights*." He does not develop the suggestions. See "A Coda," in *The Only Kangaroo Among the Beauty* (Baltimore and London, 1979), 327–28, and 331.

14. Jane Langton, *The Transcendental Murder* (1964), reissued as *The Minute Man Murder* (New York, 1974).

15. *The Mill on the Floss*, ed. Gordon S. Haight (Oxford, 1980), 377.

16. Ibid., 378, 386, 431–44, 444–45.

17. Ibid., 383, 436.

18. Ibid., 456–59.

19. Ibid., 411, 452, 459.

20. Bianchi, 170. The poet, amused by the behavior of Elizabeth Holland's family when water flooded the house cellar in the winter of 1884, for instance, was reminded of *Mill on the Floss*, "though 'Maggie Tulliver' was missing, and had she been there her Destiny could not have been packed in the 'Bath Tub' " (L, 3:814).

21. The phrase is Sewall's in *The Life*, 2:682.

22. Ibid., 1:19.

23. As Ellen Moers remarks in *Literary Women*, "Who but Emily Dickinson . . . cared for George Eliot's poetry? or took care to call her Mrs. Lewes?" (61).

24. *The Scarlet Letter* (Boston, 1850), 304, 307, 312–13.

25. Ibid., 194–96, 198–99, 201.

26. Keller discusses "Mine—by the Right" as one of Dickinson's "most exclamatory, explicitly theological poems," demonstrating "her strong assertion of the right to individuality . . . secured for her by her faith. The Puritan system . . . has secured rights for her as a woman that nothing else could do" (25). Charles Anderson's view of the poem is that it is "rapturous," describing a state of "extreme ecstasy." See *Emily Dickinson's Poetry* (New York, 1960), 184. Susan Juhasz, stating that the rhetoric is "essentially celebratory," finds the "joy" that the speaker experiences "is entirely involved with [her] right to possession," and the "tone is one of unmitigated delight"; there is "no Amherst setting," but "a situation of imagination." See *The Undiscovered Continent* (Bloomington, 1983), 101.

27. Bianchi, 41.

28. "The Three Voices of Poetry," in *On Poetry and Prose* (New York, 1957), 103–4.

29. Moers, 65.

30. The first edition of *Jane Eyre: An Autobiography*, published without the name of the author, Charlotte Brontë, was "edited by Currer Bell" when it appeared in 1847. There are autobiographical elements in the book.

31. The context for the letters to Samuel and Mary Bowles seems to have been an altercation between them and Austin Dickinson. Bowles wrote on May 15, 1861, to Austin:

... there is a point where friendship must stop in burdening you. I should hardly have talked to you as I did . . . and it did require great effort,—but it is too late to repent. . . . I want you to understand and appreciate and love Mary—to do this, you must make some allowances for her pecularities,—and judge her by what she means, rather always than by what she says. Her very timidity and want of self-reliance gives her a sharper utterance. . . . I think she was somewhat disappointed in her Amherst visit. . . . Of course the fault was mainly hers, but it was also partly mine. . . . The mischief I shall endeavor to remedy here, and without annoying you any more. But I am sore-distressed and weary at heart. My nature revolts at a divided, contradictory loyalty.

See Leyda, 2:28.

Emily Dickinson, in the first letter to Bowles, is apparently advising him that he (and she) should take "the high road." The second letter, then, would be a comment on the advice; Bowles made an effort that cost "breath" to "take" the pearl—the valued friendship? the spirit of reconciliation or forgiveness?—and he must act resolutely once again, i.e., strike the East, where Austin lives. But see Sewall, *The Life*, 2:478–81, for a different reading of the letters to Bowles.

32. Sewall, *The Life*, 2:466. Whatever the differences between the Dickinson and Bowles couples, the friendship between Samuel Bowles and Susan and Austin continued, as did the friendship between Emily Dickinson and Samuel and Mary Bowles.

33. Leyda, 1:366–67.

34. Ibid., 2:41.

35. See Johnson, 2:455. Dickinson's verses in which a bereaved husband meditates on questions of dream contra reality, and fiction contra faith, after his "Bride had slipped away—" for "Belief's delight" (#518, c. 1862), have also been suggested as an elegy on "Mrs. Browning." See John Evangelist Walsh, *The Hidden Life of Emily Dickinson* (New York, 1971), 255. Walsh tends to be disregarded, in part because of his preoccupation with what he thinks are Dickinson's plagiarisms; but the manuscript books, showing that the poet included #518 and #593 in the same fascicle, would support reading both poems as elegies written for Elizabeth Barrett Browning.

It is also said, however, that poem #518 is "best understood as being homoerotic." A psychoanalytic critic states that the poem's directness is "startling" and that "one must lean over backward not to suspect at least a homosexual trend" in the verses. See, among others, John Cody, *After Great Pain: The Inner Life of Emily Dickinson* (Cambridge, Mass., 1971), 149.

36. "One Way of Love," 11.7–10.

37. "One Word More," 11.1–4, 32–33, 59–62, 109–14, 129–32, 143, 187.

38. Walsh cites so many pairing of words or images which E. B. B. and Dickinson used in common that he believes he can charge the latter with both borrowing and stealing (98–102). See Ellen Moers's defense of Dickinson's use of Mrs. Browning "in the best T. S. Eliot sense" of tradition and an exemplary analysis of Dickinson's "Rearrange a Wife's affection" (#1737) for important differences between the poets (57, 59–60, 62). Genevieve Taggard initially observed that there were parallels between lines by E. B. B. and Dickinson; Taggard also first noted echoes of Browning's "monologue style" in Dickinson's "I cannot live with you" (#640). See *The Life and Mind of Emily Dickinson* (New York, 1930; reprinted, 1967), 150–51, 310–11. Taggard accepted the affinities between the poets as natural.

39. *Aurora Leigh* (New York, 1857), Book 6: 11.478–84, 222–23.

40. Moers, 58.

41. Leyda, 1:253.

42. *The Riddle of Emily Dickinson* (Boston, 1951), 260–61.

43. Herbert Wells, *Introduction to Emily Dickinson* (Chicago, 1947), 127.

44. Sewall, *The Life*, 1:133.

Chapter 6: Trifles

1. Poems quoted in this chapter are from *The Poems of Emily Dickinson*, ed. Thomas H. Johnson (Cambridge, Mass., 1955).

2. Wallace Stevens discusses a concern similar to that of Dickinson in "I found the words." See "Imagination as Value," in *The Necessary Angel: Essays on Reality and the Imagination* (New York, 1965), 140.

3. "The Idea of Order at Key West," in *The Collected Poems of Wallace Stevens* (New York, 1954), 130.

4. Falstaff unwittingly says to Poins, who is planning a ruse against him and wants to speak privately about it with Hal, "God give thee the spirit of persuasion and him the ear of profiting" (*Henry IV*, Part 1, Act 1, sc. 2). See also Hal's advice, upon his having assumed the crown, that Falstaff leave gormandizing and "Reply not to me with fool-born jest; / Presume not that I am the thing I was; . . . I have turn'd away my former self" (*Henry IV*, Part 2, Act 5, sc. 5).

5. Jey Leyda, *The Years and Hours of Emily Dickinson* (New Haven, 1969), 1:203.

6. The painting was by Sir George Beaumont. Wordsworth's third stanza reads:

> Ah! THEN, if mine had been the Painter's Hand,
> To express what then I saw; and add the gleam.
> The light that never was on sea or land,
> The consecration, and the Poet's dream.

7. Speaking before the United States Congress on July 18, 1854, in defense of the "virtues" of "the mechanics of the country," Edward Dickinson referred to the "noble sentiment of the poet: 'Honor and shame from no condition rise; / Act well your part, there all the honor lies' " (see Leyda, 1:307–8). Emily Dickinson would, however, have known Pope's poetry without encouragement from her father. She had mentioned "transpositions" of *The Essay on Man* when she was at Mount Holyoke Seminary in the fall of 1847 (L, 1:54).

8. "Emily Dickinson, Marianne Moore," in *Festschrift for Marianne Moore's Seventy-Seventh Birthday*, ed. [Thurairajah] Tambimuttu (New York, 1964), 52.

9. *Birds of America*, ed. T. Gilbert Pearson (Garden City, N.Y., 1936), 3:198–99.

10. Leyda, 2:131, 133, 145.

11. The Franco-Prussian War was in the news.

12. Leyda, 2:189.

13. The allusion is to Matthew 11:26: "Even so, Father: for so it seemed good in thy sight."

14. Thanking Susan Gilbert Dickinson for "Tenderness" in a letter written during early December 1865, the poet begins: "Sister, We both are Women, and there is a Will of God—Could the Dying confide Death, there would be no Dead—Wedlock is shyer than Death" (L, 2:445). There seems no question in Emily Dickinson's mind about her having outgrown childhood.

15. *Connoisseurs of Chaos* (New York, 1965), 118–19.

16. R. P. Blackmur, for instance, writes: "In Emily Dickinson we seldom see a completely mature verse, though we often see elements of such a verse. Perhaps we see her own adolescence *and* her own maturity peep through. Both are fragmentary. We cannot say of this woman in white that she ever mastered life—even in loosest metaphor; but we can say that she so dealt with it as to keep it from mastering her— by her protestant self-excruciation in life's name." In *Emily Dickinson: A Collection of Critical Essays*, ed. Sewall (Englewood Cliffs, N.J., 1963), 85.

17. *The Life of Emily Dickinson* (New York, 1974), 2:607.

18. Higginson, after the first visit he made to see Dickinson, noted: "She often thought me *tired* & seemed very thoughtful of others" (L, 2:376).

19. Pound's classic imagist poem, "In a Station of the Metro," consists of two lines. The first draft of the couplet, according to Pound, was thirty lines long. See Hugh Kenner, *The Pound Era* (Berkeley and Los Angeles, 1971), 184, 197.

20. Dickinson's first poem on the experience of seeing a hummingbird, "Within my Garden, rides a Bird" (#500, c. 1862), is twenty lines in length.

21. There is no other Dickinson poem that she chose to send to as many correspondents. It went first with a poem on the oriole and the comment, "I hope they are not untrue," to Helen Hunt Jackson in 1879. In early 1880, the poet sent a copy to Mrs. Edward Tuckerman, friend, neighbor, wife of the professor of botany at Amherst College, and sister-in-law of Frederick Tuckerman (who also wrote poetry); in November 1880, Dickinson sent it along with three others and the astute request, "Reprove them as your own," to Higginson. She also sent the poem to Mabel Loomis Todd in October 1882 and to Thomas Niles in April 1883 (L, 2:639–40; 3:655, 681, 741, 769–70).

22. Williams observes that Dickinson has the characteristic in common with Marianne Moore. See *Selected Essays of William Carlos Williams* (New York, 1954), 123.

23. Dickinson included the poem as "a chill Gift—My Cricket" in a letter of mid-March 1883 to Thomas Niles (L, 3:768).

24. "Landscapes," in *Collected Poems 1909–1962* (New York, 1963), 138.

25. *Emily Dickinson's Poetry* (Chicago and London, 1972), 151.

26. Dickinson first alluded to *Paradise Lost* in a letter written in January 1850: "War Sir—'my voice is for war!' " Satan, speaking to the fallen angels, says "Peace is despaired, / For who can think submission! War then, war / Open or understood, must be resolved" (Book I, 11.660–62). In the early spring of 1886, she referred to the landscape of Hell and called Milton "the great florist" (L, 1:79, 3:900).

27. The poem was left in penciled draft (see note on alternate wording in Johnson, 3:957).

28. *The Life*, 2:721.

29. Louisa May Alcott's stories are well known. Frances Sargent Osgood (1811–50), whose best poems describe her daughters and their friends, became one of the most popular and most admired of American poets in Dickinson's youth. In what is one of the worst poems Dickinson ever wrote, "I met a King this afternoon" (#166, c. 1860), she describes "a Barefoot Estate": a freckled boy in palm-leaf hat, his blue jacket faded, and his companions ragged, on an "excursion" in a wagon (the horse "an estimable Beast, / But not at all disposed to run!"). One critic thinks that "the little King" is the poet herself "disguised," but it is a period piece describing boys of the kind Mark Twain would transmute into characters for the great novel, *The Adventures of Huckleberry Finn* (1884).

30. In a note written shortly after the letter, the poet says to the sister-in-law: "we remind her we love her—Unimportant fact, though Dante did'nt think so, nor Swift, nor Mirabeau" (see L, 2:509).

31. See *The Poems of Emily Dickinson: An Annotated Guide to Commentary in English, 1890–1977*, ed. Joseph Duchac (Boston, 1979), 212.

32. Dickinson's daring to cross the gender line in several of her monologues and some of her notes (especially those to the children and their mother next door) is one basis for the view that the poet was uncertain about her sexual identity. Thanking Ned for an unspecified favor ("an Embassy," "an Ambassador"), for example, she borrowed " 'And pays his heart / For what his eyes eat only!' " from Shakespeare's speech for Enobarbus when he tells the Romans that Antony cannot say no to woman. She adds, "Excuse the bearded Pronoun." The note is signed "Aunt Emily" (L, 3:894). Ned, who was twenty-four at the time, must have appreciated the humor. She was ill and was probably thanking him for food she was unable to eat or for flowers.

33. She included this verse among five poems that she sent to Higginson in January 1876, and mentioned having read the correspondent's "Childhood Fancies" that had appeared in the new issue of *Scribner's Monthly* (L, 2:546–47).

34. Edward Dickinson, attending a commencement celebration at Yale in 1850, brought home as a souvenir a reprint of *The New England Primer* (Leyda, 1:178). The poet clipped the illustration for the letter "T" and pasted it above a note and a poem she sent to Susan Dickinson in 1860. The poem begins "We don't cry—Tim and I, / We are far too grand— / But we bolt the door tight to prevent a friend—" (#196, c. 1860). The primer reads: "Young Timothy / Learnt sin to fly." The illustration is of "a youth pursued by an upright wolf-like creature with forked tale." The note reads "My 'position'!" and is signed "Cole." There is also a P.S.: "Lest you misapprehend, the unfortunate insect upon the left is Myself, while the Reptile upon the *right* is my more immediate friends and connections" (L, 2:360). The poem is said to be an example of "seeming regression to childhood" and "the split-off masculine identifica-tion which the poet is not quite willing to accept consciously as part of herself" (see Duchac, 581).

35. Dickinson wrote six poems primarily to the bee; there are at least another eight in which the bee shares the attention with a fly, or flower, or a "bachelor," for instance; and she mentions the bee in more than thirty other poems. Under the heading "Bumble Bees," Joseph Lyman copied the following (n.d.) from one of Dickinson's letters:

> We had merry talk about them the other day. Austin wanted me to say what is their music. So he buzzed like one. I mocked the wee hum they make down in the calix of a holly hock. I'm sure I don't know much about bumble bees tho' I have seen them a hundred times go thump down on a buttercup head & never come out. But Father came out from the sanctity of his Sunday nap and said he was glad to see the little people enjoy themselves.

Quoted in Sewall, *The Lyman Letters* (Amherst, 1965), 79.

36. She sent the poem to Elizabeth Holland in late May 1877.

37. The phrase is Arthur Symons, describing himself in 1905 "as one who devot-edly practiced 'the religion of the eyes.' " He added that "if he watched carefully the flux might momentarily resolve itself into an arrangement" (Kenner, 70).

38. Choosing work taken primarily from *The Poems of Emily Dickinson*, ed. Mar-tha Dickinson Bianchi and Alfred Leete Hampson (Boston, 1930), the latter then

brought out a smaller volume, *Poems for Youth* (Boston and Toronto, 1932), which went through thirty-three printings. In the preface, Hampson says: "To these children [Ned, Martha, and Gilbert], she [the poet] was not merely an aunt, but an enchanting playfellow, a confederate, an understanding friend, . . . sending across the lawn to their mother and to them countless little notes and poems, from which those given here have been chiefly chosen" (n.p.). There are seventy-eight poems in the book, but the editor does not designate which of them went to Susan Dickinson alone and which to the children, except for "Some keep the Sabbath going to Church" (#324, c. 1860), which was "Sent to her little niece who was left in her care on Sunday mornings before she was old enough to go to church." Among the poems included are "I know some lonely Houses off the Road," "A narrow Fellow in the Grass," and "The pedigree of Honey," as well as "The Sky is low, the Clouds are mean," the first description of the hummingbird ("Within my garden rides a Bird"), "An Everywhere of Silver," and "The Grass so little has to do." Other poems included were, for instance, "A bird came down the walk" (#328, c. 1862); " 'Hope' is the thing with feathers" (#254, c. 1861); "I like to see it lap the Miles" (#585, c. 1862); "I'll tell you how the Sun rose" (#318, c. 1860); "I'm Nobody! Who are you?" (#288, c. 1861); "It will be Summer eventually" (#342, c. 1862); "Two Butterflies went out at Noon / And waltzed upon a Farm" (#533, c. 1862); "Lightly stepped a yellow star" (#1672, n.d.); and "The Bee is not afraid of me" (#111, c. 1859).

A Letter to the World, an edition of forty-four of Dickinson's poems chosen "for young readers" was published in 1968 (London and New York). The selection, with an introduction by Rumer Godden, includes seventeen of the poems that appear in *Poems for Youth* and a number of different ones. Among the poems Godden selected: "I never lost as much but twice," "Because I could not stop for Death," "A Route of Evanescence" (titled "Humming Bird"), "I know some lonely Houses off the Road," and "A narrow Fellow in the Grass."

Chapter 7: Points of View

1. Poems quoted in this chapter are from *The Poems of Emily Dickinson*, ed. Thomas H. Johnson (Cambridge, Mass., 1955).

2. Christopher E. G. Benfey, *Emily Dickinson and the Problem of Others* (Amherst, 1984), 5. See also Benfey's comments on "Experiment to me": "The fantasy here, treated lightly, is that of human hollowness, of inner emptiness." Pointing out the echo of "Meet" in its homonym "Meat," Benfey examines Dickinson's interest in complicating the relation of body and soul as one of outside and inside. He also explores "I like a look of Agony" and "I measure every Grief I meet" as examples of an inquisitive sadism and a skepticism that curbs the "rage for proof" when we seek to know other people (86–93).

3. Clark Griffith, *The Long Shadow: Emily Dickinson's Tragic Poetry* (Princeton, 1964), 291; and Dwight H. Purdy, "Dickinson's 'What Soft Cherubic Creatures,' " *The Explicator*, 33, 8 (April 1975): Item 67.

4. Eleanor Wilner, "The Poetic of Emily Dickinson," *ELH*, 39, 1 (March 1971): 135, and Frederick L. Morey, "The Fifty Best Poems of Emily Dickinson," *Emily Dickinson Bulletin*, 26 (First Half 1974): 18.

5. Barbara Clarke Mossberg, *Emily Dickinson: When a Writer Is a Daughter* (Bloomington, 1982), 145–46.

6. F. DeWolfe Miller, "Emily Dickinson: Self Portrait in the Third Person," *New England Quarterly*, 43, 1 (March 1973): 119–25.

7. *The Poetical Works*, vol. 1 (Hildesheim and New York; reprinted, 1977), 1:5 and 69, 40 and 58, 67 and passim.

8. Ibid., 69, 17–18.

9. Ibid., 71, 56, 188–89 and passim.

10. Rebecca Patterson, *The Riddle of Emily Dickinson* (Boston, 1951), 147, and Albert Gelpi, *The Tenth Muse: The Psyche of the American Poet* (Cambridge, Mass., 1975), 234–35.

11. Patterson, *The Riddle*, 191.

12. "Vesuvius at Home: The Power of Emily Dickinson," *Parnassus: Poetry in Review*, 5, 1 (Fall-Winter 1976): 69.

13. Wallace Stevens, "The Idea of Order at Key West," in *The Collected Poems of Wallace Stevens* (New York, 1954), 128–30.

14. In a different tone, she describes "an Indian Woman with gay Baskets and a dazzling Baby, at the Kitchen Door." The passage is Whitmanesque: "I asked her what the Baby liked, and she said 'to step.' The Prairie before the Door was gay with Flowers of Hay, and I led her in—She argued with the Birds—she leaned on Clover Walls and they fell, and dropped her—With jargon sweeter than a Bell, she grappled Buttercups—and they sank together, the Buttercups the heaviest—" (August 1880, L, 3:668).

15. *Dairy of Alice James*, ed. Leon Edel (New York, 1964), 138–40.

16. William Howarth, *The Book of Concord* (New York, 1982), 117.

17. She enclosed the poem in a letter he dated "1871?" but Johnson thinks was written in late 1872. She thanks Higginson for the "Lesson" and says "I will study it though hitherto / Menagerie to me / My Neighbor be." The letter is signed "Your Scholar" (L, 2:501).

18. See *The Poems of Emily Dickinson: An Annotated Guide*, ed. Joseph Duchac (Boston, 1979), 149–51.

19. Benfey, citing "His Cheek is his Biographer" and "The Hollows Round His eager Eyes," points out that Dickinson makes frequent use of the trope of the human face as biographer or biography (3).

20. "Emily Dickinson's Literary Allusions," *Essays in Literature* 1, 1 (Spring 1974): 65–66. Pollak's comment is in relation to "It always felt to me—a wrong." In her book on Dickinson, Pollak writes that the poet "believed that language has the potential to order emotions that are inherently disordered, that to comprehend an experience is to alter its effect, and that many experiences can never be adequately comprehended." Pollak thinks "this later assumption freed Dickinson to create a poetic self who is arguably the most complex character in American literature." See *The Anxiety of Gender* (Ithaca and London, 1984), 27.

21. Martha Dickinson Bianchi, *Emily Dickinson Face to Face* (Boston and New York, 1932; reprinted, 1970), 283.

22. Richard Sewall says of this poem in relation to Dickinson's "lover": "The anguish of their original encounter and its failure would never leave her, . . . [and] *he* must make himself aware of the price she had paid, drop by drop, of her heart's blood." Sewall concludes, however, that "this is the page [of the biography] many have tried to write and will continue to until there is new evidence" (*The Life of Emily Dickinson*, 2:508–10).

23. E. C. Gaskell, *The Life of Charlotte Brontë* (New York, 1857), 1:95. The factory was at Liversedge.

24. Johnson dates the poem 1866 in relation to the death of Laura Dickey, a close neighbor, on May 3, 1866 (see L, 2:453). "The Bustle in a House" (#1078) is also, I think, a response to the event.

25. Having realistically described "old lady Dickinson" in her casket and the ambience of flowers in the rooms at the Homestead, a neighbor wrote that "as Vinnie expressed it, it was the last party mother would give and she was glad to have her and everything about her pretty." The poet, "looking pale and worn," attended the burial service. See Leyda, 2:383–84.

26. About April 1861 (L, 2:372), the poet asked Susan Dickinson to lend her "Life in the Iron Mills" by Rebecca Harding, whose narrator set forth the first theory of realism for readers of American fiction.

Chapter 8: Words Engender Poems

1. *The Life of Emily Dickinson* (New York, 1974), 507.

2. Poems quoted in this chapter are from *The Poems of Emily Dickinson*, ed. Thomas H. Johnson (Cambridge, Mass., 1955).

3. The poem went to Samuel Bowles, Sr., of whom Dickinson said after his death that "He was not ambitious for redemption—that is why it is his" (L, 2:609).

4. Asking Higginson "Are these more orderly? I thank you for the Truth," she included the two poems in her fourth letter to him. (She had initiated the exchange in April.) "I think," she said, "you called me 'Wayward.' Will you help me to improve? I suppose the pride that stops the Breath, in the Core of the Woods, is not of Ourself." Was she ambiguously testing him again or writing about her own pride? Since he was especially interested in her solitariness, she played it for all it was worth: "Of 'shunning Men and Women'—they talk of Hallowed things, aloud—and embarrass my Dog—He and I dont object to them, if they'll exist their side." Then (and she was never more mischievous): "I think Carlo would please you—He is dumb and brave—I think you would like the Chestnut Tree. I met it in my walk. It hit my notice suddenly—and I thought the Skies were in Blossom—" (L, 2:414–15).

5. Sewall, *The Lyman Letters* (Amherst, 1965), 78.

6. Shira Wolosky observes that "My Life had stood—a Loaded Gun—" has "prompted many interpretations, which invariably posit Dickinson's psychic life—with regard to poetic, sexual, and/or aggressive energy—as the poem's subject." She then reviews the various readings and argues that "the poem's final recalcitrant stanza—the proof text of any reading" seems "a description of the Deity . . . who, like the Gun, has power over life and death, and like the Gun, is himself immortal." She *Emily Dickinson: A Voice of War* (New Haven and London, 1984), 92–95.

Commenting on the progress of the "notoriously difficult poem" to "the very center of the Dickinson canon" in the last ten years, Christopher E. G. Benfey also remarks "in passing" that he reads "My Life had stood—a Loaded Gun" and "A Word made Flesh" as allegories of the body. Both, he says, "are centrally concerned with expression and finitude." *Emily Dickinson and the Problem of Others* (Amherst, 1984), 33, 95–96.

7. Martha Dickinson Bianchi, *Emily Dickinson Face to Face* (Boston and New York, 1932; reprinted, 1970), 37.

Chronology

1830   Emily Elizabeth Dickinson is born December 10 at the Homestead, Amherst,
        Massachusetts. Second child of Emily Norcross and Edward Dickinson.
1833   Lavinia Norcross Dickinson born February 28; mother and child ill; Emily
        visits Grandfather Joel Norcross and Aunt Lavinia Norcross for month in
        early summer.
1834   Aunt Lavinia marries Loring Norcross, first cousin.
1835   Begins primary school; father appointed treasurer of Amherst College.
1838   Father elected representative to General Court of Massachusetts.
1840   Enters Amherst Academy; family moves to North Pleasant Street.
1842   First extant letters (to older brother, Austin, at Williston Seminary); birth
        of cousin Louise Norcross.
1844   Depression after death of friend Sophia Holland, age fifteen; goes for
        month's stay with Lavinia and Loring Norcross in Boston; friendship with
        Abiah Root.
1845   "Very unwell" (possibly tuberculosis?), not "confined" to school; begins cor-
        respondence with Abiah Root.
1846   In school for eleven weeks; again ill, "rides and roams the fields" for health;
        Grandfather Norcross dies; again visits Norcrosses in Boston; father buys
        piano and she begins music lessons; learns to bake bread; resumes study;
        Joseph Lyman lives with Dickinson family.
1847   Finishes with seventh-year class at Academy; enters Mount Holyoke Female
        Seminary; student for fall and winter terms; birth of cousin Frances
        Norcross; death of Olivia Coleman.
1848   At home for health during spring, completes summer and final term at
        Mount Holyoke; friendship with Ben Newton ("preceptor"); death of Jacob
        Holt.

237

1849   Lavinia Dickinson at Ipswich Female Seminary; many household chores;
        Newton leaves Amherst.

1850   Friendship with Susan Gilbert and George Gould; Amherst College *Indicator* publishes prose satire "Magnum bonum"; Leonard Humphrey, principal
        of Amherst Academy, dies.

1851   Lively times; Lavinia's *Diary;* visits brother teaching school in Boston.

1852   First poem published in *Springfield Republican;* meets Josiah and Elizabeth
        Holland; father elected representative to Congress.

1853   Newton dies; Austin enters Harvard Law School, becomes engaged to Susan Gilbert; beginning of lifelong correspondence with Hollands; visits
        them in Springfield.

1854   Terminates correspondence with Abiah Root; visits Hollands; Austin passes
        bar examination; father loses campaign for reelection to Congress.

1855   Visits Washington and Philadelphia; Austin joins father's law firm; mother's
        first long illness begins; family moves back to the Homestead.

1856   Decides "to be distinguished." Austin and Susan married.

1857   No letters, if any, written by poet survive from this year.

1858   Probably begins assembling hand-sewn books (fascicles) of fair copies of
        poems; receives gift of sermon by the Reverend Charles Wadsworth; becomes friend of Samuel and Mary Bowles; first of three "Master" letters to
        unidentified man.

1859   First extant letters to "little cousins," Louise and Frances Norcross; Lavinia
        Dickinson in Boston to help during serious illness of Aunt Lavinia, and
        poet's housekeeping duties increase.

1860   Mother recovers from four years of illness; Aunt Lavinia dies; visit to Eliza
        Coleman in Middletown, Connecticut.

1861   "Terror" in September; Susan and Austin's first son, Edward (Ned), born.

1862   Initiates correspondence with Thomas Wentworth Higginson; makes fair
        copies of 374 poems during year; Lieutenant Frazar Stearns killed in Battle
        of New Bern: "I felt a Funeral in my Brain."

1863   Samuel Bowles: ". . . to the 'Queen Recluse' my especial sympathy"; Loring
        Norcross dies; father receives honorary degree from Amherst College.

1864   Having assembled more than eight hundred poems in forty fascicles, poet
        abandons practice. "Some Keep the Sabbath Going to Church" appears in
        New York Round Table. Goes in February to Boston for eye examination by
        Dr. Henry Williams; moves in April to Cambridgeport boardinghouse in
        Boston to receive treatment for visual problem and be cared for by Norcross
        cousins; returns home November 28.

1865   Returns in April to Boston for further treatment by Dr. Williams; remains
        until mid-fall; resumes household duties.

1866   Martha, Susan and Austin's second child, born.

1868   Hollands go to live in Europe.

1869   Margaret Maher comes to work at Homestead.

1870   Higginson visits poet; Hollands return from Europe, pay visit.

1872   Father resigns as treasurer of Amherst College.

1873   Second visit from Higginson; Austin named treasurer of college; father
        elected to Massachusetts General Court.

1874   Father dies in Boston; Otis Lord becomes family adviser.

1875   Mother stricken with paralysis; Gilbert, Susan and Austin's second son, born; Otis Lord named justice of Supreme Court of Massachusetts.
1876   Helen Hunt Jackson visits.
1877   Mrs. Otis (Elizabeth Earley) Lord dies.
1878   "Success is Counted Sweetest" published in *A Masque of Poets;* mother falls, breaks hip, is bedridden; Samuel Bowles dies; correspondence with Judge Lord; Helen Hunt Jackson visits.
1880   Lord visits; Wadsworth makes unexpected second of two visits, after interval of at least twenty years.
1881   Lord visits; Mabel Loomis and David Peck Todd move to Amherst; Josiah Holland dies.
1882   Wadsworth dies; Lord visits; Lord is critically ill, recovers; correspondence with James D. and Charles H. Clark begins; mother dies.
1883   Lord visits; Gilbert, age eight, dies of typhoid fever. Poet suffers "nervous prostration": "the Crisis of the sorrow of so many years is all that tires me."
1884   Lord dies. Poet experiences "revenge of the nerves": "unconscious for the first time in my life."
1885   Helen Hunt Jackson dies.
1886   Emily Dickinson dies May 15 at the Homestead.
1890   *Poems* by Emily Dickinson, edited by Mabel Loomis Todd and T. W. Higginson.
1891   *Poems* by Emily Dickinson, second series, edited by T. W. Higginson and Mabel Loomis Todd.
1894   *Letters of Emily Dickinson*, 2 vols., edited by Mabel Loomis Todd.
1896   *Poems* by Emily Dickinson, third series, edited by Mabel Loomis Todd.

Index

Adventures of Huckleberry Finn, The (Twain), 232 n. 29

Agoraphobia, 2

Ahmed Arabi Pasha, 217 n. 8

Alcott, Louisa May, 232 n. 29

Amherst, Mass., 12–13
    Eugene Field on, 215 n. 7
    Susan Gilbert Dickinson on, 215 n. 7

Amherst Academy, 11–12, 222 n. 35

Amherst College, 53, 222 n. 32
    as Dickinson family concern, 27

Amherst College *Indicator*, 15

Anderson, Charles, 226 n. 15, 229 n. 26

Anorexia nervosa, 2, 102

Anthon, Kate Scott. *See* Turner, Kate Scott

Antony, Mark, 233 n. 32

Antony and Cleopatra (Shakespeare), 127

"Any Wife to Any Husband" (R. Browning), 116

Arnold, Matthew, 29

Aurora Leigh (E. B. Browning), 86, 123–24

Ballads, 225 n. 6

Banks, Nathaniel, 96

Barrett, Elizabeth. *See* Browning, Elizabeth Barrett

Battle-Pieces (Melville), 59

Beaumont, George, 231 n. 6

Beecher, Henry Ward, 29, 222 n. 32

Bees, 164–66, 233 n. 35

Bell, Currer. *See* Brontë, Charlotte

Belladonna, 66, 70, 71, 223 n. 60

Benfey, Christopher E. G., 225 n. 5, 234 n. 2, 235 n. 19, 236 n. 6

Bianchi, Martha Dickinson, 24, 69, 70, 71, 216 nn. 31, 32, 223 nn. 52, 57, 61, 65, 227 n. 2, 229 n. 20, 233 n. 38, 236 n. 7

Bingham, Millicent Todd, 70, 216 n. 33, 218 n. 24, 219 n. 27, 223 nn. 42, 62, 225 n. 11

Blackmur, R. P., 232 n. 16

Blind, Mathilde, 35

Boltwood, L. M., 226 n. 19

Born, Bertran de, 115

Boston, Mass., 18

Bowles, Charles, 120

Bowles, Mary, 61, 118, 120, 225 n. 10, 229–30 n. 31, 230 n. 32
Bowles, Samuel, 19, 29, 32, 37, 50, 56–63 passim, 84, 117–20, 188, 197, 211, 218 n. 19, 221 n. 23, 225 n. 10, 229–30 n. 31, 230 n. 32
  death of, 221 n. 27
  as "that man," 219 n. 8
Bowles, Samuel, Sr., 36, 236 n. 3
  as "that man," 44
Brontë, Branwell, 30, 31
Brontë, Charlotte, 4, 30, 31, 63, 100–108 passim, 116, 228 n. 13, 229 n. 30
  ED poetic tribute to, 100, 217 n. 11
Brontë, Emily, 4, 116, 228–29 n. 13
Brontë, Maria, 9
Brown, Annie Currier, 69, 223 n. 59
Browning, Elizabeth Barrett, 4, 49, 86, 120–27 passim, 132, 229 n. 13, 230 n. 38
  ED elegies for, 230 n. 35
Browning, Robert, 4, 24, 60, 86, 115–24 passim, 222 n. 39, 230 n. 38
Bryant, William Cullen, 148
Burnett, Frances Hodgson, 29

"Caliban Upon Setebos" (R. Browning), 116
Calvin, John, 188, 189
Cameron, Sharon, 220 n. 17
Capps, Jack, 225 n. 8
Champagne, 22
Charades, 13
Charles VII (France), 172
Church, Horace, 149
Cider-making, 21
"Circumstance" (Spofford), 227 n. 2
Civil War, ED poems of, 48–60, 222 nn. 33, 34, 36, 38
Clark, Charles H., 35
Clark, James D., 35
Clemens, Samuel L. See Twain, Mark
Cody, John, 64, 67, 220 nn. 11, 15, 222 n. 44, 223 n. 50, 224 n. 70, 230 n. 35
Coleman, Eliza, 86, 94
Coleman, Olivia, 86
Consumption, 12, 86
Crosthwaite, Jane, 225 n. 12
Currier, Elizabeth Dickinson, 69

Dancing, 14
Dandurand, Karen, 217 n. 12
Dante Alighieri, 115, 122, 233 n. 30
Darwin, Charles, 39
David, 167
DeQuincey, Thomas, 94
Desdemona, 127–29
Dickens, Charles, 19, 33, 142
Dickey, Laura, 12, 236 n. 24
Dickinson, Austin (brother), 3, 9, 13–15, 18, 38, 50, 63, 89, 95, 99, 118–19, 135–37, 177, 233 n. 35
  boyhood chores of, 21
  career of, 28–29
  death of, 29
  as ED "love object," 44
  eye problems of, 65
  and Mabel Todd liaison, 217 n. 8
  marriage of, 29, 118. See also Dickinson, Susan Gilbert
  and tensions with Bowleses, 229–30 n. 31
Dickinson, Edward (father), 3, 10–19 passim, 23, 27–28, 62, 65, 95, 138, 144, 222 n. 35, 233 nn. 34, 35
  before Congress, 231 n. 7
  death of, 38, 70
  political career of, 27–28, 216–17, n. 4
  public service of, 27, 28
Dickinson, Edward ("Ned") (nephew), 69, 70, 119, 140, 160–61, 167, 177, 233 n. 32, 234 n. 38
  epilepsy of, 167
Dickinson, Ellen E. (cousin-in-law), 216 n. 26
Dickinson, Emily
  on adultery, 112, 114. See also Eliot, George; Prynne, Hester
  and Amherst, Mass., 12–14
  anonymity of, 1–2
  appearance of, 15, 215 n. 16
  on bees, 164–66, 233 n. 35
  on the Bible, 167
  on Boston, 18
  childhood of, 10–12, 34, 147
  as children's poet/correspondent, 4, 159–67, 233–34, n. 38
  chores of, 21–22, 96–97, 216 n. 26

and Civil War, 48–60, 220 n. 20, 221 nn. 22, 27, 31, 222 nn. 32, 33, 34, 35, 38. *See also* Stearns, Frazar

and correspondence with important men, 29, 35–36, 42

daily rounds of, 6–26, 91–95, 211–12

death and, 8, 16, 46–47, 83–91, 191, 195–96. *See also* Stearns, Frazar

death of, 3, 239

and dramatic monologue, 4, 82–90, 115–16, 129, 134, 168, 169, 185, 187, 189, 197, 208, 224 n. 3

and duty, 16–17, 39, 111

early verse of, 15

education of, 11–12, 83–84, 88–89, 231 n. 7

eye problems of, 19, 61–75, 143, 144, 222 n. 45, 223 n. 50, 224 n. 72, 226 n. 22

and fainting ("lying unconscious"), 47–48

on food, 22, 136

funeral of, 45

girlhood beaus of, 13–14, 16, 17

and God, 8, 23, 81, 82–83, 108, 174–75, 200–201. *See also* Dickinson, Emily, and religion

ill health of, 40, 47–48, 56, 58

and illnesses of childhood, 12

influence of other writers on, 99–132, 142. *See also* Brontë, Charlotte; Browning, Elizabeth Barrett; Browning, Robert; Eliot, George; Hawthorne, Nathaniel; Pope, Alexander; Shakespeare, William; Wordsworth, William

and Lavinia D. as close friend, 15

and lesbianism, 2, 44, 220 n. 11, 229 n. 13, 230 n. 35

letters of, 25, 37, 134–50, 159–60, 165, 176–77, 218 n. 14. *See also* Dickinson, Emily, and correspondence with important men; "Master" letters; *and individual correspondents by name*

and love of Shakespeare, 3, 11, 33, 127

medications of, 223 n. 60. *See also* Belladonna

and mental instability, 2, 43–48, 64, 208

as musician, 12, 100

as nature poet, 150–55, 178–79, 187, 197, 202–4, 209

as nurse to mother, 93–98, 226 n. 22

oeuvre of, 31, 71, 226–27 n. 23

under ophthalmologist's care, 61–62

and Otis Lord marriage proposal, 39

"plagiarisms" of, 122–26, 230 n. 35

"pregnancy" of, 224 n. 4

psychological resilience, 24, 37, 212

public persona of, 2, 6, 71

reclusiveness of, 45, 143, 219 n. 28

and religion, 8, 11, 13–14, 23, 167, 199–202, 216 n. 30

and romantic love, 36–41, 218 n. 23

schooling of, 11–12, 83–84, 88–89, 231 n. 7

sexual activity of, 38–40, 224 n. 4

sexual imagery in poetry of, 40, 106, 165–66

and sexual repression, 2

"terror" of, 42–75, 87, 119, 223 n. 67, 227 n. 24

travel of, 12, 19, 32

and "unrequited love," 43–44, 64, 97

in white, 2, 71–72

POEMS:

"A Bee his burnished Carriage" (1339), 165

"A Bird came down the Walk" (328), 178

"A Drunkard cannot meet a Cork" (1628), 204

"A Dying Tiger—moaned for Drink" (566), 52

"A face devoid of love or grace" (1711), 204

"A Light exists in Spring" (812), 139

"A little East of Jordan" (59), 7

"A Mien to move a Queen" (283), 172

"A narrow Fellow in the Grass"
    (986), 163
"A Pang is more conspicuous in
    Spring" (1530), 156
"A Rat surrendered here" (1340),
    164
"A Route of Evanescence" (1463),
    151
"A single Clover Plank" (1343), 165
"A Tongue—to tell Him I am true!"
    (400), 129
"A transport one cannot contain"
    (184), 77, 195
"A Weight with Needles on the
    pounds" (264), 194
"A word is dead" (1212), 209
"Again—his voice is at the door"
    (663), 189
"All forgot for recollecting" (966),
    128
"An Everywhere of Silver" (884),
    150
"Because I could not stop for
    Death" (712), 85
"Bee! I'm expecting you!" (1035),
    165
"Before I got my eye put out" (327),
    73, 101
"Behind Me—dips Eternity" (721),
    201
"Color—Caste—Denomination"
    (970), 59
"Crisis is a Hair" (889), 205
"Deprived of other Banquet" (773),
    103
"Dont put up my Thread and Nee-
    dle" (617), 72
"Drama's Vitallest Expression is
    the Common Day" (741), 77
"Experiment to me" (1073), 168
" 'Faith' is a fine invention" (185),
    194
"Fate slew Him, but He did not
    drop" (1031), 182
"Further in Summer than the
    Birds" (1068), 152
"Grief is a Mouse" (793), 192
"He fumbles at your Soul" (315),
    179

"He gave away his Life" (567), 53
"He preached upon 'Breadth' till it
    argued him narrow" (1207), 179
"He scanned it—staggered" (1062),
    175
"Her Grace is all she has" (810),
    183
"Her smile was shaped like other
    smiles" (514), 183
"His Cheek is his Biographer"
    (1460), 183
"His Heart was darker than the
    starless night" (1378), 183
"His little Hearse like Figure"
    (1522), 164
"How many times these low feet
    staggered" (187), 89
"How News must feel when travel-
    ling" (1319), 194
"I asked no other thing" (621), 8
"I cannot dance upon my Toes"
    (326), 207
"I fear a Man of frugal Speech"
    (543), 181
"I felt a Funeral, in my Brain"
    (280), 46–58 passim, 208, 220
    n. 17, 221 nn. 22, 25, 31, 224 n. 69
"I found the words to every
    thought" (581), 133
"I heard, as if I had no Ear" (1039),
    209
"I know some lonely Houses off the
    Road" (289), 162
"I like a look of Agony" (241), 168
"I like to see it lap the Miles" (585),
    203
"I measure every Grief I meet"
    (561), 190
"I never lost as much but twice"
    (49), 82
"I never saw a Moor" (1052), 8
"I never told the buried gold" (11),
    202
"I rose—because He sank" (616),
    104
"I stepped from Plank to Plank"
    (875), 123
"I thought that nature was enough"
    (1286), 188

"I tie my Hat—I crease my Shawl" (443), 56

"I was a Phoebe—nothing more" (1009), 131

"I watched the Moon around the House" (629), 169

I would distill a cup (19), 217 n. 11

"If your Nerve, deny you" (292), 206

"I'm ceded—I've stopped being Theirs" (508), 80

"I'm Nobody! Who are you?" (288), 178

"I'm saying every day" (373), 79

"I'm 'wife'—I've finished that" (199), 124

"Image of Light, Adieu" (1556), 209

"Inconceivably solemn!" (582), 58

"It always felt to me—a wrong" (597), 173

"It dont sound so terrible—quite—as it did" (426), 51

"It would have starved a Gnat" (612), 101

"It's easy to invent a Life" (724), 108

"It's little Ether Hood" (1501), 201

"I've known a Heaven, like a Tent" (243), 202

"Lightly stepped a yellow star" (1672), 8

"Like Eyes that Looked on Wastes" (458), 229 n. 13

"Many cross the Rhine" (123), 8

"Me prove it now—Whoever doubt" (537), 110

"Mine—by the Right of the White Election!" (528), 113

"Much Madness is divinest Sense" (435), 147

"My life closed twice before its close" (1732), 84

"My Life had stood—a Loaded Gun" (754), 209

"My Triumph lasted till the Drums" (1227), 141

"Nature—the Gentlest Mother is" (790), 203

"Not with a Club, the Heart is broken" (1304), 193

"Of Brussels—it was not" (602), 203

"One dignity delays for all" (98), 196

"Papa above!" (61), 79

"Put up my lute!" (261), 121

"Read—Sweet—how others strove" (260), 81

"Revolution is the Pod" (1082), 55

"Shall I take thee, the Poet said" (1126), 135

"She dealt her pretty words like Blades" (479), 109, 141

"She rose to His Requirement—dropt" (732), 185

"Silence is all we dread" (1251), 182

"Speech is one symptom of Affection" (1681), 182

"Tell all the Truth but tell it slant" (1129), 49

"Tell as a Marksman—were forgotten" (1152), 174

"That after Horror—that 'twas *us*" (286), 205

"The Bat is dun, with wrinkled Wings" (1575), 151

"The Bible is an antique Volume" (1545), 158

"The Bustle in a House" (1078), 7

"The Devil—had he fidelity" (1479), 158

"The Ditch is dear to the Drunken man" (1645), 184

"The first We knew of Him was Death" (1006), 54

"The Grass so little has to do" (333), 92

"The Hollows round His eager Eyes" (955), 183

"The immortality she gave" (1648), 25

"The last Night that She lived" (1100), 195

"The lonesome for they know not What" (262), 120

"The parasol is the umbrella's daughter" (1747), 186

"The Rat is the concisest Tenant"
  (1356), 164
"The Show is not the Show" (1206),
  177
"The Sky is Low—the Clouds are
  mean" (1075), 141
"The Thrill came slowly like a
  Boon" (1495), 195
"There is a finished feeling" (856),
  220 n. 16
"There is no Silence in the Earth—
  so silent" (1004), 182
"There's a certain Slant of light"
  (258), 153
"These are the Nights that Beetles
  love" (1128), 157
"They dropped like Flakes" (409),
  55
"They leave us with the Infinite"
  (350), 196
"They shut me up in Prose" (613), 9
"They talk as slow as Legends
  grow" (1697), 195
"This is my letter to the World"
  (441), 208
"This World is not Conclusion"
  (501), 200
"Those Cattle smaller than a Bee"
  (1388), 158
" 'Twas just this time, last year, I
  died" (445), 87
"Under the Light, yet under" (949),
  155
"We don't cry—Tim and I" (196).
"We learn in the Retreating"
  (1083), 54
"We like a Hairbreadth 'scape"
  (1175), 206
"What I see not, I better see" (939),
  130
"What is—'Paradise' " (215), 8
"What shall I do when the Summer
  troubles" (956), 10
"What Soft—Cherubic Creatures"
  (401), 109
"When I was small, a Woman died"
  (596), 55
"You said that I 'was Great'—one
  Day" (738), 107

"Your thoughts dont have words
  ery day" (1452), 211
Dickinson, Emily Norcross (mother),
  10–11, 22, 27, 62, 65, 203–4, 226
  n. 19, 236 n. 25
  death of, 39, 76, 236 n. 25
  poor health of, 76, 93–94, 97, 215-
    16 n. 20, 226 n. 22, 227 n. 24
Dickinson, Gilbert (nephew), 161–62,
  164, 234 n. 38
  death of, 40, 69
Dickinson, Lavinia (sister), 10, 13, 14,
  18, 20, 23, 62–72 passim, 90–97 pas
  sim, 127–37 passim, 215 n. 16, 217
  n. 13, 226 n. 22, 236 n. 25
  closeness of to ED, 15
  household chores of, 21–22, 93
  rebelliousness of, 14–15, 215 n. 12
Dickinson, Martha ("Mattie") (niece),
  40, 160, 161, 167, 234 n. 38
Dickinson, Samuel Fowler (grandfather), 27
Dickinson, Susan Gilbert (sister-in-
  law), 3–4, 18, 19, 38, 43, 44, 62, 63,
  95, 100, 118, 126–27, 188, 217 n. 8,
  231 n. 14, 233 n. 34, 234 n. 38, 236
  n. 26
  as focus of ED "lesbianism," 44,
    220 n. 11, 229 n. 13
  marriage of, 29
Dickinson, William (uncle), 12
Dimmesdale, Arthur, 113–15
Donne, John, 99, 155
Donoghue, Denis, 147
Dramatic Lyrics (R. Browning), 117
Duchac, Joseph, 233 nn. 31, 34, 235
  n. 18
Dudley, Eliza Coleman, 23
Dwight, Edward Strong, 14
Dwight, Lucy Elizabeth, 23

Earnshaw, Catherine, 229 n. 13
Eastman, Charlotte Sewall, 63
Eberwein, Jane Donahue, 228 n. 4
Eden, 167
Edwards, Jonathan, 164
Eliot, George (Mary Ann Evans), 4,
  109–11, 112, 149, 229 n. 13
  poetry of, 229 n. 23

Eliot, T. S., 99, 116, 131, 155–56, 230 n. 38, 232 n. 24
Ella (Frazar Stearns's beloved), 50, 56
Emerson, Ralph Waldo, 1, 16–17, 21, 29, 35, 84, 95, 142
  death of, 39
Enobarbus, 233 n. 32
Erle, Marian, 124, 125
Essay on Man, The (Pope), 100, 231 n. 7
Evans, Mary Ann. *See* Eliot, George
Exotropia, 64–65
Eyre, Jane, 100–108, 228 nn. 11, 13

Falstaff, 130, 136, 231 n. 4
Fearful Responsibility, A (Howells), 34–35
Field, Eugene, 214 n. 7
Fiske, Helen. *See* Jackson, Helen Hunt
Footprints (Todd), 217 n. 8
Ford, Emily Fowler, 215 nn. 10, 16
Ford, Thomas W., 48, 220 n. 20, 222 nn. 33, 36
Franco-Prussian War, 231 n. 11
Franklin, R. W., 36, 48, 52, 70, 226 n. 23
French, Daniel Chester, 29
Frost, Robert, 178, 198

Gall, Sally M., 227 nn. 4, 25
Garbowsky, Maryanne M., 227 n. 2
Garrique, Jean, 142
Gaskell, Elizabeth C., 30, 95
Gelpi, Albert J., 219 n. 3, 228 n. 10, 235 n. 10
Gilbert, Sandra M., 215 n. 19, 219 n. 1, 224 n. 3
Gilbert, Susan. *See* Dickinson, Susan Gilbert
Gladden, Washington, 35–36
Godden, Rumer, 234 n. 38
Gould, George, 44
Green, Clara Bellinger, 69
Griffin, Clark, 220 n. 18, 234 n. 3
Gubar, Susan, 215 n. 19, 219 n. 1, 224 n. 3
Gulliver's Travels (Swift), 158–59

Hal, Prince, 136, 231 n. 4
Hale, Edward Everett, 35
Hampson, Alfred Leete, 233–34 n. 38

Harding, Rebecca, 236 n. 26
Hardy, Thomas, 221 n. 26
Harper, Michael S., 225 n. 6
Haskell, Abbie Ann, 16
Hawthorne, Nathaniel, 4, 111–14, 142, 159
Haymaking, 6, 8
Henry IV, Part I (Shakespeare), 130
Higgins, David, 219 n. 8,
Higginson, Anna, 224 n. 71
Higginson, Mary, 45–46
Higginson, Thomas Wentworth, 20, 24, 25, 29–49 passim, 56, 61, 67–78 passim, 84, 86, 112, 115, 118, 123, 132, 135, 143, 178–79, 208, 216 n. 31, 217 n. 13, 227 n. 2, 232 nn. 18, 21, 233 n. 33, 235 n. 17, 236 n. 4
  at *ED*'s funeral, 45
  on *ED*'s mental capacities, 45–46, 224 n. 71
  wounded in action, 58, 74
Holland, Elizabeth, 22, 32, 34, 35, 38, 70, 93, 97, 138–50, 217 n. 8, 228 n. 11, 229 n. 20, 233 n. 36
  vision problems of, 143, 144–46
Holland, Josiah G., 22, 32, 35, 36, 138, 142, 144–45, 149
Holland, Sophia, 84, 88
  death of, 83
Holt, Jacob, 83, 84
Homestead, the, 19, 22, 23, 27, 93
Housecleaning, 7, 8, 97
House of the Seven Gables, The (Hawthorne), 112
Howard, William, 226 n. 14
Howart, William, 235 n. 16
Howe, Annie Holland, 68
Howells, William Dean, 34–35
Howland, William, 14–15, 215 nn. 12, 17
Humphrey, Leonard, 83, 84, 86
Hunt, Edward B., 44
Hunt, Helen Fiske. *See* Jackson, Helen Hunt
Huntington, Frederick D., 35, 36

Imagism, 151, 197, 232 n. 19
"In a Station of the Metro" (Pound), 232 n. 19

Iritis, 66
    James Joyce and, 71, 223 n.64

Jackson, Gerald W., 66, 67, 223 n.48
Jackson, Helen Hunt, 1, 29, 34, 44, 68,
    232 n.21
    ED elegy for, 25–26
Jacob, 7
James, Alice, 178
Jane Eyre (C. Brontë), 63, 100–108, 116,
    228 n.11, 229 nn.13, 30. See also
    Eyre, Jane
Jenkins, J. L., 33
Jenkins, Sally, 167
Jenkins, Sarah Maria, 23
Jesus, 164
Joan of Arc, 171–72
Joan of Arc (Southey), 171
Johnson, Thomas H., 47, 48, 52, 219
    n.3, 235 n.17, 236 n.24
Joyce, James, 71, 223 n.64
Joyce, Lucia, 223 n.64
Judas, 167
Juhasz, Suzanne, 221 n.25, 225 n.5,
    229 n.26

Keats, John, 86
Keller, Karl, 229 nn.13, 26
Kenner, Hugh, 232 n.19, 233 n.37
Kimball, Benjamin, 40
King Lear (Shakespeare), 127
Knight, Charles, 95

"Last Ride Together, The" (R. Brow-
    ning), 86
Lair, Robert, 224 n.70
Langton, Jane, 229 n.14
Lawler, Margaret O'Brien, 19, 143–44
Lesbianism, 2, 44, 220 n.11, 229 n.13,
    230 n.35
Lewes, George Henry, 112
Leyda, Jay, 107, 222 n.39, 226 n.18
"Life in a Love" (R. Browning), 116
"Life in the Iron Mills" (Harding), 236
    n.26
Life of Abraham Lincoln (Holland), 144
Life of Charlotte Brontë (Gaskell), 30, 95,
    214 n.4, 217 n.11, 236 n.23
Life of George Eliot (Blind), 35

"Life of the Birds" (Higginson), 143
"Ligeia" (Poe), 45
Lincoln, Abraham, 54
Linton, Catherine Earnshaw, 229 n.13
Longfellow, Henry W., 142, 217 n.8
Longsworth, Polly, 219 n.28, 220 n.11
Lord, Otis Phillips, 36, 38–41, 76, 97,
    218 n.25, 219 n.27, 222 n.32
    death of, 40
    on Frazar Stearns, 53
    as "that man," 44
    widowing of, 38
"Love in a Life" (R. Browning), 116
Lyman, Joseph, 14, 44–45, 63, 64, 71,
    210, 216 n.31, 233 n.35

Macbeth (Shakespeare), 127
McClellan, George B., 55, 222 n.35
Maher, Maggie, 19, 97
Malvern Hill, battle of, 55
Manassas, battle of First, 55
Manic depression, 2, 208, 221 n.22
Man Without a Country, The (Hale), 35
Martin, Wendy, 216 n.20
Masque of Poets, A (Jackson [ed.]), 1
Massachusetts Agricultural College, 28
"Master" letters, 36–38, 43, 96, 218–19,
    n.25
Melville, Herman, 7, 56, 59, 211, 214
    n.3, 222 n.37
Men and Women (R. Browning), 116,
    121
Merchant of Venice, The (Shakespeare),
    138
Merrill, James, 78
Middlemarch (Eliot), 112
Miller, F. DeWolfe, 235 n.6
Miller, Ruth, 219 n.8, 222 n.38, 227
    n.25
Mill on the Floss, The (Eliot), 109–11,
    229 n.20
Milton, John, 158, 232 n.26
Mirabeau, Honoré-Gabriel de Riquetti,
    233 n.30
Moers, Ellen, 124, 225 n.9, 229 n.23,
    230 n.38, 231 n.40
Moi, Toril, 214 n.6
Monologue, dramatic, 829, 225 n.6

Moore, Marianne, 218 n. 20, 231 n. 8, 232 n. 22

Morey, Frederick L., 234 n. 5

Moses, 173, 175

Mossberg, Barbara, 221 n. 31, 234 n. 5

Mount Holyoke Academy, 215 n. 16

Mount Holyoke Seminary, 12, 231 n. 7

Mudge, Jean McClure, 226 n. 14

Nash, Ogden, 159

New Bern, battle of, 49, 221 n. 23

New England Primer, The, 164, 233 n. 34

"New Hampshire" (Eliot), 155

Newton, Ben, 16, 35, 39
    death of, 84

Niles, Thomas, 35, 232 nn. 21, 23

Norcross, Frances, 22, 47, 49, 56, 61–62, 72, 90

Norcross, Joel, 10, 83

Norcross, Lavinia, 10, 12, 90, 98

Norcross, Loring, 90

Norcross, Louise, 22, 47, 49, 56, 61–63, 67, 71, 72, 90, 95, 96, 221 n. 27

O'Brien, Margaret. *See* Lawler, Margaret O'Brien

Old Curiosity Shop, The (Dickens), 19

Olmsted, Frederick Law, 29

"One Way of Love" (R. Browning), 121

"One Word More" (R. Browning), 122

Osgood, Frances Sargent, 232 n. 29

Othello (Shakespeare), 127–29

Paradise Lost (Milton), 158, 232 n. 26

Parties, 13

Patterson, Rebecca, 127, 220 n. 10, 235 nn. 10, 11

Paul, Saint, 173

Personae (Pound), 115, 116

Phillips, Wendell, 29

Photophobia, 65, 66

Pierce, Edwin, 137

"Pippa Passes" (R. Browning), 116, 117

Pisan Cantos, The (Pound), 155

Poe, Edgar Allan, 45, 75, 122–23, 194, 235 n. 20

Poins (*King Henry IV, Part 1*), 136, 231 n. 4

Pollak, Vivian R., 187, 225–26 n. 13, 229 n. 13, 235 n. 20

Pollitt, Josephine, 218 n. 19, 219 n. 7

Pope, Alexander, 100, 141–42, 231 n. 7

Porter, David, 220 n. 19, 224 n. 69

Portia, 138

Pound, Ezra, 115, 150, 155–56, 232 n. 19

Practical Guide to the Study of Diseases of the Eye: Their Medical and Surgical Treatment (Williams), 61, 65, 66

Prynne, Hester, 113–15

Ransom, John Crowe, 215 n. 19, 221 n. 26

Rasselas (Johnson), 10

Recent Advances in Ophthalmic Surgery (Williams), 65, 70

Reeves, James, 221 n. 25

Reynolds, Jerry Ferris, 222 n. 45

Rich, Adrienne, 175, 235 n. 12

Robinson, E. A., 198

Rochester, Edward, 100–108, 123, 228 nn. 4, 11

Romeo and Juliet (Shakespeare), 127

Root, Abiah, 32, 83, 84, 86, 88, 216 n. 30

Rosenthal, M. L., 227 nn. 4, 25

"Rudel to the Lady of Tripoli" (R. Browning), 116, 117, 120, 127

Russ, Joanna, 215–16 n. 20

St. Armand, Barton Levi, 221 n. 22

Sand, George (Amantine Lucile Aurore Dupin), 9, 49

Satan, 20, 158, 167, 232 n. 26

Scannell, Dennis, 177, 185

Scarlet Letter, The (Hawthorne), 112–14

Schaurek, Eileen Joyce, 223 n. 64

Scott, Winfield Townley, 219 n. 8

Scribner's Monthly, 149, 233 n. 33

Sewall, Richard, 37, 61, 64–65, 112, 149, 159, 199, 215 n. 16, 216 nn. 21, 27, 218 n. 22, 221 n. 30, 222 nn. 33, 40, 45, 46, 223 n. 68, 226 n. 20, 227 n. 24, 235 n. 22

Shakespeare, Judith, 18, 215 n. 19

Shakespeare, William, 3, 4, 11, 14, 33, 38, 95, 127–30, 132, 138, 142, 188, 233 n. 32

Shepard, Mary, 226 n.19
Sherwood, William R., 219 n.3, 221 n.31
Shiloh, battle of, 55
Shurr, William H., 107, 219 nn.3, 8, 224 n.4, 228 nn.12, 13
Sleigh rides, 13
Smith, Adam, 14
Soliloquy, dramatic, 225 n.6
Solomon, 93
"Song of Myself" (Whitman), 52, 98
Sonnets from the Portuguese (E. B. Browning), 124
Southey, Robert, 30, 31, 171–72, 235 n.7
Spencer, John, 16
Spofford, Harriet Prescott, 100, 227 n.2
Stearns, Frazar, 49–51, 53, 56, 221 nn.22, 27, 30
Stephen, Saint, 173
Stevens, Wallace, 6, 136, 202, 231 n.2
Suicide, 175
Swift, Jonathan, 158, 159, 233 n.30
Symons, Arthur, 233 n.37

Taggard, Genevieve, 210 n.5, 239 n.38
Tell, William, 174–75
Tempest, The (Shakespeare), 127
Tennyson, Alfred Lord, 14
Thoreau, Henry David, 21, 108, 142, 178
Todd, David, 217 n.8
Todd, John Emerson, 221 n.25, 228 n.10
Todd, Mabel Loomis, 68, 217 nn.8, 13, 219 n.28, 223 n.54, 232 n.21
   and liaison with Austin Dickinson, 217 n.8
Transcendentalism, 17
Tuckerman, Alice Cooper, 93
Tuckerman, Mrs. Edward, 232 n.21
Tuckerman, Frederick, 232 n.21
Tuckerman, Margaret, 93
Tulliver, Maggie, 109–11, 229 n.20

Turner, Kate Scott, 44, 117, 118–19, 127
Twain, Mark (Samuel L. Clemens), 159, 218 n.19, 232 n.29
Twombly (Lavinia suitor), 15, 215 n.13

Villette (C. Brontë), 228 n.13
Vision of the Maid of Orleans, The (Southey), 171

Wadsworth, Charles, 35, 36, 84, 180, 218 n.19, 219 n.3, 226 n.18
   death of, 39, 43
   as "that man," 43–44, 224 n.4
Walden Pond, 21, 108
Walsh, John Evangelist, 220 n.9, 223 n.60, 230 nn.35, 38
Wand, Martin, 64–65, 222 nn.45–46
Ward, Theodora, 47, 220 n.17, 221 n.29
Waste Land, The (Eliot), 155, 156
Watts, Emily Stipes, 214 n.3
Weisbuch, Robert, 157, 220 n.15, 232 n.25
Wells, Henry, 129
Wheaton Female Seminary, 15
Whicher, George F., 219 n.3, 222 n.33
Whitman, Walt, 17, 52, 59, 98
Whitney, Maria, 221 n.27
Williams, Henry W., 61–70 passim, 223 n.49
Williams, William Carlos, 151, 232 n.22
Wilner, Eleanor, 234 n.4
Wine-making, 21
Winters, Yvor, 225 n.12
Wolosky, Shira, 48, 49, 220 n.20, 222 nn.33, 36, 236 n.6
"Woman's Last Word, A" (R. Browning), 116
Woolf, Virginia, 18, 214 n.6
Wordsworth, William, 30, 139–40, 231 n.6
Wuthering Heights (E. Brontë), 229 n.13